Loretta Young

Loretta Young

An Extraordinary Life

Joe Morella and Edward Z. Epstein

Delacorte Press / New York

Published by
Delacorte Press
1 Dag Hammarskjold Plaza
New York, N.Y. 10017

Manufactured in the United States of America
First printing

Library of Congress Cataloging in Publication Data
Morella, Joe.
Loretta Young: an extraordinary life.

1. Young, Loretta, 1913– . 2. Moving-picture actors
and actresses—United States—Biography.
I. Epstein, Edward Z. II. Title.
PN2287.Y6M67 1986   791.43'028'0924 [B]   86–6181
ISBN 0-385-29397-6

Prologue

Scenario: A beautiful woman with four young children, abandoned by her husband, rises to meet life's challenges. The children all become successful. One daughter in the brood is fired with extraordinary ambition and possesses the intelligence, beauty, and discipline necessary to make all her dreams come true. She wants to be a film actress, and beyond that, a star. Eventually that youngster becomes even more than a movie star: she becomes a symbol of glamour and achievement, both on and off camera. Her life story contains elements of romance, mystery, controversy, heartbreak, and triumph. She overcomes life-threatening illness. Her courage and faith are an inspiration to others. She charts her own course in a long and extraordinary life decades before women's lib. She evolves into a legendary figure. Fiction? Not at all. It is the true story of Loretta Young.

In the tradition of fictional family sagas, the Youngs always were—and have remained—a tight-knit group, "a small and exclusive union." That they are devoutly Catholic and a mutually supportive and protective family unit made each of them a key figure in Loretta Young's development.

From the time she was a child, Loretta's large, luminous blue-gray eyes and radiant face bespoke a poignant vulnerability, especially onscreen. Appearances, however, were deceiving, for behind the angelic look and soft-spoken facade lay a will of steel. Loretta Young was determined to be not just an actress but a *star,* and she disciplined herself to accomplish just that. What her determination produced is a star so enduring that it still shines.

She achieved every professional goal, but her personal life held many disappointments. There was a teenage elopement and divorce, followed by a romantic search for Mr. Right, a quest that spanned a decade. Spencer Tracy and Clark Gable are two men who figure prominently in her story. Gable's involvement with Loretta spawned one of Hollywood's most indestructible legends: that their romance produced a child. Over the years there has been so much gossip and speculation on this story that it almost seems as if any evidence to the contrary would be neither welcomed nor believed.

Through the 1930s Loretta Young was headstrong and rebellious, and she led a personal life which—while discreet—was often as colorful and dramatic as that of any of Hollywood's more publicized sex symbols.

Then, in 1940, her life-style and image changed after her marriage to Tom Lewis, a handsome, successful advertising and broadcasting executive. For years Loretta was the one star who seemed to have it all—she was wife and mother, while maintaining a successful career. More amazingly, she maintained her femininity and her strong religious and moral convictions in an industry notorious for corrupting those traits.

She once observed that getting anywhere in life is the result of "self-discipline, work—and I mean *hard* work." She was relentless, pushing herself constantly. She appeared in ninety motion pictures in twenty-five years while making scores of radio appearances and maintaining a heavy schedule of civic and charitable activities. Ultimately her determination and talent were rewarded by her peers. After two decades in pictures she won an Oscar. Then, lured by the incredible potential for reaching millions of people, she turned to the new medium of television. She swept through the doorway of her "living room" each week in a trademark entrance that earned her a place in television history. For

eight years she displayed enormous versatility performing in
over two hundred episodes of her anthology series. She was
the first Oscar winner to be awarded an Emmy—and went on
to win several Emmys more. Her public adored her. Only the
insiders knew the truly harsh personal sacrifices she had made
for her career.

Few actors achieved the phenomenal and enduring success
of Loretta Young. But perhaps more than any other Hollywood figure, Miss Young engenders wildly varied opinions
and feelings from those who have known her intimately over
the years: *"The Steel Butterfly"*; "A kind and loving woman";
"A chocolate-covered black widow spider"; "A saint"; *"The Iron
Madonna"*; "A great humanitarian."

Yet whatever people think of her, no one can deny that
Miss Young's on- and off-camera activities have made her one
of America's most admired and respected women. Perhaps
the secret of her success has been the slogan "I Can Do It."
Miss Young inherited her valuable trait of perseverance,
along with her beauty and intelligence, from another remarkable woman. A woman whose soft, gentle southern voice
masked a strong will. A woman whose life was every bit as
extraordinary as her daughter Gretchen's . . .

Book One

I was very lucky. I had a marvelous family behind me. A wise mother. If you can have this wonderful, moral background behind you, you have a chance of achieving something solid.
—*Loretta Young*

One

The early 1900s in America was a time of optimism, a time when all things seemed possible—if one was willing to work for them. *Work hard and success will be achieved.* This was the ethic to which many subscribed, and in some cases it actually was proven true.

The "work," however, was to be left to the men. Young women, by convention, were instructed that there was only one respectable career for them—marriage. Everyone knew that women could find fulfillment only through the love of and devotion to a man. Gladys Royal was no exception.

As a teenage girl, Gladys Royal could well have been the model for artist Charles Dana Gibson's idealized American beauty, the Gibson girl. Her striking good looks were in the classic mold—she was tall and slender, and she possessed high cheekbones, huge, luminous eyes, a strong jawline, and a perfect complexion. So it was to be expected that when Gladys fell in love, as she did with startlingly handsome John Earle Young, nature would swiftly take its course.

Young's job, as an auditor for the Denver, Rio Grande and Western Railroad, required a great deal of traveling. That was fine; Gladys was used to traveling. She had been born in Los Angeles, then raised in Kentucky and Tennessee. The Royals were of French and English background; the Youngs were English-American. Gladys and John were married in 1907, when both were nineteen.

Their first child, Polly Ann (called Pol), was born in Denver on October 25, 1908. The second, Elizabeth Jane (called Betty Jane or Bet), was born two years later in Salida, Colorado, on July 11, 1910. The Youngs were living in Salt Lake City when Gretchen Michaela Young was born on January 6, 1913. Twenty-one months later, on October 7, 1914, brother Jackie—the only boy in the brood—was born.

Four little children were an all-consuming responsibility, and the Young union had more than its share of problems. Gladys Young had her hands full. She was a woman of strong character, but her resilience was put to the test on many occasions by the actions of her husband. ("John was not a mean man, but he was a weak man. He was handsome, much too handsome for his own good," observed Gladys many years later.) In addition to beauty, Gladys possessed brains, ambition, drive, and determination. She would need all these traits to survive, for in 1916 a traumatic event altered the course of their lives.

One day John Young—then twenty-seven—didn't come home. At the time Polly Ann was eight, Betty Jane six, Gretchen three, and Jackie only one-and-a-half. In later years an explanation worthy of a Loretta Young film was given for the desertion—amnesia. Gladys, however, candidly rebuffed this fantasy: "He just left," she said.

Even more shocked than Gladys was John Young's mother, Laura. John's sister, Mrs. Grace Claybaugh, later stated: "He crucified our mother when John left them."

To three-year-old Gretchen, John Young's disappearance was almost incomprehensible. Because children tend to view the world as basically an enlargement of their own home experience, the events that followed their father's defection undoubtedly shaped the children's attitude toward life and its pitfalls. And while John Earle Young seemed sadly deficient as a parent, Gladys Royal Young was superb. She set an example for her progeny by demonstrating what resilience and fortitude could accomplish. The woman possessed enormous inner strength—a quality she cultivated assiduously in her children. Refusing to cave in to the heavy blow her husband had dealt them, she took her four children and traveled to Los Angeles to be with her family, determined to build a life for them there.

"Uncle Trax was sitting on the front porch and he saw a woman and four bedraggled kids walking down the dusty road from the streetcar," Betty Jane Young recalled. "Hollywood was a one-horse town in those days, with only a few paved streets, and it was hot and Uncle Trax was sorry for the group trudging along. 'Look at that poor woman with those kids,' he said. Aunt Colly came to the door just then, looked, and cried, 'Why, that's Gladys,' and they ran out to meet us."

Ernest Traxler was married to Colleen Royal, Gladys's sister. They had children of their own, and gladly took in the Young brood until Gladys could make other arrangements. The ever-resourceful twenty-seven-year-old woman went to a local Catholic bishop and persuaded him to lend her one thousand dollars—a considerable sum in those days—so that she could open a boardinghouse. Selecting a house on Ninth and Green streets in downtown Los Angeles, and buying furniture on time from a local department store, Gladys launched into a business about which she knew little. She soon learned.

Traxler was employed at the time as a supervisor and assistant director at the Famous Players–Lasky studio (later to become Paramount). Because of the transient nature of the business, he knew many people at the studio who needed lodgings, and would send them to Gladys. Gretchen would later remember that her mother was very "selective of her guests" and preferred people with children.

All the Young children pitched in to make the boarding-house successful. Polly Ann has recalled, "We all helped around, and I guess we got along pretty well right away. We carried in things from the table and helped in the kitchen." But, she conceded, "we really didn't kill ourselves at it, even when we got a little older." Despite the demands of running the boardinghouse the Young family continued to attend Mass regularly, while Gladys strove to instill in her children her philosophy of life: utilize one's God-given instincts and work *hard.* And Gladys always practiced what she preached.

Financial problems continued, however, and Gladys was receptive when Uncle Trax made a suggestion: "The kids are beautiful. Why not let them earn some money by working as extras in the flickers?"

"The flickers"—even in 1917, its infant days, motion pictures were big business. Only four other industries in the United States—railroads, clothing, iron and steel, and oil—were ranked higher at the time (automobiles lagged behind, in sixth place).

The motion picture business, although still young, was already notorious for the fast-talking, sometimes less-than-reputable characters pulling the strings and calling the shots behind the scenes. Nothing, however, could dim the aura of glamour and excitement surrounding the movies. They had captured—and were holding—the interest of the world.

Cecil B. DeMille had arrived in Hollywood only four years earlier to make *The Squaw Man.* Mary Pickford (née Gladys Smith) was the reigning female star, beloved and idolized throughout the world. This adulation was reflected in the salary she was earning, ten thousand dollars a week. Charlie Chaplin was already a legend, too, and annually earned seven times the salary of the President of the United States. Because income tax was then only around three percent, there was a lot of money spent conspicuously in the film community, and a lot of unscrupulous people had been lured there by the promise of getting rich quickly.

Gladys Young, however, had no reason to be concerned about any of this; indeed she had no reason even to be aware of it. Both she and her brother-in-law would always be there to keep an eye on little Jackie and the girls, and so she viewed appearing in flickers as a fine and legitimate way to bring some much-needed cash into the household. Traxler's young daughter, Colleen, was in fact a "kid extra," and Traxler soon got work for the Young children as well.

He brought Gretchen to director George Melford, who was shooting a Famous Players picture—*The Only Way,* starring Fanny Ward and Theodore Roberts. The story goes that Traxler took Gretchen directly from her backyard playground to see Melford. The director looked at the child and said, "Wash her face and bring her back tomorrow." (The Young family delighted in telling that anecdote in ensuing years.) The child was four when she made her motion picture debut playing a little girl who had to weep piteously on an operating table, earning $3.50 for the day's work.

These were silent pictures, of course, which meant that scenes for different films were shot side by side on adjoining sets and directors were yelling out instructions as cameras were cranked by hand. Musicians were frequently hired to play mood music. The motors of the bright, hot klieg lights were always humming and snapping loudly. There were garishly dressed, gorgeously glittering ladies and gentlemen in heavy makeup all over the lot. All in all, it was pretty heady stuff for a four-year-old, *any* four-year-old. But even at four, a child knows what he or she is happy—or unhappy—doing. And Gretchen was *happy* as a performer. She was a natural.

Gladys Young recalled, "Gretchen always knew how to present herself. I remember when she was four and people who came to the house would ask her to dance with them. She'd always say, 'I will, but first I must put on my best dress.'"

Over at Universal they were hiring kid extras for *Sirens of the Sea,* shooting on location at Catalina Island off the coast from Los Angeles. Gladys took all four of the children and got them work on the film. Betty Jane has recalled that the man in charge of the commissary was drunk, and "we lived on hard-boiled eggs and tea for two days."

Such extra work, however, did not provide a steady income, and the family continued to struggle financially while Mrs. Young devoted her energies to her boardinghouse. It was located in a neighborhood of downtown Los Angeles that was then in a transitional stage—that is, it was not a traditional boardinghouse area, but rather a neighborhood of fine, huge, stately homes starting to lose their luster. A neighboring family, the Lindleys, wanted to bring up little Jack. Mrs. Young agreed, and although the Youngs remained close to Jack, he was in fact brought up by the Lindleys, adopted their family name, and is known as Jack Lindley.

Gretchen was not unaware of her family's financial struggle during these years. She was rigidly schooled about the value of a dollar. Mamma was, in adult Gretchen's words, "mother, father, and family breadwinner." And while there was an absence of cash in the household, she remembers that "we always had a rich abundance of all things money can't buy." She was referring to love, trust, discipline, religious training. And she claimed they also "had lots and lots of fun!"

In 1917 Gretchen was an extra in *The Primrose Ring*, starring Mae Murray, the petite blonde famous for her "bee-stung" lips. As the story goes—the kind of true story that could only have happened in Hollywood—Mae Murray spotted Gretchen on the set and was instantly taken with the child's beauty.

"Who is she?" she asked. "She looks as I did when I was a child! What a wonderful daughter she would make for me!"

Miss Murray wasn't just wishing in vain. She was one of the biggest stars of the silent screen, a self-made goddess who believed her beauty and talent entitled her to everything the world had to offer. If Mae Murray spotted a pretty little girl she wanted for a daughter, then the studio—which always

made every effort to keep its money-making treasure happy
—would somehow have to arrange it.

"I'll adopt her!" declared Miss Murray ecstatically.

After Gladys Young explained to the impulsive star that
this wouldn't be possible, it was arranged for Gretchen and
cousin Colleen to "visit" with Miss Murray and her husband,
film director Robert Z. Leonard, at their estate. The "visit"
extended into an eighteen-month stay.

During that year and a half, Gretchen and Colleen were
Mae Murray's "daughters," living the lives of princesses.
They had a governess, and took ballet lessons (Gretchen
wanted to be a ballerina). Their ballet instructor was Ernest
Belcher (father of Marge Belcher, who later married Gower
Champion). Young Gretchen saw firsthand how a queen of
the silver screen was catered to and coddled. But the percep-
tive child also observed how erratic a star's behavior could
be, how her moods could fluctuate unpredictably.

Then one day Mr. Leonard decided abruptly, "no more
children." Mae was going to New York to make a film; he
was busy with his own commitments. It was time for
Gretchen and her cousin to be removed from the screen
star's life and returned to their mundane homes in Los Angeles.

Re-entry to the Young house was not smooth for Gretchen.
She was not happy to again be one of a group, and the others
teased her about her "ballerina-princess" pretensions. According to an intimate of Miss Young's, the experience in
Mae Murray's home left its mark. Now she most definitely
wanted to be a star.

Back with her mother and sisters, Gretchen met a child
with whom she became friends. Josephine Saenz (nicknamed
Josie), a few years older than Gretchen, was the daughter of
Dr. and Mrs. Jose Sainte-Saenz. He was a practicing physi-
cian, the Los Angeles Consul for the Dominican Republic,
and a very wealthy businessman who owned a chain of phar-

macies. (Josie and Gretchen have remained close friends to this day.)

There is no doubt that Gretchen was strong-willed and determined from an early age. "I'd thought of myself as a great big motion picture star from the time I was six. I didn't like being lost in a crowd of kid extras, so I started to pretend I was a star."

At times it must have been difficult for the Young and Traxler families to accept Gretchen's ambition, but they did so with good humor. According to one of the family's favorite stories, eight-year-old Gretchen once haughtily said to her aunt, who was busy with housework, "Someday, Aunt Colly, when I'm a star, I'll buy you a new broom."

At the time the house was filled with children. Since Gladys preferred families with children at the boarding-house, there were always lots of children to play with in addition to her sisters and cousins.

A favorite game around the house was dibbies, a movie star-oriented diversion. Gretchen has explained: "You would have to get up early in the morning to 'dib' the movie star you wanted for your boyfriend that day. We had a black-board, and I would always put dibbies on Ronald Colman. He was the epitome of romance, even for an eight-year-old."

Gretchen returned to the silver screen in 1921, when all the Young children were employed as extras in *The Sheik,* starring the biggest male star of the day, Rudolph Valentino.

"We were out on the desert someplace," Polly Ann has recalled, "and Mamma managed to get the only tent that had a bath. It was a canvas tub affair but everybody else was sore because we had it. We used to try to stay up as late as we could at night because Valentino would play the guitar and sing."

The matinee heartthrob also used to play with a pet snake. "He'd wind it around his neck and scare everybody to death with it," remembered Polly.

By this time Gretchen had earned an affectionate nickname

from her siblings: Gretch the Wretch. But not even her sisters' well-meant put-downs could deter her from what she wanted most in life—to become a major screen idol. "I was a very wanting child," she has recalled. "I was forever wanting something, and for whatever I wanted, I prayed. . . . I took for granted: you wanted; you prayed; you got."

But there were moments in Gretchen's early life when she was brought back down to earth, sometimes rather abruptly. At one of the parochial elementary schools she attended, she had been forced to wear a uniform. When she transferred to another school, she did not have to wear a uniform—but uniforms were all she had.

The other students cruelly made fun of her. Miss Young has remembered, "The day that one of the girls asked 'Haven't you any dresses at *all?*' her tone really shriveled my pride and I came home crying."

But Gladys Young would not tolerate tears. In a no-nonsense way, Mrs. Young explained the facts of life to little Gretchen: there was no money to buy dresses, but she could take pride in having uniforms that were always clean and neat. "She expected me to adjust to the fact that the uniforms had to be worn," Miss Young has said. "She made me feel proud of their cleanness. She made me proud to be different. And I know that this gave me an independence which has helped me in my work and in my life." Despite this pride, it is probable that Miss Young's later interest in owning and wearing beautiful, expensive clothing arises from her schoolgirl trauma.

Because her family lived in Hollywood and sometimes worked in films, Gretchen often had firsthand experiences with stars, unlike other youngsters in America. One Saturday afternoon, while Gretchen stood on a street corner, waiting for a traffic signal to change, Ronald Colman drove up in his roadster.

"For a minute I didn't know whether it was part of my daydream, and I just stood with my mouth hanging open," recalled Gretchen. "He must have felt me staring at him, because he looked at me and then he smiled. I was thunderstruck. The signal changed and off he went, and I just stood there for about five minutes. I remember thinking after he drove off that when I was a big star—and I was always sure I was going to be a Big Star, not just an actress—I was going to smile at everyone who looked at me."

At this point Mrs. Young didn't discourage her daughters' dreams. She enrolled Betty Jane in the Miriam Nolker Dramatic School for Girls—a respected organization, not one of the many fly-by-night schools around Hollywood that made empty promises of getting girls into films. The Nolker School curriculum resembled a finishing school's, concentrating on such things as posture, deportment, and articulation. One of Betty Jane Young's older classmates was a blue-eyed blonde named Jane Peters. Jane would later change her name to Carole Lombard.

By this time Mrs. Young had succeeded in obtaining a divorce from the vanished John Earle Young so she could marry George Belzer, a boarder at her boardinghouse. Belzer was a man Gladys and her children could depend on —staid and reliable, with a steady job as an accountant. Gladys married Belzer in 1923.

Some intimates say that Gretchen's "big star" behavior at home was responsible for Mrs. Belzer's enrolling all her daughters in the Ramona Convent boarding school in Alhambra, California, not far from their home. One might also assume that Mrs. Belzer had decided it was time for some stability in the girls' education, since they had all changed schools so frequently.

Boarding school was an unwelcome surprise for Gretchen. Often lonely at the convent, Gretchen would creep into Bet's room at night and crawl into her sister's bed. Gretchen coped with these austere convent days by daydreaming of how wonderful things were going to be once she became a real movie star.

The years at the convent school were not totally wasted, however. While there, Gretchen learned "the inflexibility of rules," she says, "and I learned that gentle tones and good manners, as exemplified by the sisters, are not the badge of a Milquetoast."

Gretchen would subsequently adopt this "gentle tones, good manners" approach and combine it with a will of steel.

The Young sisters eagerly looked forward to weekends and vacations, when they could go home to visit their mother. They enjoyed staging plays and sketches for their family, emulating their idols of the time, the Francisco Sisters. "We copied the way they did their hair and tried to talk like them and everything," recalled Gretchen years later.

Pol and Bet left boarding school and returned home, occasionally doing bit roles in films. They attended the Immaculate Heart School in Hollywood, while Gretchen returned alone to Ramona Convent for one more year.

The convent experience did not alter Gretchen's goal: she still wanted to be an actress, and had faith that God would eventually present her with the opportunity to follow through on her dream.

In the Belzer household, meanwhile, things were happening at a fast and furious pace. Mamma, at the age of thirty-six, had had another baby girl, named Georgina (later called Georgianna). Gladys also began attending art school at the Chouinard Art Institute and became interested in interior decorating.

Gladys's eldest daughters, Polly Ann and Betty Jane, had blossomed into beautiful and popular teenagers, attending elegant tea dances together in hotel ballrooms.

"Tea dances" were the vogue in the nineteen twenties— these were afternoon get-togethers for the young set, usually in hotel ballrooms, complete with full orchestras providing the music for dancing. "Pol" and "Bet," surrounded by their friends on the dance floor, danced the Charleston, the Black Bottom, and all the other popular numbers.

It was at the tea dances that the Young sisters met Milton Bren, a second assistant director at M-G-M. The studio was doing a college comedy starring Billy Haines, and Bren was casting around for extras for a dance sequence. Betty Jane recalled, "He came to a tea dance and took us back to the studio."

Through friends the girls obtained other bit parts and extra work at the studios. It was around this time that Betty got her first "big break": Carl Laemmle, Jr., picked her to play in one of his college pictures at Universal. "Junior" Laemmle wrote and directed a popular "collegian" series of films, and was famous in Hollywood for filling his movies with exceptionally beautiful young women.

"I got fifty dollars a week," recalled Betty Jane. "But that didn't mean much, because we had no car and I was too young to drive anyhow, and it meant I had a two-hour bus ride every day to the studio."

Polly Ann and Betty Jane were constantly courted by handsome young men in the industry. The Belzer home seemed like a happy clubhouse for young people. Gladys had very wisely encouraged the girls' social lives to be centered around their home.

After her work at Universal, Betty Jane was offered a contract at Paramount, where the studio changed her name to Sally Blane. "Sally Blane sounded all right at the time," Betty Jane recalled, "because I'd been doing those flip collegian things."

During 1927 Sally quickly became one of the most popular and well-liked starlets in the business. At Paramount she appeared in *Casey at the Bat,* then filmed *Dead Man's Curves* opposite dashing Douglas Fairbanks, Jr., at FBO studio, known later as RKO.

Fairbanks today fondly recalls the Young girls. He dated Sally and Polly Ann as friends, but never, he says, in the "romantic" sense. "We used to go to dances on Friday, and so forth. Sally and Polly Ann, they were my favorites. Gretchen was just a little kid with pigtails. When I first knew her she was about fourteen or so, and always trying to 'horn in' on us older kids of seventeen, eighteen, nineteen. 'Where are you going?' she would always ask. 'What are you going to do?' She was the 'kid sister.' "

In the midst of her sisters' burgeoning careers, Gretchen looked on impatiently, "no longer a child, not yet a woman."

"I dreamed my dreams and sat by the telephone," she recalled. "Ours was the fastest-answered telephone in town!"

Then came the call that all aspiring starlets dream about—but it wasn't for her! Over the years, many variations of this tale have surfaced. Sally Blane has recalled that one day First National studio called the Young household, asking Polly Ann to read for a part. Polly Ann was shooting on location at the time, however, so Gretchen took the call instead. "She didn't say, 'Pol isn't here,' " recalled Miss Blane. "She just put on long stockings, went over, and got the job."

Director Mervyn LeRoy, the man who made the telephone call, remembers a less calculating version. According to LeRoy, he was trying to reach Sally Blane, not Polly Ann. "Her mother answered the telephone and told me Sally was away, making a picture in Denver." Disappointed, LeRoy told Mrs. Belzer, "That's too bad. I'm about to start a picture and I had a part I thought she would be right for."

As LeRoy tells it, Mrs. Belzer then replied, "Well, obviously Sally can't do it. Her picture just started shooting a few days ago. But I do have another daughter."

LeRoy was dubious. "Is she pretty?" he asked. "Can she act?" (LeRoy later noted, "In Hollywood in those days, that was the order in which you asked about the talent of potential leading ladies. Today, whether for good or evil, the questions are reversed.")

Mrs. Belzer eagerly replied, "I think she's just as pretty as Sally, maybe even prettier. And yes, she can act too."

In retrospect this story sounds a bit farfetched. Mrs. Belzer *always* referred to her children by their given names, not by their stage names. And she certainly was not a "stage mother" who would promote the career of her school-age daughter.

An even more ridiculous account was later circulated in Miss Young's official studio biographies. They would claim it had been Gretchen's younger brother Jack who took the call. "Polly Ann's not home," he reportedly said, "but Loretta is and they look just about alike."

Miss Young herself has confirmed that, indeed, she took the fateful call herself. According to her account, when Mervyn LeRoy asked to speak to Polly Ann, Gretchen explained that her sister was working on location and wouldn't be back until the next week.

LeRoy wanted Polly Ann for a scene that was to be shot in two days. "I took a deep breath," recalled Gretchen. "So what if Pol was four years older? I was taller!"

Gretchen offered her own services as an actress to LeRoy. "Who are *you?*" he asked.

"I'm Gretchen, and I'm an actress too. And I'm available."

LeRoy was unsure. But as a Hollywood director he knew that survival in the movie industry meant occasionally taking such risks. "Come on out to the studio, Gretchen," he finally told the young girl. "Since you're an actress, too, let's have a look at you."

The most likely version of the story is that after Gretchen received the phone call from LeRoy, she simply left for First National studios without telling the director her true identity. When she got to the studio, she told the man at the gate she was "Miss Young" and that Mr. LeRoy was expecting her. When LeRoy finally saw the scrawny girl, he was amused. Obviously, he could not use her in the role for which he had wanted the eighteen-year-old Polly Ann. He was so taken by the youngster's enthusiasm, however, that he found a place for her as a child extra.

Once on the set, Loretta "appraised the other 'kids' in the scene," she recalled, "and watched the star, Colleen Moore." Loretta was truly fascinated by Colleen Moore, who was everything the young girl dreamed of being.

"I watched her like a hawk," Miss Young has remembered.

And yet, in Gretchen's eyes Miss Moore was not beautiful, elegant, graceful, or queenly, all of which Young had thought essential for stardom. And Moore's eyes were different colors —one blue, one brown. One thing Gretchen had to admit to herself, however, and that was that Miss Moore *was* a star. And Gretchen just "had to know why."

Her conclusions: Miss Moore "was like electricity! She sparkled with enthusiasm. She had a happiness about her. She talked to everybody and anybody, and she let anybody tell her any old idea anybody thought up, and she listened as though she cared!"

While Gretchen was watching Colleen Moore, Colleen Moore was watching Gretchen. Miss Moore (now Mrs. Homer Hargrave) still remembers when she first noticed the young actress. "She was a beautiful child. She had huge gray eyes. She watched everything, studied everyone. She seemed to be all business, and I got the studio to make a test of her. When we looked at the test, they said, 'But her teeth stick out!' 'Good Lord,' I said, 'she's only fourteen—haven't you ever heard of braces?' So the studio got her braces and a retainer."

Then there was the matter of her name. The studio executives thought Gretchen's name sounded too "Dutchy." "I liked everything about her but her name," says Mervyn LeRoy. "To me she was not a 'Gretchen'—that name always struck me as very hard. Teutonic. This girl was light and airy, flowerlike and dainty. I wanted a name more in keeping with her appearance and her personality.

" 'How about Loretta?' I said.

" 'I like it,' she said, without any hesitation.

"Thus, Loretta Young was born that day in my office. She was my first discovery."

Loretta's account, however, is not nearly as romantic as LeRoy's. As Loretta recalled, she was summoned to the office of executive Al Rockett, politely told she was being put under contract to First National, and that her name had been changed by Colleen Moore. Gretchen was agreeable, of course, and contracts were drawn up for her mother to sign.

Years later, Colleen Moore was on the set of a movie Loretta was making and heard her tell an interviewer, "Colleen named me—she named me after her patron saint."

Miss Moore recalls, "I interrupted. 'No, Loretta. I didn't name you after my patron saint—I don't even know who my patron saint is. I named you after a favorite doll.' "

As a child, Miss Moore had been entranced by a fairy tale about Gasparilla, the pirate, and the beautiful princess Laurita. Colleen had named her favorite doll Laurita. When the studio executives were trying to decide on a new name for Gretchen Young, Colleen Moore suggested Laurita. "Too foreign," they said. The decision was to make it Loretta.

Two

"Loretta Young" was not an overnight sensation. She was under contract, but was still used only as a bit player.

Through this transitional period, Loretta was not greatly concerned about her looks. She realized that becoming a star wasn't dependent on beauty alone.

Her cleverness was an asset every bit as important as her good looks. Sally Blane has told of a movie scene in which Loretta and a group of girls were to run first to one end of a long corridor, then the other. Cameras were stationed at both ends to film the girls' reactions.

"Loretta would run like the devil so that she'd be sure to be in front and get her face on the screen. Then she'd slow down and let the others pass her so that when they ran the other way, she'd be out front again. Isn't that bright? You see," Sally has stated, "the instinct to survive was built in."

This ability to set herself apart from the crowd—and get away with it—was rare and coveted. In ensuing years, people would resent Loretta's independence and confidence. Obviously, had she seemed even somewhat insecure, she would have been much easier to manipulate.

Loretta herself has often commented on her early determination: "From somewhere I always got some idea which kept me from being lost—at least in my own estimation. I ran faster than the other kids if we were supposed to run in a scene; I lagged if we were supposed to walk; I sat down if all the rest were standing; I stood tall if all the rest were seated. I simply moved against the crowd, and if all it got me was a reprimand from the director, well, that's better than no attention, isn't it?"

John Engstead was a budding young photographer working at Paramount. "A friend of mine was Sally Blane—pretty, vivacious, and too happy to put up the big fight for stardom," Engstead recalled, his observation bringing into focus the difference between Miss Blane and her more ambitious younger sister. "Sally acted in a few movies, but her main profession was posing for publicity pictures, which is how I got to know her."

Engstead got to know all three Young sisters and their mother. He has remembered, "One Saturday afternoon Sally came in to see her publicity man. Dragging along behind her was her thirteen-year-old sister Gretchen, pigtailed and so shy she wouldn't open her mouth. A year later, I saw Gretchen completely transformed."

Once under contract, Loretta left school after completing the eighth grade and continued her education with private tutors. As is the case with many show business children, Loretta's academic education was, in her words, "subnormal."

Loretta was not an avid student; her interest was focused solely on the movie business. She was impatient for her career to take off, jealous of actresses like Janet Gaynor, who were getting roles Loretta felt she could play.

Young once again worked with Colleen Moore, this time playing a young adult in *Naughty but Nice* when she was fourteen. Although Loretta was only a teenager, she photographed as someone much older and more sophisticated. And since these were silent pictures, her voice would not betray her age.

Precocious Loretta felt that she and Colleen Moore had much in common. Colleen, too, had been determined to become a star from a very early age, having to work harder than most because she could not rely on good looks alone to pay her way.

Also, Miss Moore was a loving person—another trait Loretta felt they shared—and possessed the colorful imagination so essential for an actress.

However, Colleen Moore was not the star Loretta chose to emulate. That honor befell Corinne Griffith, a great beauty of the day who was both very glamorous and very wealthy. Griffith was one of the biggest stars of the silent screen, and youthful Loretta's living ideal of a proper movie queen.

"But she couldn't live forever, could she?" observed the ambitious young actress, and she went about doing everything she could to make herself look and act like Corinne Griffith.

Loretta's recollections of herself at this time make her sound like a baby Eve from *All About Eve*. As Loretta recalls, she "haunted [Griffith's] sets when she was working, trailed her all over the lot. . . . I copied her makeup, her hairdo, her mannerisms, her voice, her walk." And within the severe limitations of her budget, she also tried to copy her clothes.

For a while Loretta felt she was succeeding in being the "young" Corinne Griffith. Then one day Al Rockett called her into his office and told her, "No matter how hard you try, you'll never be anything but a second-rate Corinne Griffith. Why don't you try to make something first-rate out of Loretta Young?"

Rockett's words hit the girl like a sharp smack in the face. Her ego was crushed. But when the hurt and humiliation subsided, she realized he was right—and Loretta Young was never a person to ignore good advice.

At home, meanwhile, the rest of the Young family did not quite take Gretchen's budding career as seriously as "Loretta" did. Gordon Oliver, a former actor, retired television executive, and friend of the Young family for over fifty-five years, recalls, "They moved around a lot in those days." Oliver remembers the Belzers having rented houses on Oxford Street, Wilton Street, and West Fifth Street. Each place became "the clubhouse." With fond recollection he adds, "You must remember they were beautiful girls, and a lot of us young fellows would stop by the house to try to date them and take them out dancing."

Even then, he recalls, Mrs. Belzer was a handsome, charming woman—but the girls were knockouts! "They were all making films at the time," Oliver remembers. "Sally was doing better at first," even though, in his opinion, Polly Ann was the better actress. But as Oliver puts it, she just "didn't get the breaks."

Although Gretchen had a contract and was working at the studios as were both Bet and Polly Ann, she was still only a fourteen-year-old adolescent, while her sisters were seventeen- and nineteen-year-old women with active social lives.

One of the young men Polly Ann dated was Marion Michael Morrison (called "Duke"), a student and football player at the University of Southern California. After breaking up with Polly Ann, Duke met Gretchen's pal, the very young Josie Saenz, and it was love at first sight. Josie was four years younger than Duke. (The Saenz family opposed Josie's choice, and kept the couple apart for some years.) But Josie was two years older than Gretchen, who was still, in Mrs. Belzer's opinion, too young to date.

"I guess I was Loretta's first date," says Gordon Oliver. Every time he visited the Belzer household, "there was Loretta, kind of posing, competing with her older sisters. One night when I stopped by, neither Polly Ann nor Sally were around and Mamma said, 'Oh, take Gretchen.' " Oliver took her dancing at the Cocoanut Grove, where the rest of the gang was sure to be. Prohibition liquor was not served publicly—at least not legally—so there was no age restriction for youngsters in clubs or dance halls. More importantly, it was an era of "gangs," "crowds," "cliques"—group dating was the vogue.

The clique to which Sally and Polly Ann belonged would be the envy of anyone, especially if she was an aspiring young actress like Loretta Young. One of Sally's friends was nineteen-year-old Carole Lombard. One of Polly Ann's pals was twenty-three-year-old rising star Joan Crawford (who admitted to being nineteen).

One night Crawford stopped by the Youngs' house to pick up Sally and Polly Ann. The gang was going dancing at the Grove and young Gretchen begged to tag along. When Mrs. Belzer said, "Take Gretchen," the older girls reluctantly agreed.

At the Grove the table of beauties was the center of attention, and many of the young men focused on the sparkling newcomer. Crawford turned to the Young sisters and said, "This is the last time we take Gretchen."

Although still very young, Gretchen was successfully competing with her sisters both socially and professionally, and soon her career would overtake theirs.

Loretta's "adult" career began with *Her Wild Oat,* starring Colleen Moore, and *The Whip Woman.* Though the films' titles sound silly, the people who made these now forgotten movies were top-drawer talents and in Hollywood's vanguard.

They were hardly a staid or stately group. Marshall ("Mickey") Neilan, director of *Her Wild Oat,* was a notorious ladies' man, typical of the roaring twenties pleasure-seeking Hollywood roué. A talented singer and actor in addition to being a director, Neilan was an unpredictable carouser who often disappeared for days on end, holding up production until he returned and resumed his responsibilities without a word of apology. He could not have failed to make an impression on a sheltered, convent-educated fourteen-year-old.

"Girls in studios are exposed to more temptation than other girls face," Loretta later observed. "They are not protected from life the way other girls are. Things are said to them or in front of them that aren't exactly proper, to put it mildly." Loretta didn't like it, but she didn't let it bother her. "I put it all outside," she has said, noting, "I think my mother deserves a lot of credit for bringing up three girls decently in Hollywood."

Loretta was exposed to another group of top-flight artists in her next film, *The Whip Woman*. It was produced by Allan Dwan, a man of immense talent and taste, who was instrumental in furthering the careers of many top actresses, including Gloria Swanson and, later, Carole Lombard.

The star of *The Whip Woman* was Estelle Taylor, no stranger to front-page headlines as the wife of legendary prizefighter Jack Dempsey. Taylor's leading man was Antonio Moreno, a handsome Latin of whom actress Aileen Pringle once said, "Obviously he's never had an idea above the waist."

During production of *The Whip Woman* Loretta was noticed by another actress in the cast—Hedda Hopper, a chic middle-aged woman who had made headlines on her own (long before she started writing them) by marrying the elderly stage star DeWolf Hopper while still in her teens.

Many years later Miss Hopper would observe of Loretta, "Even as a child, she knew what she wanted; I was fascinated to see how her career developed, since I was there before she *had* any career."

Loretta's career was taking off during a time which many experts regard as Hollywood's heyday—a time when today's soda jerk could be tomorrow's screen idol. "To F. Scott Fitzgerald it was the Lost Generation," Miss Hopper noted. "To Hollywood it was the Golden Twenties. Everything turned to money. Girls were plucked from the ribbon counter, from Hungary without their being able to speak a word of English; small-town clerks and collar-ad boys all were fitted into the Hollywood mold."

The "Hollywood mold" was carefully cultivated by the Hollywood publicity machine, and at First National, as at other studios, publicity was all-important. An integral part of the publicity buildup were photos of the stars, often taken in provocative poses. But Loretta Young's instincts and family upbringing obviously helped her in navigating the perilous waters of Hollywood promotion this early in the game.

"I wouldn't do drape art," Miss Young remembered. "Drape, you know, is wearing a piece of chiffon, getting as close to striptease as you can. I wasn't at all diplomatic. I just refused to come to the studio." Young later claimed she didn't know why she refused but speculated that she just had an innate sense that drape art wasn't right for her. It's a good example of her unerring feelings about her screen image.

Over at M-G-M, Herbert Brenon was directing Lon Chaney in the circus film *Laugh, Clown, Laugh,* but hadn't yet found the young girl "just right" to play the leading character of Simonetta. After dozens of starlets had been tested, Brenon spotted Loretta in *The Whip Woman* and decided to give her a crack at the role. The picture was scheduled to begin production in early 1928, so Brenon would have to make his decision quickly.

Since the story required Simonetta to appear in revealing circus costumes of leotards and tights, Loretta's extremely thin physique was a potential problem. But her face—her liquid eyes—was perfect for the part, and Brenon was uncertain what to do.

When he screened Loretta's test for friends, everyone agreed that Loretta's face was so beautiful no one would notice her legs.

One can imagine the height of Loretta's elation when Al

Rockett told her she had the role. She would be playing opposite the already legendary Lon Chaney in a major film at M-G-M. A modern parallel would be a teenager who, after making two minor appearances, is then signed to star opposite Laurence Olivier.

Loretta's extreme youth was not an asset. This was five decades before the dawn of Brooke Shields as the first child–leading woman. Some people have said Loretta fibbed about her age, claiming she was sixteen. She had a birthday on the set, and one report later claimed she said it was her seventeenth. In fact she turned fifteen on January 6, 1928, while still in the middle of shooting *Laugh, Clown, Laugh.*

The problem of her thinness, meanwhile, had been solved by the wardrobe department. "I had the most divine figure that ever walked in front of a camera, courtesy of the studio," recalled the adult Miss Young. "It was all pads—false hips, false front, false behind."

The golden opportunity of this major role came equipped with painful thorns. This was a *leading* role, and required a skilled actress. A certain standard of technical expertise was expected, and Loretta had no previous experience for a part of this magnitude.

One of Loretta's costars in the film was Nils Asther. He and Loretta were playing a scene together in which the young girl was to gaze at him with longing passion. The scene was not going well, and Asther decided to take matters into his own hands. He supposedly suggested to Loretta that while gazing at him she think of a gooey ice cream sundae. His advice apparently produced the desired effect and Loretta delighted in telling the story in later years.

Director Brenon, however, was not as kind or patient as Asther. Brenon expected Loretta to deliver a solid performance, and it must have come as quite a shock to the young girl when the director incessantly bombarded her with harsh criticism.

It was a baptism by fire. Brenon had the reputation of driving established stars crazy. Stars, however, could at least yell back at him, using his own language. But Loretta was neither a star nor vulgar. At this point she became desperate. Many days she ran off the set weeping uncontrollably, after Brenon had screamed at her.

But Loretta never cried to her mother. "Loretta cried, and cried plenty, but she wept alone in her dressing room," recalled an observer.

Though this often delayed production, Loretta wasn't fired or replaced. Obviously Brenon and the front office liked what they saw on screen. If they hadn't, Loretta Young—hardly a box office name—would have been out of a job.

Brenon's bluster, however, continued at an almost hysterical level. One day, during a difficult and highly emotional scene, Brenon yelled at Loretta, "You should be ashamed—such a pretty girl, but such a rotten actress. If I hadn't already shot so many of your scenes, I'd chuck you right out of the picture. But maybe I won't need to do that. Maybe we could finish with your sister, Sally Blane; she looks just like you and is a better actress."

Loretta's face flushed. Lon Chaney took Brenon aside. "Go easy, Herb," he told the director. "Aren't you a little hard on the poor kid?"

Brenon turned to him and replied, "It's the only way, Lon. It will make an actress out of the girl."

This may have been true, but the price Loretta had to pay was a heavy one. Brenon destroyed whatever self-confidence the youngster had and she remained "terrified throughout the picture."

Nothing she did seemed to please the director, and his sudden fits of violence were something she had never experienced before. At one point during shooting he threw a chair at Loretta, missing his target but terrifying the girl.

Loretta herself has stated, "He shouted at me that I was terrible. I knew I was and that didn't make it any better."

Her pride was shattered; he had humiliated her in front of everyone.

Loretta walked off the set and did not return for several days. But she was then uneasy about her defiance. She later recalled, "I once called a director everything I could think of and then spent the next three days figuring out how I could get back on the set." She also remembered, "I blew up. I proceeded to weep myself into a state of hysteria violent enough to turn the most temperamental prima-donna green. Production had to stop for three whole days because of me. I sat home in injured dignity until I'd forced an apology." But Loretta conceded, "It was a great waste of effort. They weren't impressed. They were pained at my pettiness."

Their egos were not "pained," only their pocketbooks. But the film was well into production and M-G-M needed to finish it on schedule. Loretta was cajoled into returning to work by Lon Chaney, who said to the youngster words to the effect, "Listen, kid, this is a hard game. They know you can do it or you wouldn't be here. Now, come on, let's try again. Besides, nothing like this is worth breaking your heart over. Work is what's important. Tears won't change things one way or another. Don't cry—no director's worth it."

But the experience left a deep, deep wound.

When shooting was over, Brenon told Loretta, "I know I gave you a very rough time on this picture. But I'm not interested in you, just in your performance. You gave one."

The message was clear—personal feelings about Loretta had nothing to do with Brenon's treatment of her. The end result—the performance—was all that mattered to him. But it didn't soothe the fifteen-year-old girl. Her experience with Brenon was so alien to anything she had encountered—so different from the kindly Mr. Rockett, the flip and amiable Mervyn LeRoy, the responsive Colleen Moore, and the family feeling at First National—that it almost completely devastated her.

Even though she was passing herself off as a Hollywood

sophisticate, she was still an adolescent emotionally. This was the shock therapy of the "big time," and Loretta had not been prepared for it. However, with her typical resolve, she devised a method to survive. She later revealed, "For four long years after *Laugh, Clown, Laugh,* my pride made me wear, like a sort of costume, an air of self-confidence. I couldn't bear it if anyone knew I had hardly any self-confidence at all. I had to make believe I had it—I knew I couldn't ever be a star without it."

Laugh, Clown, Laugh was viewed primarily as a typical Lon Chaney vehicle, another showcase for the amazing abilities of "The Man of a Thousand Faces."

But Loretta Young's contribution to the picture was not totally overlooked. Powerful Hearst columnist Louella Parsons singled her out for praise—a very important break for a budding career. Parsons had found "childlike Loretta Young . . . promising," and that was money in the bank. But Parsons also compared her to another actress, Betty Bronson, and that couldn't have pleased Loretta very much.

After *Laugh, Clown, Laugh* Loretta was lent to Paramount, for *The Magnificent Flirt,* in which she'd portray Florence Vidor's daughter. At Paramount was Bet's pal, John Engstead. He now met "Loretta"—not "Gretchen." "Her shyness had completely disappeared. The pigtails had been replaced by a bun at the nape of her neck and the dress had changed from calico to a long sequined affair, with bust pads filling out what nature hadn't gotten around to."

Engstead also noted, "Beautiful Loretta was smart enough to learn quickly the trick of posing for still photographs. But only the important ones—she kept as far away as she could from those silly gag pictures." Engstead meant the "Miss Valentine," "Miss New Year's Eve," kind of publicity photo which often got wide pickup, but also typed the actress.

Though her self-confident airs may have fooled people at Paramount, Loretta's "star" behavior was not appreciated at home. "The breaks were coming my way," she remembered. "I took them, every one of them, as my due—and behaved accordingly." In those years, Loretta has said, she easily could have won "the undisputed title of Miss Obnoxious." Her sisters, however, devised small ways for pricking her overinflated ego. They would address her as "Your Highness" or "The Princess," and on occasion would bow when Loretta entered a room.

Pol and Bet had had quite enough of Gretch the Wretch and her constant pretentiousness. Each evening at dinner she treated them to the same sort of scene—a nonstop litany of self-praise, complaints about the way things were going at the studio, and afterwards "retiring" to her room for her beauty sleep, announcing what time she'd like to have breakfast in the morning.

The older girls decided that if words could not get through to her, perhaps actions would.

They made a huge, ugly star out of old newspapers and pasted it on the door of Gretchen's bedroom. Little sister had always been very vocal about that magic day when a golden star would shine from her dressing room door.

That night when Gretchen swept upstairs after dinner, she stopped dead in her tracks in front of her bedroom door. When she saw the star, she was devastated. She instantly got the message, and she did not recover quickly.

One of her sisters revealed years later, "Gretch said that we hurt her deeply, and I guess we did." At the time, Loretta pretended to ignore the star; weeks went by without any comment. The girls and Mamma realized they had made their point, perhaps a bit too well. Loretta was temporarily subdued. She had not acknowledged the star, but instead quietly continued to live with the talisman pinned to her door. Knowing her as well as they did, the family realized that she had dealt with this as she had dealt with every previous blow to her ego—she swore to overcome it. She would not let anyone know the hurt, and would instead rise above the pain.

Finally, after several weeks, Loretta's sisters took the star down. Just as she had not acknowledged its presence, she did not now acknowledge its disappearance. But Loretta revealed years later that she was grateful when it was gone. It took her years to tell her sisters that she understood what they had done and, indeed, was grateful to them.

But at the time this prima donna behavior of Loretta's continued to be a difficulty for the Youngs. Even Loretta later admitted that the usual adolescent problems of her own children were nothing in comparison to the trouble she had given her mother when she was a teenager. When she didn't get an expected fur coat at Christmas time, she was so upset that, in her words, "I succeeded in completely ruining the holiday for the whole family."

Loretta was earning a great deal of money—two hundred and fifty dollars a week—and she yearned to live like a star. One day she announced to her mother that she was buying a Venetian-style bedroom set for her own room. Mrs. Belzer, a woman of innate good taste, must have been horrified, but remained silent and lived quietly with the hideous furniture for six months.

Loretta appeared in six films in 1928, an amazing feat by modern standards. After *Laugh, Clown, Laugh* and *The Magnificent Flirt,* she made *The Head Man.* Then *Scarlet Seas,* starring Richard Barthelmess, one of the ten top stars of silent pictures.

Offscreen, Loretta had the same romantic fantasies of the characters she portrayed. But when it came to playing love scenes onscreen, Loretta discovered she was not as sophisticated as she pretended.

"The first time I did a love scene, I was so self-conscious I could hardly stand it," she recalled. "The scene was with Richard Barthelmess, who was an idol of mine. His mere proximity was enough to set me to shaking, to say nothing of his taking me in his arms and kissing me.

"He sensed how wrought up I was. He asked, 'Are you embarrassed?' I managed to squeak, 'Terribly.' He said, 'You mustn't be. This is just another scene. Just part of the day's work.'

"I suppose every beginner goes through the same thing and lives to see the scenes as part of the business of acting and nothing else."

Barthelmess's career was about to take an abrupt nosedive, however, as the grand silent era of movies finally came to an end. "Talkies" had caught on, and big stars who didn't have "microphone voices" were on the precipice of professional doom.

"I was caught up in the panic that hit Hollywood at that time," recalled Loretta. "Top stars who looked like they would last forever were discarded overnight."

The Squall, her first of six pictures in 1929, was to be Loretta's testing ground for the new era. "The most crucial test I ever went through was for *The Squall.* If I did not come through that sound test, I knew that I would join that great lost legion that was counted out when sound came in." But Loretta's voice would prove to be perfect for the new dimension of sound in films.

Alexander Korda directed Loretta and the promising young actress Myrna Loy in *The Squall.* Miss Loy played the lead, and had to wear a thick layer of dark makeup to make her look Gypsy-Hungarian. Actor Carroll Nye was also in the cast, and quickly became a close friend of the Young sisters.

He remembers Loretta as "a sweet kid who liked to have spelling bees on the set. Polly Ann was the 'little mother,' Sally was the 'sexpot,' Georgianna 'the baby.' But Loretta was the ambitious one."

The script for *The Squall* was ludicrous. For both Loy and Loretta, however, the picture served a valuable purpose: it proved to the industry that both actresses were perfect "talking ladies."

Despite the idealized vision people have of Hollywood in

the roaring twenties—flappers, starlets, and bathtub gin—
Loretta's memories of it are quite different. "In those days,
you didn't have fun on the set. You had 'fun' if you did your
work well. There was no such thing as kidding around or
joking. It was a dead-serious business."

Actors and actresses worked long, hard hours in those days
before the actors' unions. Players sometimes worked six days
a week, day and night. Ralph Bellamy claims "it was really
seven. You'd come to work Saturday morning at the usual
time and work all day, all night, through the night, until the
leading lady fainted Sunday noon."

There was also no set minimum time between calls. If an
actor finished filming at midnight, his next shooting call
could be anytime, sometimes as early as six A.M., and often
even earlier. Actors crossed from one film to another, and
leading players often appeared in up to twelve pictures per
year.

With this kind of work schedule, Loretta saw little of her
family. But one of the happiest birthday parties Loretta recalls occurred when she came home late from shooting one
night to discover a tiny cake and candles on a little table, with
a note reading, "Dear Gretch, I waited up as long as I could.
Wake me up when you get in. Happy Birthday!" She woke
up sister Bet and together they had a midnight party.

Of all the studios, Warners had the worst reputation for
overworking its stars. Joan Blondell recalled walking off the
lot to check herself into a hospital, suffering from such total
exhaustion that her eyes would not stop blinking and she
could not stop stuttering.

Although Loretta was always cooperative and willing to
work, the pace was draining, and years later she told John
Engstead of the physical toll of those hectic years. Engstead
has noted, "Loretta played leads in one picture after another.
The California law stipulates that a minor can only work four
hours a day and cannot work after five o'clock, and that a
teacher must be present at all times. Whenever one of Loret-

ta's productions was behind schedule, the business manager would ask her to work at night. Eager to be helpful, she would agree. She was told to go back to her dressing room and start changing out of her studio clothes until the teacher left for home. Loretta would then rush back to the set and work until nine or ten o'clock and sometimes all night on Saturday. The reward for these long months of working nights was a complete physical breakdown."

Loretta voluntarily checked herself into the hospital, suffering from exhaustion. A studio executive visited her at the hospital. "The man said she was scheduled to start a film the next Monday," recalls Engstead. "He was sorry, but if she couldn't make it she would be taken off salary. And that's what happened. But the long hours lying in the hospital gave Loretta time to think. It dawned on her that it wasn't the old team spirit that motivated the studio executives; it was only money. When she recovered and returned, it was an entirely new girl that drove through the studio gates."

From that moment on, Loretta started dealing with businessmen *as* businessmen.

Although not yet a star, Loretta was now assigned leading lady roles at First National, and the studio decided to team her with a recently signed young male star whose dash and good looks would be a perfect complement.

The actor was a Young family friend: the handsome twenty-one-year-old crown prince of Hollywood, Douglas Fairbanks, Jr. Studio executives hoped Fairbanks and Young could rival Fox's hot team of Charles Farrell and Janet Gaynor.

Fairbanks had recently become engaged to Joan Crawford, who had developed into one of M-G-M's hottest properties. Metro, to cash in on the highly publicized relationship between Crawford and Fairbanks, had already teamed the two in *Our Modern Maidens,* but Fairbanks's picture with Loretta, *The Fast Life,* made it into the theaters first.

It was *Our Modern Maidens* that was the big hit. Nonetheless, First National went ahead and teamed Loretta and Fairbanks again in *The Careless Age*.

"There weren't any great demands put on her in those early days other than to be graceful, which she was naturally," Fairbanks remembers, "and she worked hard at her job." He recalls that Loretta wore braces on her teeth, and she kept wearing them for years, although "she took them off for pictures, of course."

At first, Fairbanks continues, "we didn't like each other at all. I remember wondering, 'What's wrong with me? Why am I being saddled with this "kid"?' " Fairbanks still thought of Loretta as Gretchen, "the kid sister," and he says that she probably thought of him as "pretty snooty. 'Oh, the fellow who's going with my sisters.' And we both tolerated each other.

"She was trying to be older than she was and I was putting her down. But eventually, by the third picture, we got on very well indeed, and we had a joke that we were going to keep her at the age of nineteen for the rest of her life, because when she was only fifteen or sixteen she pretended to be nineteen. When she was twenty, twenty-one, twenty-two, she still said she was nineteen. And that became a running joke with us. I still say today when I see her that she looks just about nineteen or twenty. We became very good friends indeed."

They made *The Forward Pass* together, a college musical costarring the entire USC football team. Loretta sang in this film, surprising everyone with her sweet soprano voice.

Reviewers weren't ecstatic about the Fairbanks-Young team, but the public was. Loretta made more films with Fairbanks—six in all—than with any of her other leading men. Fairbanks came across onscreen with all the style and flair he was expected to deliver. It was usually Loretta's beauty, however, not her ability as an actress, that was singled out for notice.

Warner Bros., meanwhile, had merged with First National studios and moved into First National's Burbank facility. They brought with them Darryl F. Zanuck, who had been with Warners since 1922, and put him in charge of production for the new Warner Bros.–First National organization. Douglas Fairbanks remembers Zanuck as bright and astute, not cut from the same mold as other producers of the day. Much of Loretta's professional life would be directly influenced by Darryl F. Zanuck, who would change her attitudes about the front office and her expectations of top-level executives.

In 1929 Zanuck produced the all-star musical *The Show of Shows,* Warner–First National's answer to M-G-M's blockbuster, *Broadway Melody.* Sound had clicked, but there were still only eight hundred theaters in the country equipped for "talkies," while there were twenty-two thousand showing silent pictures. To promote sound and introduce their roster of contract players, studios were all producing huge musical extravaganzas.

In *The Show of Shows* Loretta and Sally Blane were among a number of "sister acts" introduced by Richard Barthelmess. The girls sang a cute song, but surprisingly, Loretta's singing ability was never utilized in future films. It was also in this production—"A Cast of 77!"—that John Barrymore "Speaks for the First Time!"

At this point, Betty Jane's career as Sally Blane was taking off. She had starred in such pictures as *Rolled Stockings, Eyes of the Underworld,* and *Wolves of the City,* and was featured with the current singing sensation Rudy Vallee in *Vagabond Lover* over at RKO.

Polly Ann, too, was finally getting attention. The previous year she had appeared opposite heartthrob John Gilbert in *Masks of the Devil,* an Irving Thalberg production at M-G-M. Now there were full-page pictures of Polly Ann—coiffed, made up, and costumed à la Clara Bow—in leading fan maga-

zines. It was announced that M-G-M was planning to sign Polly Ann Young and groom her for stardom.

In 1929 both Sally and Loretta were voted Wampas Baby Stars. *Wampas* was derived from the initials of the group that sponsored the event, the Western Association of Motion Picture Advertisers, and starlets voted Wampas Baby Stars were considered prime candidates for stardom. The 1929 group also included Jean Arthur, Anita Page, and Helen Twelvetrees.

Actually, the annual Wampas event was just a great publicity stunt. Advertisers knew that pretty girls, especially in bathing suits, would always get their pictures in the paper. Previous Wampas stars included Colleen Moore (1922), Clara Bow (1924), and Lupe Velez (1928). Thus far, 1926 had been the most successful year for Wampas girls. Six of the thirteen Wampas selections of that year had gone on to stardom: Joan Crawford, Janet Gaynor, Mary Astor, Dolores Del Rio, Fay Wray, and Mary Brian.

Loretta was now sixteen and established at Warners as a leading lady, complete with all the attendant accoutrements: her own studio-assigned makeup man, hairdresser, and wardrobe woman.

Around this time she was lent to Samuel Goldwyn Productions for *The Devil to Pay,* starring opposite her childhood heartthrob, Ronald Colman. Constance Cummings, just then starting her career, had originally been set to star opposite Colman. But producer Goldwyn didn't think she looked British enough for the role—"Too chubby," he said—so he tested Loretta.

"It seems he wanted someone skinnyish, since he thought an English lady should be skinny and tall. That was the only recommendation I had," Loretta remembered with characteristic candor and humor.

Once on the Goldwyn lot, Loretta managed to get into the projection room and saw Constance Cummings's screen test. "She was so marvelous that I got this terrific inferiority complex," recalled Loretta. "It's possible I looked more the part, but I didn't have her talent. I panicked." Nevertheless, Loretta was assigned the female lead and Miss Cummings a smaller role.

This story illustrates Young's astuteness. She made it her business to get into the screening room to see what others had done with the part and what was expected of her.

Filming on *The Devil to Pay* soon hit a snag. Loretta would perform flawlessly in rehearsals with Colman, but once the camera started rolling she would go blank. She finally confided to her speech coach that she had had a terrible crush on Colman for many years. Word got back to the actor and he handled the situation adroitly.

"He wooed me enough to fulfill all my romantic dreams about him," Loretta has said, "and still not enough to encourage me beyond our eight hours on the set." Of course, as Miss Young notes, "being a sixteen-year-old in those days of purity, a touch on the hand was ecstasy."

When filming was over, Colman continued to be kind to the youngster. He would occasionally invite her to social gatherings at his home, but never encouraged her romantic fantasies.

Loretta was fast becoming a star, and the speed of her meteoric rise made her difficult. "I was a willful, stubborn girl," she has recalled, "accustomed to following my impulsive desires." This was not a melodramatic overstatement; her mother's attempts to keep her in line were constantly met with firm resistance.

It was around this time that Loretta met a young Jesuit priest, Father Patrick Ward. She would later report that he did not speak to her flatteringly, as most people speak to a star. He spoke to a foolish young girl going her headstrong way down a bewildering road filled with dangerous curves.

" 'Don't you know,' he said, 'that God didn't give you your talent just so that you could glory in it for the gratification of your ego? It was given to you to develop for His glory. You are in a position to be an example to others. You have no right to lead a selfish personal life. For whether you want it this way or not, as a movie star you will be an example. You dare not be a *bad* example.' "

But before the priest's words could sink in and ostensibly take effect, the impatient and headstrong Miss Young would have to endure possibly the harshest trial of her teenage life.

I thought I knew what I was doing.
—Loretta Young, 1930

Three

He was a very tall, extremely handsome young man, with many of the traits Loretta's errant father had possessed, including a charming personality, an unpredictable nature, and the aura of excitement.

Loretta was now a young woman with a normal female's physical desire and curiosity about the opposite sex, and nature simply took its course.

Grant Withers was dashing—a quality constantly underscored in his publicity. He was the "matinee idol" type that Hollywood was so adept at exploiting. And according to fellow actor James Cagney, he was also "a very talented fella." Although his name means little today, in 1929 he was a hot property among youthful moviegoing audiences.

Withers, born Granville Withers in Pueblo, Colorado, in 1905, came from a reasonably well-to-do family. His grandfather, Gus, owned the local newspaper, *The Pueblo Chieftain.* His father, Ernest Withers, and mother, Nona Newton Withers, lived in a huge two-story brick house on Elizabeth Street, where Grant and his brother, Newton, were born. After attending grade school in Pueblo, Grant was sent to Kemper

Military Academy, then to Centennial High School. At Centennial High, Coach Kettering was happy to have the tall boy on the football and basketball teams, while the dramatic teacher, Miss Heller, cast him as the hero in all the school plays.

Grant Withers was a ladies' man from adolescence into adulthood. He had married and fathered a child by the time he was twenty. But small-town life was not for Grant; he wanted the freedom and thrills found only in the big city.

He had been a police reporter and fire warden in Pueblo before coming to Hollywood, and although his publicity said Withers was a nationally known hero, the truth is, he came to Hollywood as a member of a champion drill crew fire brigade. The team had won a drill competition and their prize was a trip to the FBO lot in Hollywood.

The novelist Elinor Glyn had turned her attention to screen writing, and the self-proclaimed arbiter of sex appeal was continuously on the lookout for people who had "that certain something" so desirable in the movies. One day on the FBO lot Glyn pushed her way through a visiting crowd of burly young firemen to get to a particularly handsome man standing six feet three, with dark, curly hair and blue eyes. Glyn delivered the classic line "How would you like to be in the movies?"

She obtained a bit part for Grant in the currently shooting *Three Weeks,* which was based on her own successful novel. Withers stayed on in Hollywood through the midtwenties, quickly working his way from bit roles to leading man.

His devil-may-care attitude and personality were the perfect reflection of Hollywood in the twenties: a winning combination of charm and aggressiveness, and, like Loretta, he was a star of the silent screen, so his ability to act was not a prerequisite.

Within a relatively short time Withers was starring opposite such top leading ladies as Dolores Costello and Corinne Griffith. Offscreen he appeared the answer to every young girl's dream, although at twenty-five, he was already divorced and the father of a five-year-old son.

"Grant was a gorgeous-looking man," reminisced Joan Blondell. "You couldn't be a full-blooded woman and not respond to Grant. He was like Prince Charming."

But appearances can be deceiving. Hubert Voight, head of M-G-M's New York publicity office, had been lured to Hollywood to head up the publicity operation at Warner Bros.–First National. Voight recalls Withers as "a nasty character." The young Withers also had a reputation at the studio as a heavy drinker.

The front office cast Withers opposite its budding ingenue. Loretta was peeved when she learned her next film was to be a programmer. Hadn't she just co-starred opposite Warners' leading star, John Barrymore, in the comedy *The Man from Blankley's?* It was type casting: the wildly unpredictable Barrymore was playing a drunk and Loretta a young governess.

In *The Second-Floor Mystery,* Withers was to be top-billed, since he was a bigger star than she. His latest film, *In the Headlines,* was a big hit and he was the darling of the fan magazines. Like Loretta, Withers had made an easy transition to talkies, and he was being promoted as "the talking William Haines."

Up to now Loretta had read about "love," seen fellow actors "in love," delivered lines about "love," and exhibited all a young girl's curiosity about "love," but she had never really known love. Her involvement with Withers was a road Loretta had never traveled before.

Apparently the emotions in the scenes Loretta and Grant played before the camera were not turned off after the director yelled "Cut!" By September 1929 there were published reports that the sixteen-year-old Loretta and the divorced Grant were "engaged." But this was columnists' speculation. No such announcement was made by Loretta's family. Her mother and sisters were deeply concerned over Loretta's headstrong behavior and opposed her choice of suitor.

Loretta was envied by others—not only was Withers "a dreamboat," but his star was on the rise. He was set to start filming *Tiger Rose* with Lupe Velez, and then star opposite Billie Dove in *The Other Tomorrow.*

Carroll Nye recalled, "When Loretta was sixteen she asked me if she should marry Grant Withers. I said no. But she was crazy about him—the worst case of puppy love I ever saw."

Subsequent revelations proved that Loretta had been no prude. She and Withers had secretly rented a flat at the El Royale Apartments on North Rossmore; furthermore, they had even furnished it.

Loretta celebrated her seventeenth birthday on January 6, 1930. On January 26 she and Withers carried out their secret decision. The couple chartered an airplane—considered the chic, "in" way to travel since Lindbergh had crossed the Atlantic in *The Spirit of St. Louis* only three years earlier.

Loretta and Grant looked like a *Vogue* ad as they boarded their little plane for Yuma, Arizona. She wore a fitted leather coat, belted at the waist, with a leather flying cap, complete with goggles, hugging her head. Withers, in an ankle-length camel coat, was an Adonis straight out of the Arrow collar ads.

They were married secretly, but the idyll abruptly ended when the newlyweds returned from Yuma. Mrs. Belzer had been shocked and deeply upset by Loretta's act, and she vowed she would have the marriage annulled.

A press conference was held. A distraught but cool-headed Loretta explained that her mother was understandably upset, and Withers solemnly parroted Loretta's responses. He added, "Of course we will defer to Loretta's mother." Gladys Belzer was present, and publicity executives were pleased with the air of "class and authority" she lent the proceedings.

It was assumed by all that Loretta would return to living with her parents until things could be sorted out. But it wasn't typical of Loretta to give up what she wanted without a fight, and time would prove she had a plan.

As far as the public was concerned, the couple was married but not living together, owing to parental intervention.

Florabel Muir reported that Gladys Belzer said Loretta had been brought up in a faith which forbids elopements with civil marriages, and girls of that faith are bound not to marry divorced men.

The press also reported that Withers's mother agreed with Gladys on the inappropriateness of the wedding. Supposedly, Mrs. Withers had been instrumental in breaking up her son's first marriage.

There were mixed feelings among executives at Warners concerning the marriage. Publicity about love and marriage was always an asset in the careers of their contract players. But according to Hubert Voight, "none of us approved. It was a most unfortunate marriage." Voight says that Loretta was "head and shoulders above the other contract players at the studio in breeding and class." He states that people at the studio were very fond of her and were all sad that this lovely girl had become involved with such a carousing character.

More personal problems surfaced. Withers's first wife, Inez, suddenly sued her former husband for increased child support, bringing more unflattering publicity upon the couple.

Then, a few days after the press conference, it came to light that Loretta and Withers had defied her mother and were actually occupying their apartment at the El Royale. George Belzer, Loretta's stepfather, now interceded. He told reporters that Loretta and Withers had attempted to "fool Mrs. Belzer," and said that the couple had deceived them so they could be free to "disappear." This defiance was a shocking development.

Mrs. Belzer's attempt to have the marriage annulled because her daughter was under age had failed. It seemed Loretta and Grant had thought of everything. In California the legal age for a girl to marry without consent was eighteen, but in Arizona it was only sixteen.

On February 6, less than two weeks after the marriage, Mrs. Belzer dropped the annulment suit and with typical resolve announced, "Let the couple make the best of it."

For the first time Loretta Young's name had made headlines. This was not just a puff story publicizing a film; it was a dramatic story about her private life. A "sensational elopement," defiance of parents, a threatened annulment, her subsequent success in avoiding the annulment and staying with her true love—this was the sort of story that propelled starlets from the movie page to page one. The kind of publicity that Loretta Young and her family neither coveted nor liked, and, to this day, try to avoid.

At the time, however, the headstrong teenager told reporters flat out that she and Withers intended to remain married and were deeply in love. "I am extremely happy," she proclaimed. She made no bones about who was running her life: "I love my mother, but I love Grant and he loves me, and that's all that matters."

But she was not unaware of the effect all this might be having on her career. "I couldn't do my best work if we were not married," she said at the time. Work was certainly something Loretta and Grant had plenty of. To capitalize on the publicity, the studio teamed them in a second film, *Too Young to Marry*—a blatant reference to the leading lady's private life. The film was directed by Mervyn LeRoy, and he has recalled that during the shooting Loretta and Withers seemed very much in love.

Virginia Sale, then a young character actress and the sister of comedian Chic Sale, was also in *Too Young to Marry*. Miss Sale had come to Hollywood in 1927, about the time Loretta had signed with First National, and she says, "We all agreed that she didn't know what she had gotten into. But," Miss Sale recalls, "Loretta had a great sense of humor. And she got a lot of kidding about *Too Young to Marry*, since they were just back from their elopement."

In 1930, Loretta starred in five more pictures opposite top

male stars of the day, including Otis Skinner and Conway Tearle, while Withers played the lead in *Sinners' Holiday,* which introduced James Cagney and Joan Blondell to the screen.

Some of the titles of Loretta's pictures seemed to parallel her personal life. In *Road to Paradise,* Loretta played twins, one good, one evil. Then she did *Kismet.*

In her private life with Withers, Loretta unfortunately discovered that the warnings of her family and coworkers were justified. She cared deeply that there was a schism between her and her beloved mother, and it is not surprising that almost from the beginning there were many arguments between Loretta and her husband.

"And then little things began to mount into big ones," recalled Loretta. "I don't think I could ever explain Grant's character. He is disarmingly gentle and sweet."

One of the major problems was money. "He has not the slightest conception of the value of money. Money, to him, is just something one has in one's pockets to pass out to various people for amusements and things. One thing it is *not* to him is a source of paying bills."

The fact that Withers never had any money for the necessities of life—"only the luxuries"—could not be overlooked. With the value of money so deeply instilled in her, "I couldn't reconcile myself to Grant's charming, spendthrift ways while the bills went begging."

Loretta had not forgotten the plight of her childhood: "Things have not always been so comfortable for my family as they are now."

Although Grant and Loretta frequently argued, the marriage did not disintegrate overnight. They tried to make a go of it. Loretta desperately wanted to be able to prove she was right, that she had done the right thing in marrying the man she thought she loved.

But Loretta later said that she never felt she really knew Withers, even after a year of marriage. What Withers had done was to break up her organized life. She was a creature of routine—"certain things at certain times"—and Loretta never knew what Withers was going to do next. "One minute he would swear that he could not accept a picture that would take him on a long location trip because it would mean separation from me—even though I asked him not to. He would say that he wanted nothing more than a 'little dinner at home, just for two,' and a half hour later he would be on the telephone calling up three or four other young couples to come over and join us."

While Withers's freewheeling personality had undoubtedly attracted her at first, its charm soured rapidly. "I wanted to understand him," said Loretta, "because I was so anxious to prove to my family and the rest of the world that I had *not* been impulsive in my marriage. But every day I realized that understanding him was more difficult than I had thought."

Although she never discussed it at the time, others have referred to Withers's drinking and the personality changes it wrought. Alcohol brought out a coarseness in Withers's behavior that Loretta did not know how to handle.

From Withers's point of view, the strain of the whole adventure, combined with his own mother's interference and the career pressures on him, were all too much for a young man interested mainly in "a good time." During his marriage to Loretta, Withers's film contract was not renewed, and Loretta found herself stuck with paying *all* the bills. She denied that Grant's canceled contract was the last straw. Withers signed for a vaudeville tour, and although Loretta had already made the decision to leave him, she did not tell him so.

Withers behaved like a man in love. The first week he was on tour, he spent a fortune calling Loretta long-distance from Chicago. She threatened to refuse to answer the phone "if he continued to be so foolish." But he was persistent and demanded that the Los Angeles operator ring Loretta's phone until she answered it.

In February 1931, just over a year after their marriage,

Loretta announced that she was waiting for Grant to return from his vaudeville tour before she filed for divorce. It was over.

What had the indomitable young Loretta learned from this entire experience? "The knowledge I should have had before I took the enormous step in the first place," she said at the time. "I am convinced that it will be a long time—a *very* long time—before I'll ever think of marriage again!"

Loretta wasn't speaking lightly. She later stated, "Grant and I may have hurt each other—not may have, we did—but only through youth and inexperience, not ill will."

Withers had his side of the story. He later described Loretta Young in three words that her enemies have repeated relentlessly over the years: "The Steel Butterfly."

"I think the experience scarred her terribly," said her friend Carroll Nye. "She was just too young for a man like that."

*The game is hard and fast and grueling
and not many last.*

—*Dorothy Wooldridge*

Four

Loretta had emerged from the Withers debacle with her dignity intact. She would always emerge from *all* situations with her dignity intact.

She moved back with her family—Loretta did not need to use her marriage and subsequent separation as an excuse to leave home or as a stepping-stone to independence. More importantly, she did not look upon her mother as someone holding her back; she regarded her as a wise and loving guide. The intimacy that Pol, Bet, Gretch, and Mamma enjoyed was both supportive and fun, and Gretchen needed a great deal of support in the hectic work schedule she faced. There were eight pictures on her schedule for 1931, and such a workload left little time to dwell on unhappy thoughts. Making movies was a powerful distraction: there were scripts to memorize, endless costume fittings, and hair, makeup, and photographic sessions, all requiring intense concentration.

The job of acting—the fantasylike sets, the constant attention of people tending to her, the energy constantly required —conveniently preoccupied all of Loretta's attention.

She was loaned to RKO for *Beau Ideal.* The explosive Herbert Brenon was once again Loretta's director, but by this time she had learned how to handle both herself and Brenon, and there were no more outbursts of tears or running from the set. All was strictly business, with no delays on account of Loretta Young.

Loretta next played opposite the stunningly handsome John Wayne at Fox in *Three Girls Lost.* Loretta's childhood pal, Josie Saenz, was dating Wayne against her parents' wishes. Undoubtedly, the Saenz family could use Gretchen's recent sad experience as an example of what happens when one defies one's parents and marries the wrong man.

Too Young to Marry, released in May 1931, made money— exploiting stars' personal lives was always profitable—and Loretta's career continued to purr along smoothly.

In 1931 Loretta was named "the prettiest girl" in *The Hollywood Who's Who.* That year Jeanette MacDonald was "the best-looking woman," Ruth Chatterton "best actress," Marie Dressler "best character actress," Marion Davies "best-liked person," Garbo the "most discussed personality," and Constance Bennett the "most sophisticated woman." There were several more categories: "freshest guy" (Jack Oakie), "saddest case" (Renée Adorée), and "unluckiest person" (Anna Q. Nilsson). Irving Thalberg was voted, predictably, "best executive."

Loretta co-starred with Douglas Fairbanks, Jr., again, in *I Like Your Nerve,* and then was lent to a Poverty Row studio, Columbia, for a costarring role in *Platinum Blonde.* Needless to say, Jean Harlow, in the title role, would receive all the attention. But the picture presented Loretta with a vital opportunity—the chance to work with director Frank Capra, a man famous for his insight and sensitivity in dealing with actors. Capra's method of drawing a performance out of an actor was in direct contrast to that of men like Herbert Brenon; Capra believed in instilling his players with confidence.

As shooting on *Platinum Blonde* began, it seemed to Capra

that close-mouthed Loretta had little understanding of her character. Unlike Brenon, who embarrassed her in front of cast and crew, Capra took her aside and very quietly asked her, "What do you think of this character, Loretta?"

"Think?" she quickly blurted out. "Oh, I never think, Mr. Capra. I never think about the characters I play. I just try to do what the director tells me." The fear that Capra, too, might turn into a terror obviously lurked in Loretta's mind.

Capra very gently explained to her. "Loretta, acting *is* what you think. Acting is listening to the other person and then responding, so it is vitally important that you always know what you think."

The words made a lasting impression. Loretta acknowledges today that this was the best professional advice of her career, and came at a crucial point. Working with Capra, she slowly but surely recovered her confidence in her abilities as an actress.

Loretta worked that year with one of the all-time great actors of stage and screen, Walter Huston, in the film *The Ruling Voice*. It was high praise indeed when Huston, discussing Loretta with a reporter, said he was "impressed" by the beautiful girl's know-how. "She's very professional," he said. "Always knows her lines, always hits her mark, and is very aware, in the right way, of the camera."

The barometer in those days of how a person's career was progressing was simple: fan mail. And Loretta was receiving a goodly share. She was perceived as a younger, more beautiful Janet Gaynor, radiating a wistful, saucer-eyed vulnerability that intrigued and interested fans. As with Gaynor, the fans *liked* her, and this likability was crucial in keeping the public coming back for more.

Gossip columns and fan magazines of this era were the main publicity outlets for building stars and selling films. Fan magazines such as *Photoplay* and *Modern Screen* were as integral to the industry as the films and stars they sold. For audiences of the twenties, thirties, forties, and even fifties, fan magazines were the equivalent of *People* magazine today. Top writers like Adela Rogers St. Johns informed the public of the minute and often intimate details of the stars' private lives. Today, instead of doing an interview with the equivalent of an Adela, Louella, or *Photoplay*'s Ruth Waterbury, stars go on talk shows or *Entertainment Tonight*. But in the early history of Hollywood, the print media was king.

Regardless of whether publicity was studio-promoted, as with people like Garbo, or done with the willing cooperation of the stars themselves, such as Loretta, the public was treated to steady accounts of the actors' lives in the workplace and at home. The fanzines sometimes exaggerated, but in many cases the facts were basically correct and reporters did not need to rely on sensationalism.

The stars themselves were often the greatest fans of the gossip columns and fan magazines, regarding them as a reliable way to keep up on what was happening in Hollywood's business as well as social world.

Throughout the thirties, Loretta's image as a religious person was reinforced (undoubtedly in her own mind as well) by feature stories and photographs. She was presented as someone who attended church regularly and came from a strong religious background. Some of her portrait photographs even went so far as to show her in the vestments of a choir girl, with hymnal in hand.

Hubert Voight tells of two amusing incidents involving Loretta in typical early 1930s publicity stunts. One was the Joan of Arc episode. A huge cross had been erected on an empty lot adjacent to the studio, and the publicity boys thought it would be a great gimmick to pose Loretta as Joan burning at the stake. Loretta was agreeable. Everything was set: Loretta donned her costume, and the fire was lit. But then the wind suddenly shifted. "There was a scramble to save Loretta from actually getting burned," remembers Voight.

In a less dangerous stunt, Voight hired a number of extras,

passed them off as college professors—"in those days, I think it was about twelve dollars a day for a beard"—and Loretta Young was "voted" as "the most well-read and cultured actress in films."

Admiral Richard Byrd, who had become a worldwide legend when he explored the South Pole, visited the Warner studio in May of 1931. The visit, a widely heralded Hollywood event, included a luncheon organized at Warners in Byrd's honor.

Top executives and stars attended, including eighteen-year-old Loretta. She was not seated with Byrd or Zanuck—that honor befell actress Bebe Daniels and actor-writer-director George Arliss. But the admiral expressed particular interest not in Miss Daniels or the distinguished Mr. Arliss, but in the beautiful young brunette and stunning blonde flanking the lower end of the T-shaped table: Loretta Young and Joan Blondell.

Loretta's salary, as well as her star, was on the rise. After only four years she was earning close to a thousand dollars a week. While the Depression engulfed the American public, movie salaries soared to record heights: Ruth Chatterton and William Powell were each earning $6,000 a week, and golden girl Constance Bennett had established a new record of $30,000 a week—one which went unchallenged for many years. Broadway star Ina Claire's $50,000 per picture paled by comparison.

Loretta, whose nearly $50,000-per-year salary entitled the studio to use her in as many pictures as possible, still had a long way to go to catch up to these supersalaried stars. Considering her family's financial plight only a few years before, however, Loretta had achieved the equivalent of scaling Mount Everest. She was *rich*. "My little moneymaker" is how Loretta's mother sometimes affectionately referred to her. But all was not calm. Loretta wanted the life-style of a star to accompany her salary, and there were many tussles between her and Mamma, each a headstrong woman who knew how to get their way. For example, Loretta wanted a car and driver, while Gladys insisted that Gretchen continue to drive her own car. There was a telephone pole on a corner that Loretta had to pass every night coming home from the studio. One night, Loretta found that she was too tired to make the turn and smacked into the telephone pole. Mrs. Belzer got the message and soon agreed that perhaps Gretchen did need a car and driver.

Throughout 1931 gossip columnists continued to speculate that Loretta would reconcile with Withers. But Loretta was happy back at home, and noted to friends that nothing much had changed during her absence—the town's leading swains still paid court to her gorgeous sisters.

While Grant was back in Hollywood and "stepping out with Aileen Pringle," as one columnist observed, Loretta also began making the social rounds.

One of her dates was Ricardo Cortez, with whom she had just made a picture, *Big Business Girl.* A few years earlier Cortez had married a talented and beautiful screen personality, Alma Rubens, but the marriage had quickly turned into a nightmare. Rubens was a morphine addict, and there were frequent stories that physical violence had occurred between husband and wife. It was in Cortez's home that Alma Rubens died.

While some insiders claim that dating leading men was part of publicity, Loretta maintains she never let the studio dictate her private life.

Loretta was then linked with Warner–First National executive Irving Asher; they were often seen dancing together at the Cocoanut Grove. Loretta and Asher were a "Beauty and the Front Office" combination that was then popular. Irving Thalberg and Norma Shearer, the town's premier couple, had established the pattern.

Gossip was that when Loretta went to Reno for location filming on her next picture, she would finally file suit for divorce against Withers.

The publicity machine erected around Loretta revved up, until soon fans must have found it impossible to distinguish between what was set-up and what was real. For example, there was a puff piece showing Young and costar Frank Albertson in a photo layout entitled "He, She, and 'It.'" The two actors portrayed a young couple kissing, tickling each other, and gazing dreamily into each other's eyes. "Loretta and Frank charmingly portray two modern young folks in love," read the caption.

Other photo layouts emphasized the glamorous side of Loretta's life, particularly her extensive and elegant wardrobe. Her sophistication was constantly played up. "She's only twenty," said one article, which of course was a lie—she was only eighteen.

For another fashion feature Loretta posed in no less than ten different outfits—a portent of things to come—but fans weren't encouraged to be jealous. On the contrary, Loretta was only too happy to tell her fans "how to give your wardrobe the same touch." This was no easy task. One beaded gown worn by the actress had cost seven hundred dollars, much more than a year's salary for the average Depression-era moviegoer.

Then, in September 1931, a small piece of *real* news: "Mrs. Loretta Withers, Gretchen Young, Loretta Young—they're one and the same—recently divorced Grant Withers on the grounds of no support."

Pictures of Loretta in the courtroom presented a very poised but somewhat melancholy-looking young woman, very smartly dressed and immaculately groomed. But her eyes, those liquid eyes, spoke volumes—she was definitely no longer "a kid."

Typically, when it came to beautiful actresses, even staid justices were not immune. "I want to tell you I have seen your work in motion pictures and have enjoyed it very much," beamed Superior Court Judge Henry B. Willis as he signed the divorce decree.

Back in Hollywood, Loretta didn't try to sidestep responsibility for her actions. "I'm sorry to have made my mother unhappy and Grant unhappy," she reportedly said.

She took two weeks off to vacation in northern California, inspiring immediate speculation that she was having a romance with University of Southern California football player Paul Fretz, Jr., who lived in Palo Alto. Mrs. Belzer instantly denied the rumor, saying that Gretchen was just going to stay in Palo Alto with friends of the family for a ten-day rest.

She would need the rest. Loretta's workload was staggering, calling for six pictures in 1932.

She was not always first choice for roles—sometimes she was third or fourth choice. But her ego did not interfere with her business sense and when assigned a part, she played it.

Loretta's next film, *Taxi,* was a James Cagney vehicle: both female leads, Loretta and Dorothy Burgess, were really only window dressing for the new young star. Cagney made his motion picture dancing debut here with Loretta, during a scene in which the duo win a dance contest. Loretta portrayed his wife in the picture, and later confessed that she had developed a crush on the actor.

"We were both so young then . . . I admired him so much, though I could never tell him so. I remember having this romantic dream about him—well, my idea of a romantic dream—in which I was drowning and he rescued me. He was very gentle with me. I remember this scene when he leaned his face on my hand . . ."

She has also recalled that Cagney had "complete control of expressing the whole gamut of emotions with his eyes. He could accomplish with a glance what lesser actors need a whole bag of tricks to put over. That, too, is a lesson in control."

Sally was on the Warner lot at this time. Mervyn LeRoy cast her in *I Am a Fugitive From a Chain Gang,* which starred young stage actor Paul Muni. LeRoy originally cast Sally as Muni's wife, but apparently the real Mrs. Muni was instrumental in having Miss Blane recast in a smaller role. This was a major disappointment for Miss Blane. She was sensitive and simply didn't have her younger sister's resilience. Unlike Loretta, she couldn't use a setback to spur her on to greater heights.

At this time, Sally Blane's career was running on about an equal par with Loretta's. She was making as many films, although unlike Loretta, she bounced from studio to studio.

The same year Sally appeared in *Moon Song* with brand-new radio sensation Kate Smith; she also costarred with Randolph Scott in *Heritage of the Desert* and *Wild Horse Mesa.*

Most of Sally Blane's films have been forgotten, but at the time they were popular fare and Sally herself was as popular and well known as Loretta. Of the three Young sisters, only Polly Ann did not actively pursue a career in films.

Loretta's assignments at Warners continued to cast her opposite the studio's top commercial stars. Edward G. Robinson had the title role in *The Honorable Mr. Wong,* retitled *The Hatchet Man,* in which both players were cast as Orientals. Robinson's top billing dwarfed Loretta's, which in small type read, "with Loretta Young." The film's director, the talented William Wellman, would helm several pictures with Loretta.

In *Play Girl,* Loretta met actor Norman Foster, who was currently married to Claudette Colbert. The marriage was most unconventional, and Foster's arrangement with his wife had given rise to various explanations. The couple maintained two separate households—"two beautiful homes, each perfectly run, fully furnished, staffed with servants and situated only four blocks apart." In one, according to accounts of the day, Foster lived his "tranquil existence." In the other, "Claudette entertains her friends—often including her husband—or goes about such domestic duties as her devoted mother and aunt allow her to do."

This dual setup had the gossips clucking, and gave rise to a number of conjectures. Was the couple contemplating a divorce? Were there other men and women involved?

According to the two parties, nothing could have been farther from the truth. They were living in separate houses because they had found, over the five and a half years they'd been man and wife, that it was better for their "artistic careers."

The Fosters had an open relationship, each leading the private life he or she wanted. For the moment they were separated but saw no reason to seek a divorce. During the period when Loretta and Norman Foster made several films together, they often dated.

Loretta aroused more speculation when she chose Herbert Somborn as her next escort. Somborn was thought much too old to be Prince Charming—already in his early fifties, he was years older than Loretta's mother!

Ten years earlier, Somborn had been married to Gloria Swanson, with whom he had had a daughter. Somborn had taken charge of Swanson's business affairs, and Gloria ended up paying all the bills. She would later claim Somborn had blackmailed her.

Loretta and Somborn lunched frequently at the Brown Derby, the posh new restaurant on Vine Street which Somborn owned. It was the current number-one gathering place for Hollywood's biggest stars.

One of Somborn's friends later noted, "Herb is a man of the world and he would never be interested in just a beautiful young girl like Loretta unless she had something much better than beauty."

Some were astonished when it was announced that Loretta was interrupting her film career to appear as Juliet that summer in Los Angeles as an outdoor production. The venture never panned out.

There was no question but that there existed an untapped potential in Loretta's acting abilities. In *Life Begins* she delivered a performance of great depth, thoroughly researching her role before shooting by visiting a real maternity hospital.

Although the extra effort she had made paid off on screen,

she was "rewarded" by the studio with a potboiler—*They Call It Sin*. In addition, she had to take a salary cut, from $1,000 a week down to $800.

The wily Warner Bros. used the Depression as a ploy to force all their stars to take salary cuts. William Powell and Ruth Chatterton were cut from $6,000 to $4,000 a week; Doug Fairbanks, Jr., Kay Francis, and Edward G. Robinson from $2,500 to $1,975; Cagney from $1,250 to $1,000; Paul Muni from $1,500 to $1,200; Joan Blondell from $600 to $400. Even Constance Bennett was cut, from $350,000 to $225,000 per year. The studio, however, continued to earn huge profits during these Depression years.

In *They Call It Sin* George Brent, the studio's answer to Clark Gable, was upped to costar status. Loretta has recalled Brent as "an unconscious model of absolute control. I can't imagine him going to pieces under any circumstances." Renowned actor Louis Calhern was also featured in the picture, and Loretta's name was linked in the columns with his, not with Brent's. The pair was described in the tabloids as having "quite a romance." (Her dating men like Somborn and Calhern led to speculation that Loretta was seeking a father figure.)

The studio, however, sent Loretta and Brent on a personal appearance tour to promote the picture—they knew who the fans wanted to see!

To round out the year, Warners threw Loretta into more programmers, including *Employees' Entrance* and *Grand Slam*. Films like these were not the kind Loretta wanted to continue making.

An opportunity for a truly fine role soon presented itself. Jesse Lasky, aced out at Paramount, had set up an independent production unit at Fox. He asked to borrow Loretta for the role of the waiflike orphan in *Zoo in Budapest*, and Zanuck agreed.

Up to this point, none of the "A" movies Loretta made were built around her character; in *Zoo in Budapest*, her character was the focal point. The story concerns an orphan, Eve, who each week visits the zoo with the rest of the orphanage. One week Eve escapes from the supervisors and takes refuge with the zookeeper, Zani, played by Gene Raymond. The girl is wide-eyed, shy, and childlike—qualities radiated on screen by Loretta. The twenty-year-old Loretta had the advantage of six years acting experience while still being young enough to photograph with a childlike quality. Her slim physique also contributed to the ethereal quality she projected.

Production proceeded smoothly and the studio was excited by the results. Even before its release, word in town was that *Zoo in Budapest* would be one of the biggest hits of the year. When the picture was booked at the country's new premiere film showcase, Radio City Music Hall in New York, the movie seemed assured of success. This was Loretta's first picture to play Radio City.

At this time Fox was planning a major film version of the hit play *Berkeley Square,* with British star Leslie Howard in the lead. Loretta saw the play and was excited by it—she thought herself *perfect* for the female lead. So perfect, in fact, that when the role wasn't offered to her outright, she gladly told her bosses at Warners that she would test for it.

Meanwhile, Warners cast Loretta in *The Life of Jimmy Dolan* with Douglas Fairbanks, Jr. Costarring were Aline MacMahon and Lyle Talbot; thirteen-year-old Mickey Rooney had a minor role.

Also in the film was John Wayne, who had an unbilled bit part as a prizefighter. Loretta had gotten Duke the job when he lost his Fox contract and began making westerns at one of the minor studios. After dating for over six years, Duke and Josie had persuaded the Saenz family to allow them to marry. Loretta was to be maid of honor, an obvious tribute to their strong friendship, since Josie had three sisters who might also have been chosen.

Loretta and Gladys were going to serve as hostesses as well. The wedding would be held in June at the Young-

Belzer home in Bel-Air. Josie, Loretta, and Gladys eagerly prepared for the happy event.

As filming ended on *The Life of Jimmy Dolan,* Loretta was confident that the *Berkeley Square* role would be hers. Jesse Lasky was to produce the picture; hadn't Loretta's triumph in *Zoo in Budapest* been his triumph too? How could she not get the role?

Loretta prayed often, always ending her prayers with the words "Thy will be done." Later, however, she candidly admitted that as a youngster she "somehow always believed that God's will would always coincide with mine."

This time Loretta's prayers failed her. To her shock and sorrow she read that a British beauty, Heather Angel, had been cast in *Berkeley Square.* She did not believe it—it was just a publicity stunt, Loretta reasoned. Then Warners phoned to tell her, yes, she was going on a loanout—but to M-G-M, not Fox.

Loretta was agonizingly bitter over the loss of the part she had so coveted. She was dramatic in her anguish, and none of her family could console her. She ranted, she raved, she cried. To her "it was the end of everything—my career, my ambition, the world."

Gladys was alarmed at how deeply distraught her daughter was over losing this part. Mrs. Belzer's ability to talk common sense to Loretta was invaluable—it enabled the girl to overcome many obstacles. Their relationship had always been a source of strength for both mother and daughter.

Loretta later acknowledged that her mother was responsible for teaching her "the standard by which to judge the genuinely important things of life."

Although losing the role was hardly a calamity of life-or-death proportions, it was at the time a severe test of Loretta's faith. In her mind it was inconceivable that her prayers hadn't been heard. But with her mother's counseling she accepted the loss, although with a heavy heart, and returned to work.

The loanout to M-G-M was for *Midnight Mary,* another

programmer distinguished only by the fact that she would again be directed by Wellman. Ricardo Cortez and Franchot Tone were the male leads.

"I accepted it with total indifference," Loretta said, "but once on the set I worked very earnestly."

William Wellman was known as Wild Bill, a nickname the thirty-five-year-old director had acquired for being quick to use his fists. Often he would physically fight with cast and crew members on his films. Mike Lally was the assistant director on *Midnight Mary;* according to popular Hollywood legend Wellman once tried to shoot Lally during a production!

Despite his reputation as a brawler, Wellman was noted for drawing excellent performances from his actors. "I felt very secure when I was working with Wellman," said Loretta. "There was nothing phony or artificial about him. He was also very attractive in every way. He liked to shoot fast, in one take, and his energy went right through him and into the actors. A director is boss for a reason, and Bill was good."

Loretta, though a divorcée, was, it seems, still naïve. In one scene she couldn't understand why the gangster slaps her.

"Because you're his girl," Wellman explained.

"He doesn't have to slap me."

"Yes, he does."

Wellman never came right out and said, "Because you're sleeping with him," and Young said years later that even if she had known what Wellman was talking about she would have put it out of her mind.

In any event, the director elicited a fine performance— both he and Loretta quickly moved on to other projects, forgetting about *Midnight Mary.*

Other all-too-forgettable pictures she was assigned to that spring were *She Had to Say Yes, The Devil's in Love,* and *Heroes for Sale* (also directed by Wellman).

She Had to Say Yes teamed her with Lyle Talbot for a second time, and the duo allegedly had a brief romance during production.

The Devil's in Love, filmed at Fox, lacked a star-status leading man. Victor Jory, an actor in his midtwenties, had the male lead and was receiving top billing, since he was a Fox contract player. According to Jory, Loretta wasn't terribly helpful or responsive to him, and he concluded that this was because he was not on her level star-wise. He later revealed that in their love scenes she only feigned kissing him.

Sally Blane, coincidentally, had made a film with Jory earlier that year, called *Trick for Trick.* Sally and Polly Ann were planning a trip to Europe, and Loretta announced that on completion of *The Devil's in Love* she would join her sisters overseas.

But first there was the long-awaited wedding of Josie Saenz. On June 24, 1933, Josie and John Wayne exchanged vows. The wedding and reception, held at the Young-Belzer home, was one of the premier social events of the season. Not only were Josie and Duke close with Hollywood celebrities, including Loretta and director John Ford, but Josie enjoyed recognition by the "old guard" of Los Angeles society because of her family background.

Loretta was excited for her friend. Josie and Duke had found a charming three-room garden apartment in the Hancock Park area, and the couple was embarking on what all agreed would be an idyllic union.

Love and marriage, however, were not on Loretta's schedule, as far as she knew. Her contract at Warners was coming to an end, and there were important career decisions to be made. Although she was still very young, Loretta was already being referred to as "a survivor." After all, writers pointed out, many of Young's fellow Wampas Baby Stars had already met sad finales. Loretta was one of the very few who had not only survived but flourished.

The histories of some of her contemporaries is revealing. There had been one hundred and four Wampas Baby Stars in the eight groups selected from 1922 to 1929. By 1933 eight had entirely disappeared; one had died, four were doing "bits" or minor roles, and two had attempted suicide.

Many were still playing leads—Sally Blane, Mary Astor, Evelyn Brent, Eleanor Boardman, Mary Brian, Fay Wray, and Jean Arthur among them. It was acknowledged, however, that only eight were "first magnitude" stars: Joan Crawford, Janet Gaynor, Lupe Velez, Clara Bow, Dolores Del Rio, Marian Nixon, Colleen Moore—and Loretta Young.

Dorothy Wooldridge, a writer of the time, noted that some of the Baby Stars made an indelible mark in the motion picture industry: "Some of these marks occasionally have been a bit lurid. . . . The game is hard and fast and grueling, and not many last."

Loretta was destined to last—to last and last and last.

Zoo in Budapest had been a hit, as expected, and Loretta's professional life was finally embarking on a spectacular new phase.

Darryl Zanuck had left Warners after the studio reneged on its promise to reinstate the cut salaries of its stars. Zanuck obtained the backing of mogul Joseph M. Schenck to form a new company, Twentieth Century Pictures. The films would be released through United Artists, which Schenck headed. In addition, the new company would be located on the United Artists lot and utilize its facilities. William Goetz, one of L. B. Mayer's sons-in-law, was the third partner.

Zanuck had lured George Arliss and Constance Bennett from the Warner Bros. ranks, and he and Schenck made deals to borrow other top stars, including Wallace Beery, George Raft, Lee Tracy, and Ann Harding.

After *Zoo in Budapest* Zanuck was more confident than ever about Loretta's potential—he saw her as the natural successor to Janet Gaynor. Since Loretta's seven-year contract was expiring, Zanuck wooed Loretta to Twentieth Century with promises of star treatment, star vehicles, and a starting salary of over seventeen hundred dollars a week, almost twice what she was earning at Warners.

(Young later said that she didn't leave to sign with Zanuck, but that Warners wanted her to waive a fifty-dollar-a-week option raise and when she refused, they dropped her.)

Because Loretta was still under twenty-one, the Los Angeles court had to approve the long-term contract and her mother had to accompany her to the studio to sign it.

Before beginning with Twentieth, Loretta planned to take her first trip to Europe, where Sally was doing a film in England. But once again work interfered. A project at Columbia was offered, and she decided to accept it. The picture was *A Man's Castle,* directed by the famed Frank Borzage. Borzage had directed the legendary *Seventh Heaven* six years earlier, for which he won the first best director Academy Award, while the picture's star, Janet Gaynor, won the academy's first best actress award. Borzage had responded to Loretta's touching performance in *Zoo in Budapest;* he realized that her wide-eyed innocence would be ideal for the role of the waif Trina in *A Man's Castle.*

Her leading man would be Spencer Tracy, and the experience would prove to be a major turning point in Loretta Young's life.

*They fell madly in love while they were
making the film.*

—Hubert Voight

Five

In 1933 Hubert Voight moved from Warners–First National
to Columbia, where Loretta and Tracy were to begin filming.
"Even I—and I was director of publicity—was banned from
the set of *A Man's Castle,* the scenes were so hot."

The attraction between Spencer Tracy and Loretta Young
was evident to everyone working on the film—from the director, Borzage (a close friend of Tracy and his wife), to
costars Walter Connolly and Glenda Farrell.

Today, Spencer Tracy's personal image is welded with the
screen image he cultivated for three decades: a combination
of solid citizen and compassionate, liberal, and understanding
father. His well-publicized long-term relationship with Katharine Hepburn has given him an added aura of sophistication,
romance and glamour. The Spencer Tracy of 1933, however,
had not yet acquired any of this mystique. When he met
Loretta Young that summer, he was a thirty-three-year-old
married man with two children who had the reputation
around town of being difficult to work with. In addition, he
was plagued by self-doubt and often took solace in the bottle.

As an actor, Tracy was undisputably a genius. He would

not permit his private life to be exploited for publicity purposes, and so by Hollywood standards he was an enigma. He had arrived in Hollywood only three years earlier, having already established himself as a Broadway star.

Hollywood saw Tracy as a successor to Edmund Lowe and Victor McLaglen, the "roughneck" leading men of the time, but the Fox publicists were dismayed when Tracy refused to play the Hollywood publicity game. He shunned press agents and the fan magazine buildup, the route which had proven successful for so many actors and actresses, including Loretta Young.

To Tracy, movies were strictly business. He was an intense, moody Irishman who came from a nontheatrical midwestern background. Whereas Loretta Young's background had been fraught with financial struggle, Tracy's was full of ease and comfort. But like Loretta he had a competitive personality and a compulsive need to be number one in everything. If he knew he couldn't be the best—in a particular sport, for example—he simply chose not to compete.

After college he moved to New York, where he studied acting at the American Academy of Dramatic Arts while living in a cubicle-sized apartment on West 96th Street. Tracy's reputation for being "impatient and arrogant" won him no friends in the all-important Broadway casting offices, so he took on the grueling pace of touring with stock companies.

While on tour, he started dating the company's leading lady, Louise Treadwell, a pretty, dark-haired actress with all the stable, levelheaded qualities Tracy admired. Tracy, meanwhile, was stuck playing a series of small roles, and was turned down whenever he asked for bigger parts.

When Louise was signed as the lead for the Repertory Theater of Cincinnati, she demanded that Tracy be signed as the company's leading man. The director acquiesced.

The couple was married on September 12, 1923, and nine months later Louise gave birth to a son, John. When it was discovered the boy was deaf, it was a devastating blow to both parents—a tragedy from which Spencer never fully recovered.

In the beginning Tracy's career was frustratingly erratic. But the famed George M. Cohan liked the young actor and often cast him in his plays, encouraging Tracy to continue his career. The movies beckoned, but a screen test for M-G-M in New York resulted in the dreaded "Don't call us, we'll call you." Tracy was also tested and rejected by Universal and Fox.

But finally, in 1930, he scored an enormous Broadway success playing Killer Mears in *The Last Mile,* a gritty tale of revolt in a prison death house. Talent scouts could not ignore Tracy's triumph, and he was signed by Fox soon after.

After several of his Hollywood movies proved to be duds, however, Tracy again turned to the bottle. Usually mellow and charming, Tracy became abusive and cantankerous when he drank. Studio press agents had quite a job keeping the actor's name out of the tabloid columns.

As anyone who knew the Tracys well could have predicted, the couple shunned the Hollywood social scene. Spencer, the loner, detested nightclubs, glamorous restaurants, and Hollywood parties. He also shied away from the studio's exclusive call girl service and the nearby brothel on Wilcox Avenue, frequented often by Hollywood stars.

He loved playing polo—at which he excelled—and spent most of his idle hours at the posh Riviera Country Club, where he also indulged his passion for drinking. He palled around with Frank Borzage, Douglas Fairbanks, Sr., and Darryl Zanuck, also a polo buff. Another close friend back at Fox was Will Rogers.

Few knew that one of the main reasons Tracy had accepted the Hollywood contract was for the money. He had hoped his newfound wealth would provide a cure for his son, but all the doctors agreed that John's deafness was permanent.

To add to Tracy's misery, he feared his Fox contract would be canceled—there had been too many flop films (including

Disorderly Conduct, featuring Sally Blane). When Louise became pregnant again, the Tracys faced the prospect of having another child born deaf, but to their immense relief, their daughter, whom they named Louise, was perfectly normal.

Tracy was at odds with the studio over his next project. He had just finished Jesse Lasky's *The Power and the Glory* with Colleen Moore, but it had not yet been released. Great things were expected of the film, and Fox had rewarded Tracy with a fat new contract. Rather than hassle with his bosses, he jumped at the chance to do the Borzage picture when it presented itself. For Spencer Tracy it was to be an unexpected experience—not since touring with Louise Treadwell had he fallen in love with his leading lady.

When he signed for *A Man's Castle* Tracy was not yet a full-fledged star. He had received star billing in Fox pictures, but hadn't yet reached the stature of his contemporaries Gary Cooper and James Cagney. According to some reports in the press, other top actors had been considered for *A Man's Castle.* But this had been a publicity ploy masterminded by Borzage, who had had Tracy in mind for the role from the beginning. Borzage had a powerful script by Jo Swerling, based on a novel by Laurence Hazard. He had lined up Walter Connolly, Marjorie Rambeau, Glenda Farrell, and child star Dickie Moore for his supporting cast. The story concerned a group of down-and-outers living in one of the Depression shantytowns lining New York's East River.

Tracy and Young's attraction for each other was so intense that others in the cast felt like intruders on the set. The camera picked up Spencer's and Loretta's feelings. Executives who saw the daily rushes were ecstatic; aware that the romance developing off-screen was making a sensitive transition onscreen.

Production was still in progress on *A Man's Castle* when *The Power and the Glory* was released in the summer of 1933.

To everyone's shock, it bombed. Now Tracy's mercurial personality interfered explosively with his work.

Some insiders theorize that Loretta was attracted to Tracy at first for humanitarian reasons, rather than for any romantic interest. He was obviously a man with a serious alcohol problem, a person she might help.

In writing about Loretta, Howard Sharpe described the original attraction between Tracy and Young, although Mr. Sharpe chose to change the actor's name: "We can call him Stephan. Stephan was working opposite Loretta . . . when he was working; when emissaries of the studio . . . could find him and give him a cold shower and get him on the set in time for a scene or two. He was a perfect actor, and is, but there was head-shaking about him in that year. He who had never had time for liquor, now used it for a purpose, which he achieved magnificently: to forget the wife from whom he had separated.

"Loretta observed him with compassion, knowing his story."

One afternoon, according to Sharpe, when the picture was only a third finished and the company was breaking up, Loretta saw "Stephan" heading determinedly for the soundstage door. "She knew he was going to his hotel room, and she knew that no one would come to see him during that evening, and she knew what he would have for company. And on an impulse, she called to him.

" 'Would—would you drive me home? My car's not here and it's such a nuisance getting a studio car. I hate to ask—'

" 'I'd like to very much,' he said gratefully. 'I haven't anything else at all to do.' "

Soon, as production on *Man's Castle* progressed, the couple were often seen together in public.

"What is this we hear about Spencer Tracy and Loretta Young?" columnists asked. "Tracy has been taking Loretta around. Just what does it mean?"

Everyone knew what it meant. Tracy had met a young

woman so appealing that he defied his own strict sense of
ethics to please her. Already separated from Louise, Tracy
was a desperately unhappy man. His state of mind, by his
own admission, had nothing to do with his wife or anyone
else. It was a feeling he had little control over, a deeply self-
destructive aspect to his personality.

Tracy was living in a hotel, but friends expected him and
Louise to reconcile soon. As far as the world was concerned,
Tracy was still a married man.

Meanwhile, shooting on *A Man's Castle* continued. The
film was a love story, an intimate portrait of two people strug-
gling to survive during the height of the Depression. The
sentiments of the leading characters strikingly paralleled
those of the actors who portrayed them.

"He gives me everything anyone could want," Young's
character says of Tracy's.

"You're a heck of a woman for a guy like me—a hunk of
bones," Tracy's character tells Loretta's. He refers jokingly to
her "skinniness" throughout the film, although another character says to Young, "You're slim—there's a difference."

The Bible plays a part in the story. At one point Walter
Connolly, holding the Book, says of Tracy, "I only wish I
could get him to read it." In another scene, when Loretta is
reading the Bible, Tracy says: "I thought you didn't believe
in that stuff."

"I lied. I do," answers Loretta passionately and intensely.

Their characters are madly in love, and even to a modern
viewer the emotion between them appears real, powerful,
and unwaivering. Loretta's character cooks, cleans, and irons
for her man, always gazing at him adoringly.

Tracy's character, however, has wanderlust. Throughout
the picture a railroad whistle frequently moans, symbolizing
his yearning to move on. In one scene Tracy sits at a make-
shift window in the shack that is home to him and Loretta,
staring longingly at the sky and at the birds flying free beyond.

"Even birds can't fly all the time," Loretta notes wistfully. "They get tired and have to come home."

Early in the picture Tracy and Young have a nude swimming scene, though the audience never gets even a glimpse of flesh. In the next scene the characters go through the ritual of "getting married."

"It ain't the same as in church, but the words are the same no matter who says 'em—man and wife," declares a poignant and sincere Loretta.

All the love scenes between Tracy and Young are subtle and powerful. Never more so than in one scene, outdoors, on a busy street, when Loretta very intimately whispers something in Tracy's ear. The audience can't hear what she's saying. But the expressions on the two actors' faces say everything. No dialogue is necessary.

There are even scenes with Tracy and Young in bed together (completely clothed, of course). Loretta's character is always afraid Tracy's will leave her—but she knows she's going to have his baby.

"Even if you leave, I've got you now," she says, tense and passionate. At one point, talking about God, Loretta says to Tracy: "I ain't any closer 'n you are . . ."

It is pure love that Loretta's character feels for Tracy's. In one scene she tells him, "You don't have to make excuses to me for anything."

Loretta had never worked with anyone like Spencer Tracy before. "You never have a feeling with him that a scene is artificial," she said at the time. "He is so perfectly natural, himself, in any situation. Nothing throws him."

Loretta learned from the brilliant young actor. "Interpreting a character is like shooting at a target; it's easy to hit the outside circles, but not so easy to hit the bull's-eye. Tracy hits dead center, and he doesn't knock the target over doing it. He is my teacher of accuracy." (Katharine Hepburn said of Tracy, decades later: "Acting was easy for him. *Life* was the problem.")

Tracy and Young continued to see each other after the film completed shooting. For Loretta's benefit, Spencer transformed himself into a social animal, embracing the Hollywood life-style he despised. He bought expensive clothes to escort her to restaurants, parties, and premieres. But his guilt made Tracy surly, and on these social excursions he was rude to newsmen, often threatening to smash their cameras.

According to all accounts, Loretta was not judgmental or sanctimonious with Tracy. She understood him, and the bond between them never weakened. This was no "teenage romance." Young was only twenty but already a woman of extreme intelligence and sensitivity, possessing the same stability and levelheadedness that Spencer had loved in Louise Treadwell. In addition, Loretta was a great beauty—a girl many cameramen at the time considered the most beautiful actress in films. And Tracy was in his physical prime, still a young man although twelve years Loretta's senior.

Loretta continued to give press interviews, as was her custom, but when she commented on Tracy in some of these pieces, he complained loudly. She subsequently cooled it on the topic of their relationship when talking to the press.

The press, however, continued reporting items that greatly embarrassed Tracy. "Loretta Young and Spencer Tracy continue to discuss their 'business' during cozy, intimate luncheons or while dining and dancing at various popular late-spots around town," observed one columnist. "They seem to have such a grand time together that maybe the business—which concerns a play both hope to appear in sometime this season—is just an excuse! Both Mr. and Mrs. Tracy deny that Loretta had anything to do with their separating. But maybe she *will* have something to do with *keeping* them separated."

In a totally unexpected development, Tracy found he was suddenly hot stuff in the fan magazines. Never before had he been a romantic figure, a sex symbol, but the association with Loretta Young had suddenly made him "sexy."

The persistent column blurbs and stories were embarrassing to the Tracys' friends, who felt Louise was being made to look the fool. The situation actually placed Loretta in a most unflattering light. She bristled at being portrayed as "the other woman"; after all, Tracy had left Louise before he had ever met her.

Throughout all this neither Tracy nor Loretta had the luxury of free time to spend with each other: both were working nonstop.

Loretta's film *Midnight Mary* was released, and to her surprise and great delight it was a "sleeper"—a picture which unexpectedly performed as a blockbuster. The paying public responded to Loretta's solid performance as the heroine who rises from fallen woman to redeemed sinner. Loretta later noted that the "fates had cast me more conspicuously than if I had done *Berkeley Square.* This taught me a great lesson."

Back at Fox, Tracy was thrown immediately into two programmers. Infuriated by the studio's treatment of him, Tracy would sometimes come to the set in clothes he had worn partying the previous night; sometimes he failed to show up for work altogether, hiding away somewhere to lose himself in drink. When the bender was over, he turned up at the studio ready for work. He was disobeying Hollywood's cardinal rule, committing the worst offense an actor could commit: he was costing the studio money in production delays. But the young star couldn't help himself.

Tracy was lent to Twentieth for *The Trouble Shooter,* costarring Jack Oakie and directed by William Wellman. Again, Wellman was reported to have fist fights on the set—with both Mike Lally and Tracy. In fact he fought with Tracy on more than one occasion.

The Trouble Shooter was retitled *Looking for Trouble* before its release. Then Tracy went to M-G-M for *The Show-Off.*

That fall Loretta starred in her first Twentieth Century picture, *Born to Be Bad.* Zanuck had originally wanted to borrow Jean Harlow from M-G-M, but Thalberg had issued an edict: no more loanouts for Harlow. Loretta got top billing playing

an unwed mother opposite handsome thirty-year-old Cary
Grant. Young had always rebelled against playing divorced
or "fallen" women. She contends Zanuck held her to their
contract and forced her to make this film against her better
judgment.

Emotionally and physically drained, Loretta became ill. After a short vacation in Palm Springs to regain her strength,
she returned to work. Before signing a long-term deal with
Twentieth, Loretta had made two demands of Zanuck: one,
that she would not have to work with George Arliss, and
two, that she would have a vacation every year. She wanted
these *in* the contract but he said he couldn't put them in
writing. Then other stars would want demands in their contracts. However, he told her he would honor her requests.

"One of my first pictures was with George Arliss," Loretta
later recalled, "and I didn't get a vacation for five years."

In *The House of Rothschild*, starring George Arliss, she was
again faced with a director she didn't like or respond to.
Although Alfred L. Werker was listed as director, Arliss ran
the show. While George Arliss was respected throughout the
industry and was a top box office draw, Loretta was unim-
pressed. She was almost contemptuous of him. His attention
to detail and his painstaking devotion to technique were not
then qualities that Loretta considered essentials—she felt she
was an emotional actress, not a technical one.

To her young eyes, Arliss was a fussy old man. Loretta
would try to call attention to herself onscreen through extra
little touches which, to her consternation, Arliss would not
permit. He quietly restored the character Loretta was playing
(his daughter) to the one that had been written.

Furthermore, Arliss wouldn't permit her to play a big emotional scene with the intensity she wanted to give it; he felt
her high-pitched performance was out of key with the film as
a whole. Eventually, Loretta played the scene his way..

Making the film was an exasperating experience for Loretta, and the final product was not pleasing to her. She didn't

like herself in the picture because she didn't stand out; Arliss hadn't let her utilize her ever-growing bag of tricks to catch the camera's eye.

Years later, however, she acknowledged that Arliss had taught her a vitally important lesson: to keep her overall performance controlled by the content of the story rather than let a particular scene be played for more than it was worth.

The film was to prove a prestige hit, but Loretta would receive only third billing (after Arliss and Boris Karloff). Although she played the female lead, it was only a supporting role.

Tracy was working in a picture at Fox. In addition to all his agonies about separating from his wife and children and contemplation of divorce, Tracy was now unnerved. He'd received a threatening note demanding money—or someone would be kidnapped—either he, a member of his family, or as the staid *New York Times* delicately phrased it, "the young actress with whom his name has been linked romantically."

Nothing came of the kidnap threats. But the reports helped fuel the public's imagination about the Tracy-Young love affair.

A Man's Castle was released late in 1933 and was an immediate critical and commercial hit. The gossip columnists and fan magazines informed the public that the Tracy-Young romance was still going strong even though the film had been completed months ago.

Would the couple be teamed again? That seemed a sensible idea, but Loretta was already lined up for several pictures, as was Tracy, and the two stars were under contract to separate studios. If they had both been under contract to the same studio, a reteaming would have been inevitable.

While Loretta's work schedule was as strenuous as it had been at Warners, she was happy that her films were commercial hits. Ironically, *Berkeley Square* had been a dud, and as Loretta later noted, in Hollywood the box office receipts were all that mattered. Perhaps if Spencer Tracy's pictures had been as successful as Loretta's during this crucial time in their relationship, his feelings about himself might have lightened considerably.

The success of *Zoo, Midnight Mary,* and *A Man's Castle* made Loretta a very hot commercial property. But *Born to Be Bad* turned out to be a failure, the only Twentieth Century picture (in the brief history of that independent company) to lose money. Zanuck had given Loretta the rare opportunity to play against type, and some people today regard this performance as one of her most intriguing. But the public was befuddled by the choppy script, which had Loretta, as a sexy tramp, constantly spurning her smitten suitor, Cary Grant. Undoubtedly, the continuity had been jumbled by the censors' insistence that certain scenes be cut. In any event, Loretta never played that type of role again.

The rest of the Young family had by now returned from Europe. Sally had made two pictures in England, but noted, "I'm happy to get back to Hollywood, to the tempo I'm accustomed to." When her ship docked in New York, she said, "I'm not married or engaged, nor am I in love!"

But her younger sister *was* in love, and it was not just an exaggerated crush. Loretta had discovered what it really meant to be "in love," and there seemed no easy resolution to the situation.

A great deal was happening in the Young household. The girls were not the only ones making news. Mamma had filed for divorce from George Belzer, announcing, "For two years we have lived as brother and sister, not as man and wife." She also said that for the sake of their nine-year-old daughter, Georgianna, the Belzers had postponed a separation as long as possible. Since they lived with Loretta, it was Belzer who moved out of the house and into an apartment in Westwood. (After the divorce, Belzer did not leave the Youngs' lives—he remained Gladys's and Loretta's accountant, and of course was included in all family gatherings. "After all," says an intimate of the family's, "he was Georgie's father." Belzer remained, until his death, devoted to his daughter. However, a man who would become close to the Youngs observed that the ladies' attitude toward Belzer was not always commendable. He was called, albeit affectionately, by the nickname "Mutt.")

Sally now signed with Twentieth Century Pictures, and even Polly Ann became interested in working in films again. (Polly Ann was an extraordinarily beautiful woman; people spoke of her then, and recall her today, as *the* most beautiful of the Young sisters.) Sally resumed her Hollywood career with *No More Women* on loanout to Fox, opposite Victor McLaglen, and *Half a Sinner,* in which she was top-billed over Joel McCrea.

Meanwhile, Loretta completed *Bulldog Drummond Strikes Back,* her second picture with Ronald Colman, and was immediately lent to Fox for two pictures, including *Caravan,* a highly-touted epic costarring French heartthrob Charles Boyer. All concerned knew the film was a turkey. Loretta played a countess who falls in love with a gypsy violinist, played by Boyer. The Frenchman, however, was having considerable difficulty with English, and was further embarrassed by having to wear a rather silly-looking curly wig.

Loretta was next assigned a meaty role in *The White Parade,* a Jesse Lasky production by Fox. Polly Ann also got a part in the picture.

One day Sally's friend Dennis Smith-Bingham asked her to drive with him down to the dock at San Pedro to meet a pal who was arriving on a cruise ship from Cuba. When they got to the pier, photographers waiting for the ship to dock immediately started snapping pictures of Sally, Smith-Bingham, and the new arrival, David Niven.

Niven later recalled, "I found myself improvising about pony racing and my plans. The next day there was a picture of me in the *Los Angeles Examiner* with the caption 'British

Sportsman Arrives: Plans to Bring Over 100 Head of Polo Ponies.' "

In reality, of course, Niven was just a charming, amiable, highly intelligent young man traveling around the world with little money and no place to stay. He recalled Sally saying, "It's all arranged. Mom's got a room for you. You're going to come visit with us until you find someplace to live."

Niven was bowled over when he met the other Young sisters, recalling that even Mrs. Belzer was a beauty. "There has never been, in my experience, such a beautiful family to look at," stated Niven. "And the beauty came from within." Niven and the Young family became fast friends.

Niven "confessed one night to Mrs. Belzer and the girls that I was hoping to break into movies. I felt like an idiot doing it in front of three already established professionals, but they took it in their stride."

Loretta and Polly Ann sneaked him onto the Fox lot and inside stage 19, where they were shooting *The White Parade.* "Niven had moved in with the Youngs," recalls a friend, "and it looked like he would never leave."

During the filming of *The White Parade,* Loretta had a much-publicized feud with another actress in the cast, Astrid Allwin. In one scene, Miss Allwin had to throw water on Loretta, while Loretta later got to slap Miss Allwin. Observers recall that the actresses played their parts with gusto.

She was cast in a big-budget opus, *Clive of India,* once again teamed with Ronald Colman, under the direction of Richard Boleslavski. For Loretta it was yet another window-dressing role. "They used me for Lady Clive because I was under contract. Ronnie was far too big a star to 'need' any leading lady. I just fit the part. I looked it and I was under contract. When you are under contract, you work." An understatement. Disillusionment with Zanuck was setting in; in three of her four Twentieth Century pictures thus far, she was simply being used as a clotheshorse.

Spencer Tracy meanwhile wasn't as busy professionally as Loretta, and seemed to be suffering from his normal cycle of depressions. Still separated from his wife, Tracy had refused to acknowledge the seriousness of his relationship with Loretta. Louella Parsons quoted the actor as characterizing his friendship with Young as "casual and platonic." Helen Twelvetrees, Tracy's costar in *Now I'll Tell,* countered with "When was he sober enough to say a thing like that?"

Over the years there has been much speculation about the breakup of the Tracy-Young romance. Few realize that it lasted as long as it did; the couple had known each other for over a year. One theory is that Miss Young was waiting for Tracy to divorce his wife—after all, Loretta had married Grant Withers, who was a divorced man.

Another theory is that Tracy wanted the relationship to continue as it was, and Loretta would not hear of it. Others claim that it was Loretta who finally urged Tracy to return to his wife and children.

One fact is certain: in late summer of 1934, Tracy's mentor from New York, George M. Cohan, was on the Fox lot making a film. Although Tracy tried to avoid Cohan, the showman finally confronted the actor. Though no one knows for certain the dialogue that took place, before Cohan left California Tracy had reconciled with his wife.

Few people realize that Mrs. Tracy was not a Catholic but an Episcopalian. The myth that has lived for years, that Louise Tracy would not give her husband a divorce, is false. It was Tracy who would not divorce Louise.

Twenty-five years later Loretta Young shed indirect light on this period of her life. The always-truthful but sometimes enigmatic actress revealed that between the years of her nineteenth and twenty-fifth birthdays "I did love someone very much and I had to learn the lesson of self-denial. The man I loved could not love me."

There were many men whose names were linked romantically with Loretta's during this period (1932–1938). Most people believe the man she was referring to was Spencer Tracy. But many others contend that she was referring to another: Clark Gable.

He wasn't tending to business. Not
the business of making movies.
—William Wellman

Six

Zanuck and Schenck had secured Clark Gable's services from
M-G-M for a Twentieth Century picture—and it proved to be
a coup. *It Happened One Night,* Frank Capra's film starring
Gable on loan to Columbia, was one of the biggest hits of
1934. Now Twentieth proposed to team Gable and Young in
a film based on Jack London's classic *Call of the Wild.* And
after that film Zanuck had committed Loretta to a loanout
film at Paramount. Once again she had to postpone her
planned trip to Europe.

William Wellman was set as director of *Call of the Wild.*
Wellman had, of course, worked previously with Loretta, and
he seemed to be Gable's kind of "man's man."

Unlike most films of the day, which were shot almost entirely on studio lots, this one involved location shooting. The
cast and crew set off to spend ten days at Mount Baker, north
of Bellingham in the state of Washington. They would be in
each other's company, both on and off set, far more than if
they had been shooting back at the studio.

According to Jack Oakie, who costarred in the film, Gable

and Wellman did not get along from the beginning; the director seemed to take an instant dislike to the actor.

When the crew first arrived at the Leopold Hotel in Bellingham, they found scores of women waiting to meet and touch the famous Clark Gable. According to Oakie, Gable said, "Hold on to my arm, Shorty, and let's get straight up to our rooms!" The two men rushed through the crowd in the lobby and into the elevator, hearing one woman shriek behind them, "I touched him, I touched him!"

Wellman caught up with the men. "What's the screaming about? Who did she touch?" he asked. And Oakie answered, "Gable." Wellman sneered disdainfully.

Throughout the long, cold days on location, hundreds of women braved blizzard conditions to get a glimpse of the screen's top male star. Few, if any, realized that it had taken ten years, two wives, and an expert dentist to transform the gangling, awkward Billy Gable, a young man from the little town of Cadiz, Ohio, into the leading sex symbol of the cinema.

In 1923 Billy Gable was doing stock in Portland, Oregon. He left the young girl he loved to move in with Josephine Dillon, an acting coach thirteen years older than he. The couple moved to Hollywood and six months later they were married.

While Miss Dillon coached Billy in walking, talking, and acting, the aspiring actor continued doing stock. On tour in Houston, however, Gable met Maria Langham, a woman years older than Josephine. Ria, as she was known, was then married to her third husband, a wealthy stockbroker. Ria divorced her husband, Clark left Josephine Dillon, and the two returned to Hollywood, where Ria backed the Los Angeles production of the play *The Last Mile*.

Like Spencer Tracy, however, Clark Gable had difficulty breaking into films. He failed screen tests at M-G-M and Universal, but did a few movies at Warners under the Zanuck regime. Warners soon dropped his option (a move neither

Zanuck nor Warner ever lived down). Like Tracy, who had George M. Cohan in his corner, Gable had an experienced older actor who believed in his potential. Lionel Barrymore arranged another screen test at M-G-M and told Gable, "This time, don't smile." M-G-M was impressed, and Gable was signed.

Immediately afterwards Gable had some quick dental work done. It was a sloppy job, however, done by a second-rate dentist, and Gable would ultimately have to wear a full set of dentures while still in his prime (a secret kept from the public).

He quickly rose up the ladder on the Metro lot, starring opposite top stars like Constance Bennett, Jean Harlow, and Joan Crawford, with whom he had a blazing affair. He married Ria in June 1931, however, and stayed married to her—although his name was frequently linked with those of Jean Harlow and others.

As he became popular, Gable began availing himself of Hollywood's top call girls, preferring professionals because he didn't have to be "Clark Gable" with them.

By 1934 everyone in Hollywood accepted the fact that Clark Gable and Ria had an "arrangement." Ria, a leading café society figure, enjoyed the prestige of being Mrs. Clark Gable.

Although his fans knew Gable was married, they still regarded him as the screen's greatest lover, and his name was romantically linked with almost every one of his leading ladies. Loretta Young would be no exception.

The *Call of the Wild* company was to be housed at the Mount Baker Lodge in Heather Meadows at the foot of Mount Shukshan, just north of Bellingham. There were one hundred and seventy-five people in the cast and crew, and when they arrived at the lodge they found the snow piled ten feet high. The crew immediately began digging out, an unwelcome task they had to endure through the entire stay.

The original ten-day shooting schedule stretched into

weeks, while the weather often dipped below freezing. Loretta had brought a full-length mink coat to keep her warm but still had to wear several sets of woolen underwear.

The lodge was not large enough to accommodate everyone, so members of the tech crew were asked to move in with neighboring families. The crew spent most of its time working in the subfreezing outdoors, and soon there was dissension because of an executive order forbidding them to drink while on location.

"We didn't know the meaning of hardship compared with the technicians' troubles," Loretta later said. "Eventually Clark and I turned all our liquor over to the boys, orders or no orders. And from then on things were a little easier."

Inevitably, rumors about the stars soon began circulating. One thing was certain: William Wellman was not happy, and the cause of his unhappiness was Gable.

"We had trouble on *Call of the Wild,*" Wellman said. "Big trouble, on top of a mountain. He wasn't tending to business. Not the business of making movies. He was paying a lot of attention to monkey business, and I called him for it. Lost my easy-to-lose temper and did it in front of the company. A *bad* mistake. He was a big man. I am not. But there was a big something in my favor. His face. He made his living with it. Mine was behind the camera. He might have beaten my brains out, I don't know, but I do know that I could have made a character man out of him in the process. I think he knew that and we finished the picture speaking only when necessary and only about business."

The plot of London's book concerns a wild dog who has been domesticated but returns to his natural savage state. The scriptwriters tried to change the focus from the dog to the humans. In the story, Loretta's character is married, but her husband is presumed dead, so she and Gable's character set up housekeeping. Co-star Jack Oakie played Shorty Hollihan, Gable's buddy. Despite this cast of characters, however, almost everyone involved in the project agreed that the star of *Call of the Wild* still remained the dog, Buck.

One brutally cold night Young, Gable, Oakie, and a few others were sitting around the big oak dining table, relaxing after dinner. "It had been one of the coldest days we had had during the shooting of the entire picture," Oakie recalled. "We had to be dug out that morning, and the path leading to the street where we were shooting was flanked by snowbanks at least ten feet high. The Moose [Oakie's nickname for Gable] and I were having some brandy, trying to thaw out, when Wild Bill came in with a blast of icy wind."

Wellman wanted to retake a scene, but Gable balked. "Are you crazy?" he said. "It's *too* cold out there."

Wellman cajoled the actors, and Gable and Oakie finally agreed, as did Loretta. "If you're going to do it," she said, "so can I."

Outside, Gable played with Buck as the lights and camera were set up, but the dog was unfriendly and constantly nipped at him.

"Be careful, he bites!" said the owner-trainer, Carl Spitz.

"What's the matter with Buck?" Gable asked.

"That's not Buck," answered the trainer. "It's too cold out here for Buck. That's Buck's stand-in."

Gable became furious and began screaming at Wellman. To diffuse the impending furor, Oakie exclaimed, "Look at Loretta! She's turning purple!" Gable swept Loretta up into his arms and carried her back to the warmth of the lodge.

Back in Hollywood, gossip columns continued to hint that Loretta and Clark were having a romance.

On February 1, 1935, the cast and crew celebrated Gable's thirty-fourth birthday. By mid-February location shooting on the picture was finally finished and Gable was back in Hollywood to attend the Academy Award ceremonies with his wife and her daughter. He was stunned when he won the best actor Oscar for *It Happened One Night.*

Years later Loretta would laugh when asked about her love

By her midteens Loretta Young was already a great beauty.

With Lon Chaney in *Laugh, Clown, Laugh* (1928). Young was only fourteen, but photographed older. This was five decades before Brooke Shields made child leading-ladies fashionable.

In *Zoo in Budapest* (1933). Nineteen-year-old Loretta played a waif.

The beauteous Young brood in the midthirties: Mamma Gladys (center, seated) surrounded by her daughters (left to right) Polly Ann, Sally, and Loretta.

Loretta Young and Spencer Tracy in *A Man's Castle* (1933).

Loretta and Clark Gable in *Call of the Wild* (1935).

Loretta, in long blond wig, was the star of DeMille's *The Crusades* (1935).

A typical 1930s Loretta Young pose: mannequin-perfect.

With Tyrone Power in *Second Honeymoon* (1937). They were a team the public loved and made five pictures together.

Young and Power in *Suez* (1938). The spectacular drama was the final
pairing of the two stars.

scenes with Gable in *Call of the Wild*. "Clark Gable was memorable, all right. He wore a beard throughout the picture. Imagine getting Clark for a screen lover, and then having a scriptwriter put whiskers on him! There ought to have been a law. I had fun in that picture, however, largely because of Clark. He puts everyone at ease. He has a sense of humor, which always helps." She referred to both Gable and Oakie as "laugh riots."

Loretta had been greatly impressed with Gable's acting ability. "In his presence one is ashamed of any selfish impulse," she said. "If I ever felt myself getting 'upstage,' I would think of Clark Gable and change my ways."

When shooting on *Call of the Wild* was finally over, both stars were off to new assignments: Gable to Catalina Island for *Mutiny on the Bounty*, Young to Paramount for Cecil B. DeMille's epic, *The Crusades*.

The rumors of the Gable-Young romance would soon fade but not entirely disappear.

Because of the extended schedule on *Call of the Wild*, Loretta was weeks late reporting to Paramount for *The Crusades*, in which she had the female lead and received top billing. As was DeMille's practice, the movie had had months of preproduction and was now months into production.

DeMille had originally announced that he wanted an actress with the acting ability of Helen Hayes, the effervescence of Miriam Hopkins, the wistfulness of Helen Mack, and the charm of Marion Davies. In addition, the actress would have to be as beautiful as all four of those women combined.

Loretta wore a long blond wig throughout the picture, and looked stunning. However, her friend John Engstead, who did the still photographs of her during the film, noted that she was a changed woman.

"One evening at six o'clock I went to Loretta's dressing room," Engstead has recalled. "She was in one of the choice first-floor suites, and when I knocked, she was engaged in a telephone conversation but motioned for me to come in. Her makeup was off, there were shadows under her eyes, and she looked tired. I could not believe her telephone conversation. She was reading the riot act to some studio executive. She told him in no uncertain terms exactly what she would and would not do, made herself crystal-clear, and hung up. I was amazed by the transformation from the sweet, shy Gretchen to this strong businesswoman."

It was apparent the moguls intended to work Loretta relentlessly, but it was also apparent that Loretta was nobody's fool. She was greatly respected by her employers, but the business demanded a tremendous amount from its stars— today's screen idol could be tomorrow's has-been, virtually overnight. It happened all the time.

Immediately upon completion of *The Crusades,* Young began *Shanghai,* her second picture with Charles Boyer. Afterwards she insisted that she needed a rest and was at last going to take her European trip. She left for New York with her mother in early June and checked into an apartment at the swank Hotel Pierre on Fifth Avenue.

Loretta said she intended to see plenty of plays, but generally the prescription called for was rest before sailing on the *Ile de France* to England on June 30, for what she described as "a two-month vacation."

The press, however, would not leave Loretta alone, and shortly after her arrival in London her name was linked with that of handsome tennis star Fred Perry, with whom she attended the Wimbledon matches. Young's only comment: "I like Frederick very much, but the fact is, there isn't any love life for me now." It was a rather plaintive remark.

She had known Perry in California, and denied responsibility for breaking up his engagement with British actress Mary Lawson. Loretta also said that after her week in London she hoped to visit Paris and Italy, and that she had to be back in Hollywood by August. "You can bank on it that I'm not going back as Mrs. Perry."

For the next few months reports on Loretta petered out and became vague. Columns back in Hollywood hinted Loretta was ill and recovering from exhaustion.

Although she was personally absent from the Hollywood scene, Loretta Young was on screens across the country when three of her films were released that summer. *Shanghai, Call of the Wild,* and *The Crusades* had all opened within a month of each other.

That same summer Zanuck and Schenck merged Twentieth Century Pictures and the Fox Film Corporation into Twentieth Century–Fox. The new company announced a full-length Technicolor feature, *Ramona.* It was an old Fox property based on the Helen Hunt Jackson novel, and had been a big silent hit for Dolores Del Rio. Fox executive Winfield Sheehan had been grooming a seventeen-year-old contract player, Rita Cansino—later renamed Rita Hayworth—for the part. But after the merger Sheehan was eased out and Miss Cansino's option was dropped.

Zanuck cast ex-radio announcer Don Ameche in the male lead. (Ameche would become Twentieth Century–Fox's first studio-made star.) For the title role, Zanuck said he wanted Loretta and would hold up production until she returned from overseas (Loretta later said she "fought" to play the role).

While Loretta was away, Sally was making news over her romance with Norman Foster, whom she ran into at a dinner party in London. She had known Foster since the days he had dated Loretta, and she later revealed that she had been attracted to him even then. Apparently, however, the sparks between them didn't ignite until now.

Once back in Hollywood, Sally and Norman began talking seriously about marriage. There was a hitch however: although estranged for years, Foster and Claudette Colbert had never gotten a divorce. "As soon as Miss Colbert obtains a decree," it was reported in August 1935, "probably in Mexico or Reno, Foster will marry Sally Blane." Referring to the impending divorce, Foster said, "It will have to be outside of California, because here you have to wait a year, and that's too long."

Miss Colbert started proceedings to obtain a quick divorce, and throughout September the press kept hinting that the Foster-Blane wedding would be sometime soon. There was some speculation that the couple was waiting for Loretta's recovery and return—she was still out of town recovering from exhaustion, reports said—so she could attend the ceremony.

An official announcement of the Blane-Foster engagement was made on September 16. Sally and Norman said they were thinking of sailing to Australia for a honeymoon, but they were still uncertain as to the date, since the wedding would depend on Loretta's recovery.

How ill was Loretta? wondered many in Hollywood, especially after the following bulletin as reported by the International News Service: "Utmost simplicity will mark Miss Blane's wedding, due to the serious illness of her sister."

For some reason, through the years, many film historians have misreported the Foster-Blane wedding as having occurred in 1937. But in reality the ceremony finally took place on October 8, 1935, at the Church of St. Paul the Apostle in Westwood, followed by a small, quiet reception at the Young-Belzer home. There was no mention at the time of Loretta being in attendance at either the wedding or the reception.

Suddenly, newspapers began commenting on Loretta's "illness," and even the Associated Press ran a huge story with blazing headlines about costly sicknesses in Hollywood. "Disaster in the form of movie illness has written approximately $1 million on the red ink side of studio ledgers," reported AP. "Major casualties are: Loretta Young—out for a year through illness—four films canceled." Others cited were Freddie Bartholomew, "out for two weeks," Adolphe Menjou, "one picture delayed," and Simone Simon, "one picture

delayed." Through stories such as these confusion later arose
as to how long Loretta was actually away. She was absent
from Hollywood, in fact, only five months.

Columnist Lloyd Pantages wrote in October, "I very much
fear that Loretta Young's illness will necessitate her retirement from the screen for at least a year." But only a few
weeks later, on November 30, 1935, Loretta appeared in
public. Although her departure for Europe had been covered
with much fanfare, she had somehow managed to return to
Hollywood unnoticed. She virtually popped up, and the press
was taken off guard.

It was the first time they had seen her in months, and the
papers splashed her photographs all over their pages with
headlines proclaiming, LORETTA RECOVERS. Her name
stayed in the news for a few weeks when Gable publicly, if
not officially, separated from Ria and moved into a hotel. The
press speculated on his many romances with his leading ladies, and listed Loretta among them.

In December, Spencer Tracy got into a brawl with William
Wellman at the Trocadero. Tracy fought with Wellman (and
others), and was not as concerned over marring his good
looks as Gable might have been. On this occasion, the feisty
Wellman belted Tracy in the eye. Tracy biographer Larry
Swindell has noted, "The fight was kicked off by a remark
Wellman had made to Tracy about Loretta Young."

The next day, newspapers reported the fight with banner
headlines. One newspaper had a picture of Tracy, captioned
"Fights Over Loretta." "L. B. Mayer was furious about the
story, but not nearly so angry as Tracy," Swindell has stated.
"The story implied he was still carrying on his affair with
Loretta Young, which was far from the truth."

It was conceded by those who knew Tracy well, however,
that though reconciled with his wife, he had not gotten over
his feelings for Loretta quite as quickly as was reported.

That same month, the January 1936 issue of *Photoplay* hit
the stands. The issue had gone to press in mid-November, a

couple of weeks before Miss Young had resurfaced in Hollywood. In it ace reporter Dorothy Manners discussed the persistent rumors of Loretta Young's mysterious disappearance
from the Hollywood scene. The article, "Fame, Fortune and
Fatigue," attempted to put to rest various theories about Loretta Young's absence: she had an incurable illness; she had
been maimed in an accident; she was secretly married and
was expecting a secret child. According to Miss Manners,
Loretta was resting so she'd be strong enough for a major
operation she had to have. With an air of total authority she
declared, "This is the truth about Loretta Young's mysterious
illness."

The impact of the article was diffused by the fact that Loretta had returned from her mysterious trip healthy and ready
to return to work. At the time the magazine was on the stands
with its fanciful conjectures, Louella Parsons reported to millions, "Loretta Young, who had such a long and dangerous
siege of illness, is well again and ready to step into a motion
picture. She looks more beautiful than ever, and she has entirely recovered from the cold and cough that kept her in
seclusion for so many months."

Loretta started working almost immediately on a loanout
to M-G-M for *The Unguarded Hour* with Franchot Tone. For
the first few months in 1936 the tenor of Loretta's publicity
was basically "Everyone is glad to have Loretta back again,
looking so well and radiant."

The Hollywood social scene seemed busier than ever.
There was "informal" Hollywood, where roller-skating
would shortly be the new craze among younger members of
the film set. Ginger Rogers had even installed a portable rink
at her home in Beverly Hills because she "didn't want to
drive miles to a roller rink." And then there was "formal"
Hollywood, with its big parties, benefits, and gala balls. This
seemed more Loretta's milieu.

The eagerly awaited formal event that season was the Mayfair Club Ball, an annual benefit for the Motion Picture Relief Fund. David O. Selznick headed the club and Carole Lombard had persuaded him to let her be hostess that year. The theme of the ball was Black and White. The men were to wear tails and the women were requested to wear only white.

There was a touch of drama when Norma Shearer defied Lombard's edict and entered the room gowned in flaming red. Thalberg, of course, was her escort. Lombard was incensed and behaved horribly for the rest of the evening.

Loretta was dazzling in white fox. Her escort was Lydell Peck, Janet Gaynor's former husband. David Niven attended with his "best girl," Merle Oberon, who was impeccably gowned in a white ensemble dotted with black polka dots. Bette Davis was there with her boyish-looking husband, Harmon Nelson, while Henry Fonda escorted Jeanette MacDonald. Gable was there, as was Ria Gable, who appeared very matronly amidst all the spectacular young beauties. Clark ignored his estranged wife, directing his attention to Lombard (whose escort was Cesar Romero).

Gable and Lombard even slipped away for a ride in his new Duesenberg, but according to reports, when she invited him to a breakfast party she was hosting with friends, Gable declined, saying, "I've got a date." Lombard shot back, "With who? Loretta Young?"

It appears then, as now, even Hollywood stars believed gossip about Hollywood stars.

Gossip and innuendo faded as Loretta proceeded to tackle her career and social life with the zeal of a quarterback returning to the game after halftime.

After *The Unguarded Hour* Loretta went right into a film on the Fox lot. In return for "lending" Loretta, Zanuck now "borrowed" leading M-G-M heartthrob Robert Taylor and cast him opposite Loretta in *Private Number,* a remake of an old Constance Bennett–Lew Ayres film, *Common Clay.* For once there were no rumors of an offscreen romance; Taylor was seeing Barbara Stanwyck, and the couple's marriage was imminent.

Loretta liked *Private Number* and fondly recalled a particular love scene with Taylor: "He sat on the ground, and she was in a hammock beside him. They talked about very casual things, but from the tone of their voices you sensed their longing for each other."

Through the years Loretta has been very vocal about love scenes in her films. "I don't enjoy the groping, grabby kind of love scenes," she once said. "I don't like to play rough. It's no fun being mauled. I prefer something a little more subtle and sensitive. Also, for my taste, the less I have to say and the more I can concentrate on expressions, the more effective a love scene is." Instead of using words, she said, "I have been using my eyes."

Private Number was a memorable experience for Taylor too. "Loretta's an avowed, unapologetic perfectionist," he later noted. "When we worked together and she'd step to a mirror just before each scene for that last merciless self-analytical inspection, many's the time I was tempted to howl like a coyote. Then, seeing the finished picture, I had to admit, 'The lady was right.'"

The lady herself has explained that the mirror was "an indispensable part of my business." To Loretta, it was an "invaluable critic."

After *Private Number* came the delayed *Ramona*. Loretta wore a long, dark wig for the role, and looked like a porcelain-skinned madonna. Her delicate coloring and superb complexion were effectively captured by the Technicolor camera, and her svelte proportions were ideal for the tight-waisted, long-skirted costumes. She proved she was a spirited dancer in this film.

Costar Don Ameche was impressed with her knowledge of what went into making movies. He observed, "Loretta knew more about the technical end of moviemaking than almost any other actress I ever worked with." If the lighting wasn't exactly right, or the camera wasn't in the right place, Loretta, in her polite and ladylike manner, let the right people know.

There was real-life drama on the set of *Ramona* when a fire broke out and Loretta grabbed Ramon Lugo, the two-year-old child actor doing the scene with her, and rushed him and herself to safety.

Actors took a lot of risks making movies during these days, and in addition to making films and doing publicity, contract players were also compelled to participate in what was then known as "promotion and exploitation," appearing in advertisements for products which also carried mention of that star's latest film. Loretta's radiant face smiled from ads hawking such wares as Lux Toilet Soap: "Avoid dangerous pore-choking Loretta Young's way. . . . Use Lux Toilet Soap." These endorsements brought the stars no extra money; all this merchandising was simply part of the job.

In her private life Young avoided further entanglements with actors. She was dating sophisticated film director Edward Sutherland, former husband of Louise Brooks. Although Loretta was considered a mature sophisticate in the eyes of film fans, she was in fact only twenty-three years old. She saw Sutherland, who was many years her senior, for over a year. They were rumored engaged as early as May 1936, and Sutherland found the press comparing him to Grant Withers.

Withers had not dropped off the face of the earth after he was divorced by Loretta. He had appeared in *Goin' to Town* with Mae West and *Border Flight* with Frances Farmer. He later appeared on Broadway in *Boy Meets Girl* and *Helzapoppin,* both long-running hits. Withers made news of his own with several more marriages and divorces. (Throughout the thirties, however, in all publicity for both Withers and Loretta, the other was usually mentioned.)

When queried about her first marriage around this time, Loretta told a reporter, "Isn't it too bad I didn't have a baby? I could play with it now."

Sally was pregnant, and so was Polly Ann, who had married Pasadena socialite Carter Hermann. Polly Ann had appeared onstage at the Pasadena Playhouse, but for now she joined Sally in looking forward to motherhood.

Obviously, Polly Ann's film career had never been particularly important to her, although she had made a few films. After *White Parade* there had been *Crimson Trail, Sons of Steel,* and *The Border Patrolmen.* In addition, Polly Ann had starred opposite her brother-in-law Foster in *I Cover Chinatown.* Foster not only played the lead but also directed the film. From this point on, Foster would concentrate on his directing career, often making films with one of the Young sisters. Foster had stayed on the Fox lot after the Twentieth Century–Fox merger, and would remain there for years as a director-screenwriter.

Fox was Loretta's home lot, and from this point on there would be no more loanouts. Working at one studio had its advantages, including the chance to build a rapport with people behind the scenes.

Loretta's self-discipline was a trait which saw her through the work schedule Twentieth Century–Fox now set for her. In *Ladies in Love,* Loretta's next picture, she costarred with the woman she had once envied so intensely—Janet Gaynor. They were now friends. Constance Bennett was the third star of the picture, and French actress Simone Simon was also featured.

Gaynor and Bennett were two of the biggest female names in the business, but their box office appeal had diminished. Teaming two stars on the wane was an old showman's ploy to give a vehicle the illusion of "importance." Loretta was not overshadowed by either woman, a tribute to her own uniqueness.

To play Loretta's love interest in the picture, Zanuck featured one of the handsomest—indeed, prettiest—young men ever to appear on screen, Tyrone Power, Jr. He was a year younger than Loretta, and had garnered a huge amount of fan mail after a one-scene appearance in a programmer, *Girls' Dormitory.*

Loretta has recalled Power as "the only bashful leading man I ever had. He got over his shyness as time went on." She described him as possessing "the appealing quality that hints at just a little timidity underlying everything . . . a wholesome balance against too much cocksureness and vanity."

Zanuck had planned to cast Young opposite Don Ameche in the proposed spectacle *Lloyds of London,* but when the fan mail began pouring in for Power he decided the youngster had star quality and replaced Ameche with Power—and instructed the writers on *Lloyds* to build up Power's role. Suddenly Loretta's role became merely window dressing, and she refused to participate in the film.

Loretta had started off at Twentieth as second lead to George Arliss in a costume drama. Twelve pictures later, Zanuck was again casting her in a secondary part.

Loretta left with her mother for Hawaii, ostensibly for a vacation. It appeared, however, that Loretta was playing the Hollywood game. She was now represented by one of the town's most powerful agents, Myron Selznick, who informed Zanuck that Loretta wanted to make only four movies a year and would play only leads.

Her salary had more than doubled in three years, and Zanuck was certainly pleased with her performance both on the sound stage and at the box office. He wanted to sign Loretta to a new seven-year contract. Selznick and Zanuck began bargaining, a process that would continue for some time, since Young's present contract still had two more years.

Ty Power appeared in *Lloyds of London* opposite Madeleine Carroll (another Myron Selznick client) in the role intended for Loretta. Although he was the lead, Power received fourth billing. Carroll had been billed second, Sir Guy Standing third, and child star Freddie Bartholomew received top billing, portraying Power as a young boy.

Young returned to Fox that fall to make *Love Is News,* directed by Tay Garnett. She would again be costarred with Power. To Darryl Zanuck, the duo was a natural for reteaming—this was, after all, the era of the great "teams." In silent films it had been Ronald Colman and Vilma Banky, Garbo and Gilbert. The current blockbuster pairings were Astaire and Rogers, MacDonald and Eddy.

Power had caught the moviegoing public's fancy in a matter of months. To Loretta's astonishment and anger, she learned that Zanuck was giving Power top billing in *Love Is News.* The newcomer, whom she liked immensely, was being given the advantage of starring opposite a proven draw. From Loretta's point of view, she had every right to be furious— she'd appeared in fifty-eight films to date, and now Zanuck was responding to her loyalty by giving her second billing to a novice.

From Zanuck's point of view, however, it was good business. Power had signed with the studio for seven years, while Loretta was still refusing to extend her contract. Zanuck's maneuver was one Loretta would not forget—or forgive. And in the opinion of someone who was close to the star for years, this was yet another important point in Loretta's life where she had been "betrayed" by a man—her father had been the first. Gladys had long ago instilled in Loretta the perception of men as creatures to be wary of, not to be trusted; now Loretta's business experiences seemed to verify Mrs. Belzer's warnings.

In November, Cecil B. DeMille invited Loretta to star on his popular network radio program, *The Lux Radio Theater.* Each week DeMille hosted an abbreviated version of a famous film broadcast live to some fifty million listeners. The property might be a movie that was a few years old, or one in current or recent release. In many cases the people who had played the parts on screen repeated their roles for the radio version.

In some rare cases all of the leads from the film were on the show. Regardless, it was always an elaborate production. Actors did not merely show up and read scripts; there was a full week's rehearsal beforehand with a director. A live studio audience at showtime. Top stars received several thousand dollars for appearing on the program, a respectable stipend for a week's work. (There was conjecture that the stars who graced the Lux soap ads seemed to be more frequent guests than those who didn't.)

For her Lux radio debut on November 10, 1936, Loretta played the lead in *Polly of the Circus* (a former Marion Davies film) opposite James Gleason. Lux would prove to be a valuable showcase for maintaining the star persona of Loretta Young.

When Young and Power finished *Love Is News,* Zanuck immediately cast them together in *Café Metropole.* Inevitable rumors of a romance between Tyrone Power and Loretta Young were prominent in the press, despite Power's involvement with skating champion-turned-movie-star Sonja Henie. Power seemed to prefer foreign women who were worldly and took the role of initiator. On screen, however, Tyrone Power was always the happy-go-lucky, charming male, and the onscreen chemistry between Young and Power was immensely appealing.

George Hurrell photographed Young and Power during the years they were teamed together. "Loretta Young was one of the most inventive subjects that I ever shot," he observed. "She always had exciting ideas about the way she should be photographed. She had radiance. I don't believe that we ever, during the twenty-five years that we worked together, repeated a pose. She was a disciplined pro."

Love Is News, released in March 1937, was a smash hit—the only Loretta Young film of the thirties, in fact, to be listed as a top-ten moneymaker. Her films were always profitable, but never extravagant successes.

"Love *IS* news . . . when this romantic trio make their new kind of love!" said the ads spotlighting Young, Power, and costar Ameche. The movie posters particularly emphasized Power, proclaiming that the audience would thrill "especially over Tyrone Power, the new star sensation of *Lloyds of London* in a role even more sensational!"

The picture brought Loretta good personal notices, too, calling attention to "a comedy flair one would never suspect."

She found it fun doing comedy if it was spontaneous and she was not told by the director, "This is a wow of a line, don't muff it." She knew how she worked best: "When I try to be funny, I'm pathetic, but when I just let it come, I'm not so bad."

To further publicize the film, Loretta and Tyrone did an abbreviated twenty-four-minute radio version on Louella Parsons's *Hollywood Hotel* network program.

Loretta got top billing in *Café Metropole,* released the next month, while gossip columnists and fan magazines kept linking "Loretta and Ty." They were, after all, seen together often at premieres and photographed dining and dancing. But Gordon Oliver, an old friend of Loretta's, says, "The whole thing with Ty was just publicity."

When queried about Loretta's romance with Edward Sutherland, which continued throughout this period, Oliver says, "Eddie was too old for her. She was just a kid."

Around this time, Loretta abruptly stopped dating Sutherland. "Loretta idealizes," Sutherland said, "and she is rebuffed by the slightest intimacy. A platonic love would suit her, I think. I hope she marries again. When real love comes along, perhaps she won't be so finicky." He had chosen his words carefully, but the point was clear.

Loretta, decades later, commented on Sutherland's attitude: "I don't blame him . . . but I just didn't want to get married. I wasn't especially in love with him. I was in love with love."

And there was plenty of love in the titles of her pictures. In 1937 Loretta made *Love Under Fire* with Don Ameche. Ameche was one of those rare actors who could play both young leading men and young character parts. Loretta actually made as many films with Ameche as she did with Power, but she and Don Ameche were never considered a team.

Loretta and her mother left Hollywood after she finished shooting *Love Under Fire* in April. Sally told friends that Loretta and Mamma had gone to Bermuda instead of Europe because Loretta wanted to visit a handsome young man she had met the previous year in Honolulu. En route to Bermuda, Mrs. Belzer and Loretta stopped in New York, where they stayed a week at the Pierre.

While in New York, Loretta met with writer Irene Thirer, who reported that Loretta "talked about her career and her sisters and her sisters' babies, and how she was green-eyed with jealousy at their domestic bliss instead of being glad for them—only fooling, of course!"

Miss Thirer's article mentioned Polly Ann and Sally and said that Loretta "has enjoyed more cinema success than her equally attractive sisters, but not nearly as much personal happiness." When Loretta returned from Bermuda, she would make some real news.

Loretta had given an interview to writer Carolyn Hoyt on the subject "I'm Not Married Because . . ." She discussed children, saying that her only regret was that she didn't have any. Loretta enthused over Polly Ann's four-month-old son, Jimmy Hermann, as well as Norman and Sally's daughter Gretchen, Loretta's namesake. Sally had told Loretta, "Gretch, there's nothing like it. To feel the absolute dependence of that little creature on you. To know you're the one person in the world she trusts instinctively, turns to for everything."

Loretta made no secret of her desire for children, and soon her fans would know, too, when Hoyt's article appeared two months later in *Modern Screen*.

It was June 1937, and Louella Parsons knew something was in the wind. Louella had not become the town's leading reporter by waiting for press releases or official announcements. On June 10, Parsons had a scoop for her millions of readers around the country, setting off a wave of speculation that reverberates to this day. Even when Miss Parsons initially reported the story her choice of words was intriguing and the innuendo was strong. "Loretta Young, film star, admitted to me today she is a mother—by adoption," Louella wrote. "Two little girls, Jane, age three, and Judy, twenty-three and a half months, have been adopted by Loretta. As she confirmed the news she laughed:

" 'Yes, it is really true. They are such darlings . . .' "

"Origin a Secret," read the subheadline of the article, and Miss Young was further quoted as saying, "There is just one thing I can't tell you, and that is where I got the children, and I want to forget as soon as possible that they are not mine."

Miss Parsons noted, "And just like all new 'mothers,' she's already talking plans for Jane and Judy Young," adding subtly, "I wonder if all this can mean that Loretta is never planning to be married again."

The confusion soon began. The following day, the United Press reported that Loretta Young had become a mother by signing papers to adopt two youngsters, a three-year-old boy named James, and a twenty-three-month-old baby girl named Judy. According to the wire service, Miss Young had found the children at a Catholic orphanage the previous Christmas.

Then, three and a half weeks later, a followup story proclaimed, "Loretta Young relinquishes tot to mother." At the time, Loretta wouldn't disclose which of the two children she had to give up, saying that she would make an application to adopt another child soon. But after giving up young Jane,

Loretta would not adopt another child, keeping only the (then) two-year-old Judy.

It seemed to many that a smokescreen had been set up, and the town was abuzz with gossip. The question asked in whispers by Loretta's peers was the obvious one: Was Judy her real child? Rumors spread quickly, and speculation ran rampant.

Although for the past year and a half Loretta's name had been linked with half a dozen men, people now harked back to her alleged romance with Gable and the fact that she had disappeared for much of 1935. They recalled stories of Young's fatigue and mysterious illness, and her abrupt recovery almost overnight.

Had Loretta's "illness" two years ago been an excuse to quietly have a baby? Tongues began to wag, and when this gossip was published years later, one of Hollywood's most indestructible legends was created. People were reminded of the presumed affair with Gable. They were apprised of the *Photoplay* article, with allusions to "secret marriage . . . secret child." They were told that Loretta "disappeared for a year." People theorized then, and still do, that if Loretta had had an affair and had become pregnant, she would have had to have the baby because an abortion would have been out of the question due to her religion.

Of course, all evidence was circumstantial. When piecing together the puzzle, the truth reveals that Loretta had been gone from public view for only five months during 1935, but who wouldn't want to believe the story of the "secret child"? It's the stuff that Hollywood myths are made of.

Perhaps one reason there is such suspicion about the adopted child's natural mother is that there have been many conflicting details, such as the aforementioned Jane-James mix-up, and the fact that at the time of the adoption there was much overlapping and contradicting information fed to the public. In addition, through the years Judy's age and birthdates have changed and conflicted. If she were twenty-three and a half months old when adopted, her birthday would be in June or July. But it is usually reported as November.

Over the decades, the legend that Judy is Loretta's natural child has gathered many believers. Writer George Eels, for example, reported that a former coworker of Loretta's "claims . . . she employed a nurse, who told her, 'Loretta didn't adopt that child. She's hers.' The nurse claimed to have worked on the staff of the hospital where the child was born. 'Now, that nurse was a good Catholic woman who had nothing against Loretta, and there was no reason for her to lie.' "

Speculation about Gable having a secret child has also been bandied about for decades—he was, after all, "the screen's greatest lover." In the late nineteen thirties there was a much-publicized paternity suit. Although his first two wives were much older and there was never a question of their having children by Gable, he did try desperately to have children with his third wife, Carole Lombard. Gable even submitted to sterility tests. Naturally, this information was kept secret; Gable's studio could not risk revealing that the virility of the country's leading sex symbol was in question. The rumors of Gable's secret child, therefore, were not denied with any vehemence, since they only enhanced his reputation as a great lover.

Late in life Gable was finally able to father a child with his fifth wife. After his death, however, the "secret child" stories were given some credence by top screenwriter and Hollywood personality Anita Loos, a friend of Gable's and confidante of Lombard's. Writing about Gable's son in 1974, Loos claimed, "Contrary to press releases, the boy is not Clark's only child. A short but hectic affair Clark went through with a costar when they were far from Hollywood on location had resulted in the birth of a baby girl. She is now a Park Avenue matron, a dream of a beauty, like her mom."

Like Miss Loos's, most accounts are direct about one star

but deliberately vague about the other. There have been published rumors of "the child recovering from cosmetic surgery on her ears," and a few stories directly link Young's name with Gable's. *Call of the Wild* director William Wellman has been quoted as saying, "All I know is that Loretta and Clark were very friendly during the picture and it was very cold up there. When the filming was finished, she disappeared for a while and later showed up with a daughter with the biggest ears I ever saw except on an elephant."

Of course it must be considered that the uncharitable Mr. Wellman was notably hostile toward Gable and may have had an unrequited yen for Miss Young.

Today, a source very close to Miss Young states simply, "I couldn't swear either way if the child is Loretta's or not. If she is, it was a very courageous thing for her to have kept the child." However, the source points out that Loretta was *never* one for intimate flings ("that is *not* her type of relationship") and also has doubts about the allegation that Gable fathered the child. Gable was often a guest at social gatherings at Loretta's home in later years, and would often bemoan his lack of childen. For Gable to make such statements in social circumstances, under the close scrutiny of his peers, seems hardly a confirmation of the legend. "In my opinion," concludes the source, "neither Loretta nor Gable could have carried off such a charade."

As many top stars in Hollywood have learned, trying to refute gossip of this nature is impossible. There are even people who contend that Judy is actually Spencer Tracy's "secret child"!

There is no way to prove that Judy is Loretta's child; however, there also seems no way to dispel the contention that she isn't. One fact is certain: as the years have gone by, all concerned speak as if she were. Miss Young declared in 1937 that she wanted to forget as soon as possible that the child was not hers—and she has apparently done just that.

At the time of the original adoption announcement, single-parent adoption was an extreme rarity. Other famous single actresses—notably Miriam Hopkins and Gloria Swanson— had adopted children before Loretta, and the resulting rumors were similar. The allegation that Swanson's adopted son, Joe, was actually her son by Joseph P. Kennedy persisted for decades.

In 1937 Loretta certainly must have anticipated the deluge of gossip she would inspire by adopting a child. At no time, either during or after the adoption, did she ever deign to comment on the rumors. To her credit, she did not attempt to keep little Judy in the background; instead, she mentioned her adoringly when discussing her private life and yet sheltered her from the exploitive publicity that could have made the child one of Hollywood's "star babies." From the beginning, Judy was an integral part of the tight-knit Young family.

*Worldly, with a nice, lustrous polish
over her private emotions.*
—*Karen Hollis describing
Loretta Young, 1938*

Seven

By the fall of 1937, the spotlight had turned from Loretta's
private life back to her career. She had three films in immediate release, all major productions: *Love Under Fire; Wife, Doctor and Nurse;* and *Second Honeymoon.*

Wife, Doctor and Nurse matched Loretta with Warner Baxter
and Virginia Bruce. Baxter had been a big silent star and
winner of the second Academy Award given for best actor,
and he was still Fox's leading male star when Zanuck took
over. The studio czar was now phasing Baxter out, however,
just as he had Janet Gaynor earlier. Loretta was the box office
attraction in *Wife, Doctor and Nurse;* Baxter was too old for
the public to accept him as a real romantic lead for Loretta.

In *Second Honeymoon,* Loretta was again teamed with Tyrone
Power. She enjoyed one love scene in particular. "I love
delicate love scenes. There was one in *Second Honeymoon* on a
dock. They sat there, reminiscing about their elopement. The
audience had to imagine how they had looked and what they
had been like. The tone of their voices, more than their actual words, told the story."

Loretta's comments on scenes such as this one (and the

earlier one with Robert Taylor) give insight to her concept of what is truly romantic. It was the sentiment, the style, the thought—not the clinch—that impressed her most.

Claire Trevor also appeared in *Second Honeymoon,* and later provided fascinating insight into Loretta and the Hollywood scene of those years. Discussing promotion, Trevor said, "I hated it with a passion, because after every picture you'd have to pose for fashion stills. And you'd spend the whole day in the still department changing clothes and holding poses. And you know, when you're a young girl, that's such a bore." According to Miss Trevor, Loretta Young "was a perfect movie star; she did everything right. She'd comb her hair and then she wouldn't move. Marvelous! And one day they said to both of us, 'All right, ladies, you're finished.' It was about one o'clock. I said, 'Wow!' Off came the eyelashes. Know what she did? She called the still department. She said, 'I have an afternoon free. Let's make some stills.' That's how she was. If you're going to be a movie star, be a movie star, and work with all those people. Get your picture in the paper."

Second Honeymoon was another hit, but Loretta was not pleased with the direction her career was taking. She voiced her grievance in the press so that the front office would know she was serious. "I don't want to do another dizzy comedy for a long time," she said. "I want to do a heavy costume picture—all big, tragic emotion. The studio officials point out to me that they have been in the business a long time and know better than I do what the public wants. But nevertheless, I want to go dramatic in a big way, and I'll have to keep harping on it until they let me have my way."

Loretta's agent, Myron Selznick, was still negotiating with Zanuck, who wanted Loretta to remain with Fox and kept upping the ante. Meanwhile, Zanuck continued to cast his unhappy star in the expensive formula pictures he was using to build up his stable of male stars.

The studio tried to cook up another publicity romance be-

tween Loretta and Richard Greene, her handsome English costar in John Ford's *Four Men and a Prayer*. Zanuck was hoping Greene, publicized as a "cross between Tyrone Power and Robert Taylor," would strike the same chord with the audience as had his prototypes.

Loretta's days as "Miss Cooperation," however, were drawing to a close. Without mentioning Greene by name, she later recalled, "A certain studio wanted to get an English actor started and asked me to launch him. I was to go around to nightclubs with him and be seen everywhere with him and the studio would pay all the expenses. When this was proposed on the set one day I was in a hurry and said, 'It's a wonderful idea.' But when one of the executives saw me later and said, 'Now we want to lay this out properly,' I said, 'Are you kidding?' I was under contract to appear in the picture with him, but they couldn't make me go out with him socially."

However, Loretta did appear with Greene at premieres and nightclubs—but always in the company of another dashing young actor from England, her pal David Niven. Niven had signed a long-term contract with Sam Goldwyn, who saw him as a successor to Ronald Colman. Goldwyn, a wily showman, had told Niven, "Now you have a contract. Go around and get parts at other studios, and when you have experience, I'll give you a role in a Goldwyn picture."

Niven was lent to Twentieth for *Four Men and a Prayer*, and reportedly Loretta was instrumental in getting him the part. This was the first of many pictures Young and Niven would make together. On Niven's first day of shooting the entire Young family turned out to give him moral support.

Pairing director John Ford, a man who abhorred pretense and frills, with a star like Loretta was bound to cause waves. One day, when Ford sent for Loretta on the set, she refused to come out of her trailer, explaining she was not yet satisfied with her makeup and hairdo. The crew and Ford waited impatiently. After a while the director called a few stagehands and the men began rocking and shaking her trailer.

Years later, Ford, confronted with his behavior during this production, conceded, "I just didn't like the story or anything else about it. It was a job. I kidded them slightly."

Loretta's private life, meanwhile, continued to intrigue the public. She had dated young Alfred Vanderbilt, but no one took the pairing seriously—Vanderbilt dated all of Hollywood's beauties. She also dated handsome John McClain, and was seeing the brilliant young writer Joseph L. Mankiewicz, brother of Herman Mankiewicz.

In 1938 yet another member of the Young troupe made it onto the silver screen: "Loretta Young's littlest sister, grown up, renamed Ann Royal, is playing her first role in *Mad About Music*. Time marches on!" one magazine reported.

Georgianna was hardly "grown up"—she was only thirteen. Loretta, in fact, was only twenty-five, but by 1938 she seemed to have been around forever.

Georgianna seemed very interested in a film career, but Loretta thought she was too young to enter the movie world. "You were thirteen," Georgianna countered. Loretta conceded that was true, but said, "I don't regret it—for me. But that was in silent pictures. All you needed was a passable face."

It was at this time that Loretta went on a rare trip to New York—alone. She seemed to be asserting her independence and people close to her knew she needed a breather—her family was pushing her to sign that new Fox contract. "I suddenly realized a while ago that I've let myself be pampered, depended on others—my mother particularly—too much. Until I came east alone this time I had never bought a railroad ticket, or tipped a porter, or attended to any of those little details that children can cope with."

William Powell, at the peak of his *Thin Man/Great Ziegfeld* stardom, was in New York at this time and the press, of course, tried to create a romance between Powell and Loretta. They were, in fact, friends—they often dined out together with Josie and John Wayne.

Powell was long divorced from Carole Lombard, but still recovering from the shock of the sudden death of Jean Harlow, to whom he had been engaged.

Young and Powell created quite a stir in New York when they appeared together at the horse show at Madison Square Garden—even sophisticated society folk couldn't help but stare at movie stars. "No romance, y'understand," emphasized society columnist Robert McIlwaine. "The two just happened to be staying at the same hotel and since they're good friends, they decided to see the town together. Joe Mankiewicz is still Head Man in Loretta's young life, and Bill isn't interested in sentiment these days . . ."

But the question of why Loretta hadn't yet married was a frequent topic of gossip among insiders. "Here was a girl who, by simply existing, must mow men down," was a typical comment. "How has she escaped the hunters? Why isn't she married?"

While today no one thinks twice about a woman of twenty-five being single, it must be remembered that in previous generations the subject of marriage—especially for a woman —was an obsession.

Although Hollywood "romances" were constantly reported and even encouraged, it was never to be assumed that people were physically intimate or living together without first having married. Even if someone was divorced, the question was, Why hadn't they remarried?

Loretta wasn't coy or hesitant about such queries. "The whole thing can be summed up in a sentence," she said. "I don't want to marry—I won't marry—till I meet the man I feel I can't live without. I'm a normal girl. I've fallen in love. If it were just a question of that, I'd have married long before now."

The ever-practical Loretta further pointed out, "With me marriage has got to be for life. I can't say, 'I've made a mistake. Divorce!' My ethics, my religion, my whole outlook, forbid it. When I marry, I've got to stay married. I have no choice."

Of course, the subject of Grant Withers couldn't be ignored. "I wasn't married to Grant in the Church," she explained. "It was a civil marriage, and therefore, to the Church, no marriage at all. If I'd had to marry Grant within the Church, I might not have done it," she admitted.

Years later Joseph Mankiewicz disclosed, "She wanted to get married but I was a divorced man and she was a rabid Paulist Catholic, which is the worst kind in the world. It would have meant getting a dispensation from the Pope and you can just see me, as anticlerical as I am, trying to get that."

Obviously, if Loretta was going to marry again, it was going to be within the Church. But it didn't seem to matter that she was single; she appeared to be leading a full life. She certainly had more going for her than many of her contemporaries. She had her family, her faith, and her career. She did, however, voice concern about having more children. Judy, now three, was a constant joy to her. "I'd like to have more. If I don't have some of my own pretty soon, I'll have to adopt them."

Back in Hollywood, Loretta's home life revolved around the much adored tot, Judy. Gladys's seventy-two-year-old father, Dr. Robert Royal of Seattle, visited his famous granddaughters, and Loretta's sixteen-millimeter camera photographed precious footage of four generations of family: Grandpa Royal, Gladys, Sally and her daughter Gretchen, Polly Ann and her son Jimmy, and of course, Loretta and little Judy.

At the studio Loretta completed *Three Blind Mice,* a comedy costarring Joel McCrea and the fast-rising David Niven. Afterwards, she was given her requested respite from comedy and was assigned the role of the empress Eugénie in Zanuck's monumental production *Suez.* But once again, to Loretta's chagrin, the main focus of the story would be the man's role.

Within a year and a half, Tyrone Power had vaulted to the same height of popularity and box office value as Gable, Tracy, and other leading men who had been in Hollywood for years. M-G-M had borrowed Power to star opposite Norma Shearer in *Marie Antoinette* and now he was back on the Fox lot for another historical costume epic. In *Suez* he played the lead character, Ferdinand de Lesseps, the man who built the famous canal.

Director Allan Dwan, in a rather uncharitable assessment of his star, noted that casting Loretta as an empress was "type casting," since she usually came across as royalty in person. "Loretta was always above everything, you know," he remarked. "And she used that quality as Eugénie, of having complete control over her situation and being vastly superior to everybody. It came naturally for her to make you feel that everyone she came in contact with was far beneath her."

Loretta had admitted on an earlier occasion, "Every once in a while, I think I'd like to be a part that I'm playing." When she appeared as an empress, some people felt the part and the person had more than a little in common.

It should be noted, however, that Loretta's royal demeanor was actually her best defense against the exploitive Hollywood system. Loretta had never been available for executive "parties," as some other aspiring actresses were, and her most effective strategy was to remain aloof and unapproachable. Loretta Young is one of the few screen beauties who has never been accused, even by her most hateful critics, of taking the casting couch approach to success.

But she *has* been accused of scene stealing. In *Suez* she had powerful motivation for doing so: she felt the studio was using her to advance her costar's career. When Zanuck wanted to reshoot a scene because "Young stands out too much," Young retorted, "That is what I intended."

She collaborated with the costume designer to fashion "the largest hoopskirts ever," and she let her fingernails grow very long. Zanuck was furious. "You can't wear nails like that as Eugénie; you'll have to cut them," he demanded.

"You can make me play the role but you can't make me cut my fingernails," she replied.

Allan Dwan has said tales of Loretta's scene stealing were exaggerated. "I wouldn't have let that happen," he explained. "She was too professional. She knew that the better the final picture, the better it would be for her."

Tyrone Power was aware of Loretta's discontent. The romance rumors circulating during the filming of *Suez* were not about Ty and Loretta, but about Ty and Annabella, the third lead in *Suez*. A close friend of Marlene Dietrich, Annabella was being groomed by Zanuck for stardom—and would shortly become the first Mrs. Tyrone Power.

When Loretta groused at home about playing Eugénie in *Suez,* Sally cut her short by asking her, "What are you complaining about? I'd give my eye teeth for such a role!"

Sally would most likely have given more teeth for Loretta's next part. It was in a big Technicolor production, *Kentucky,* once again pairing her with British import Richard Greene. ("Loretta was one of the few who could share the screen believably with unbelievably good-looking men," noted one critic.)

What is noteworthy about this film today—in assessing its leading lady—is how contemporary she looks and acts. Her natural makeup, simple hairstyle, and tailored clothes are all in up-to-the-minute fashion. Many of Young's contemporaries, if judged by today's standards, are sadly dated in appearance. Such was never the case with Loretta Young—if one were to plant color photos of Young as she appeared in *Kentucky* in a 1986 *Vogue* magazine, ladies would ask who did her hair and makeup and want to know where they could buy the clothes.

An amusing footnote: in one scene in *Kentucky,* a love scene between Loretta and Greene, she visibly blushes—and,

very surprisingly, the braces on her bottom teeth are momentarily—but clearly—visible!

Everyone in the cast worked hard to make their performances effective, but it was the decidedly unglamorous character actor Walter Brennan who stole *Kentucky.* He would
win a best supporting actor Oscar for his portrayal of Uncle
Peter, "the best judge of horseflesh in Kentucky."

Loretta continued to appear on radio while at Fox. In May,
she guested on *Lux Radio Theater* again, playing opposite
George Brent in *The Girl from Tenth Avenue,* a Bette Davis
film. She also appeared on other radio programs, including
the top-rated Edgar Bergen and Charlie McCarthy comedy
show. Guest-starring on radio was an important way for stars
to plug films. In the fifties, television shows such as Ed Sullivan's were utilized for this purpose, while today, of course,
there are the talk shows. In the thirties, radio was the popular
way to reach the masses.

Lux was not the only dramatic program that featured radio
versions of films. *Hollywood Hotel* presented *Second Honeymoon*
while Loretta was out of town, with Sally Blane recreating
Loretta's screen role.

One burning question had preoccupied all of Hollywood's
top actresses for a couple of years now, including Loretta:
Who would be cast to play Scarlett O'Hara in *Gone With the
Wind?* In fact, these top stars were not only intensely pursuing the role, many had agreed to even screen-test for the
part!

Gone With the Wind was one of Loretta's favorite novels.
Loretta certainly had the right appearance for the role of
Scarlett, despite the fact that her ethereal image lacked the
fire-and-brimstone quality that the character of Scarlett required.

The final decision rested with the film's producer, the
legendary David O. Selznick. The most dynamic and talented
producer of his generation, Selznick was a whirlwind of en-

ergy, charm, and chutzpah (Benzadrine pills were at least partly responsible for his seemingly inexhaustible energy). Over six feet tall, curlyheaded, and bespectacled, Selznick was married to L. B. Mayer's youngest daughter, Irene, but had quite a reputation as both a womanizer and an inveterate gambler.

Selznick International was unquestionably the top company among the independents. In its three years of existence it had turned out *Little Lord Fauntleroy, The Garden of Allah, The Prisoner of Zenda, Nothing Sacred,* and *A Star Is Born,* the latter responsible for bringing Janet Gaynor back as a box office attraction after Zanuck had all but finished her at Fox.

The company was currently producing *The Adventures of Tom Sawyer* and *The Young in Heart,* but the most eagerly awaited Selznick International production was, of course, *Gone With the Wind.* It was already the motion picture event of the decade—before a camera had even turned. The novel, published in 1936, continued to sell at a fantastic rate.

"The only star not in contention to play Scarlett is Rin Tin Tin," quipped Robert Benchley, "and I'm not sure if she's a he or a she!" The role of Rhett Butler, of course, belonged to Clark Gable.

As early as the fall of 1937, Loretta and Selznick were "wooing" each other professionally, and not solely because of *Gone With the Wind.* Selznick's meticulous care in star selection and production values made most major actors and actresses eager to work for him.

Loretta was certainly Selznick's kind of star—ultraelegant, a great beauty, a true lady. Darryl Zanuck was livid when Loretta and his archrival were photographed "having themselves a time at the Rainbow Room" during one of Loretta's visits to New York.

By October 1938, with Loretta's Fox contract in its final days, a deal between Loretta and David Selznick seemed imminent. "Thinking of Boyer and Loretta for *Intermezzo,*" wrote Selznick at the time. To hire the duo would cost the producer somewhere in the neighborhood of $150,000, "which is a good deal more than it's worth . . ."

Selznick had already spoken to Boyer about the picture, and the French actor was interested. "Loretta has not yet approved her role because I have not yet spoken to her about it," noted Selznick in one of his famous memos. "But I don't anticipate any great difficulty with her, especially since she is most anxious to be with us . . ."

Loretta was not oblivious to Selznick's multifaceted personality. She greatly respected and admired his talent, but she also had to contend with an aspect of the man that led her years later to describe him as being "brutal" when it came to getting what he wanted.

"Concerning Scarlett," wrote Selznick in November 1938, "I think that at the moment our best possibilities are: Paulette Goddard, Doris Jordan, Jean Arthur, Katharine Hepburn, and Loretta Young . . ."

A few days later: "We're getting closer to the starting date of the picture [GWTW] that I'm commencing to grow fearful of losing any of our really good possibilities and I think we should make clear to Katharine Hepburn, Jean Arthur, Joan Bennett, and Loretta Young that they are in the small company of final contenders."

Loretta had once been asked how she would know if a man truly loved her, and not just for her stardom, her Hollywood glamour, her connections, and her bank account. "I can't answer that," she replied. "I don't know the answer. In this business, it's almost impossible to find out for sure."

During the year a new man appeared in Loretta's private life. He was a "civilian"—not an actor or someone in "the business"—thirty-one-year-old William Buckner. He was a nephew of Thomas A. Buckner, chairman of the board of the New York Life Insurance Company; it was said that his father and two other uncles also held high positions in the company.

He was attractive and apparently very wealthy—it was no

wonder the press took notice of him. Like many young men who had made their way to Hollywood, Buckner was identified by columnists as everything from "an attorney" and "a wealthy broker" to "a socialite" and "a playboy." In a town teeming with hustlers, however, there was no way to tell who was telling the truth until some blunder was made and people began asking questions.

The Young family obviously approved of Buckner. At one point he resided in the lovely guest house on the grounds of the Young home. Buckner traveled a great deal, and while away Loretta would write to him, revealing her feelings through her letters. In October she cabled him, "Darling Buck: your sweet wire Sunday seems years away." On November 19 she sent him another cable: "Darling, *Suez* opened here last night. However, I am waiting here to see it with you. Please hurry, darling."

Hollywood bachelors envied Buckner—many had been after Loretta for years, but Buckner obviously had that something extra. The only question remaining, it appeared, was when were the lovebirds going to tie the knot.

Loretta had made it no secret that when Mr. Right came along she'd go to the altar as soon as possible. "Long engagements are stuffy," she had observed on numerous occasions.

Some of Loretta's associates tried to warn her about William Buckner—he had approached them regarding financial endeavors that seemed somewhat suspicious. But Buckner was a charmer, and the Hollywood community assumed Loretta would finally be getting married again.

As to her future in films, there seemed no doubt that Loretta was determined to leave Fox after finishing off her contract.

Suez was a smash hit. Although all of the actors had given credible performances, it was the spectacle of the film itself that was drawing in audiences. *Suez* had fantastic special effects for the day, and its sandstorm and flood scenes were talked about for some time to come.

The picture was another triumph for Tyrone Power, who was onscreen almost the entire time, while Loretta appeared in only half the film. The screenwriters, of course, had rewritten history. In the film's conclusion, the empress Eugénie, who hadn't aged a day, presents her elderly lover Ferdinand de Lesseps with a commemorative medal. (There is no historical evidence that Eugénie ever had an affair with De Lesseps, and the canal took only ten years to complete.)

Loretta made it clear to Fox that she wanted out if she was to be continually cast in supporting roles such as Empress Eugénie. "It seems I've been here 150 years," she told Zanuck and Schenck. "I'll work for Mr. Schenck but not for you," she told Zanuck. "In all the years I've been here, you've never once sent me flowers or given me a bonus or even a raise. Ty Power has been on the lot one year and he's been raised twice."

Loretta wasn't bluffing.

She had to make two more pictures for Fox under her contract (though neither film would be released until 1939). *Wife, Husband and Friend* boasted a Nunnally Johnson script based on a James Cain novel and was directed by Gregory Ratoff. Warner Baxter was the leading man and Binnie Barnes and Cesar Romero had featured roles. Despite some promising ingredients, the finished picture was undistinguished.

Loretta didn't want to do *The Story of Alexander Graham Bell,* another Zanuck production, but Zanuck insisted and soon prevailed. Directed by Irving Cummings from a Lamar Trotti script, the picture would forever identify Don Ameche as the inventor of the telephone. Loretta observed that Ameche had "learned a great deal" about movie acting since his early days on the Fox lot. "He wasn't so intense. Radio actors are trained to put everything they have into their voices, and Don was still doing that. Now he has calmed down and relaxed."

Zanuck cast *all* the Young sisters in *Alexander Graham Bell*

—playing sisters. It was the only time all four were cast in the same film, and it brought the project terrific publicity: "Georgianna, the youngest of the Young sisters, is really responsible for getting all four into *Alexander Graham Bell,*" went one blurb. "This fourteen-year-old has long hankered to be a movie queen. But Loretta took a firm stand on the subject."

For months there had been talk that Loretta didn't want Georgianna in films. (She had dropped the Ann Royal alias and now was known professionally as Georgianna Young.) Loretta had obviously now withdrawn all her objections, and spoke openly about why she had opposed Georgianna's career in the first place. Loretta was definitely against Georgie starring in pictures at such an early age, "but not on the grounds her morals might suffer."

As far as Loretta was concerned, for Georgianna it had just been "too easy. She didn't have to work for it. I have been criticized a lot for holding her back, but I had a good reason. Georgie gets fifty dollars a week and she doesn't do anything to earn it."

During the year David Selznick had taken an interest in the girl and Loretta now confirmed that Georgianna had "made a few tests. She may play one of the sisters in *Gone With the Wind.* My objection was that she didn't earn this herself. Heaven knows there are plenty of girls here trying to get jobs who must be just as attractive and have just as much talent. She didn't have to go through the mill of working as an extra, of being hungry, of wanting a job. She got a job because her name happens to be Young."

The Story of Alexander Graham Bell would be Georgianna's last film, and although Sally and Polly Ann would appear in a few more programmers, this was their last major film also. Sally and Polly Ann did not actively seek more jobs, but sometimes took parts if they didn't interfere with their private lives, or if they would be working with relatives or friends. For example, after *Alexander Graham Bell,* Sally appeared in her husband's production *Charlie Chan at Treasure*

Island. Foster had successfully directed the Mr. Moto series for Fox, and now had switched over to the Charlie Chan series. Foster's work was highly regarded by his peers, and some contend that the young Orson Welles was influenced by Foster's early work.

In *Alexander Graham Bell,* Loretta portrayed Bell's deaf wife, a role she found both unique and challenging; her scenes—particularly the love scenes—called for an extraordinary amount of sensitivity, and Loretta would often recall them with fondness.

In one love scene "the word 'love' was never mentioned. It was a proposal scene. They were riding in a buggy along a country road. He was moody. He started talking about whether a man should keep on trying to make something of an idea, starving, losing out on the happiness other men had, or give up his idea, get a job, and earn enough to support a wife. She told him, very simply, that the man should keep on with his idea, because the girl would wait for him. 'She would?' he shouted, surprised, exuberant. That was all. But there wasn't any doubt about how much they loved each other."

In another scene, Loretta recalled, "My character was deaf, you remember. That in itself made her sensitive. He led her out of the bright hall into a dark room at one side to hold her in his arms, tell her he loved her. She said, 'It's so dark in here, and I do so want to hear you say it.' He said again, almost in a whisper, 'I love you.' Her fingers were against his lips, 'reading' them. The tenderness of that scene was a thrilling thing to me. More thrilling than any crushing clinch has ever been."

Henry Fonda, Charles Coburn, Gene Lockhart, and Spring Byington rounded out the first-rate cast. Fonda, another unhappy Zanuck actor, didn't even mention the picture in his memoirs.

Loretta was under enormous pressure from all sides concerning renewal of her Fox contract. The studio gave her a taste of what she would be up against with the press if their powerful public relations operation turned against her. Suddenly, printed "rumors" that her option was not being picked up by Twentieth Century–Fox began appearing in the tabloids.

Loretta's good friend Louella Parsons noted that "in spite of all the talk, I know that Loretta Young is one of the most serious-minded girls in Hollywood," adding in deference to the studio system, "When the dust clears, I am sure that she will still be on the Twentieth roster."

While Loretta toiled away on the Fox sound stages, a real-life debacle was getting ready to erupt. It would be the kind of exposure she had heretofore never experienced. This was not gossip column material but front-page scandal involving fraud, indictments, and the United States government.

*He did not ask me to invest any money
and I certainly didn't invest any.*
                    —*Loretta Young,* 1939

Eight

William Buckner was arrested by federal agents in New York on December 1, 1938, as he returned from Europe aboard the luxury liner *Queen Mary.* Buckner was charged with mail fraud in connection with a boom in Philippine Railway bonds that had been under investigation by the Securities Exchange Commission.

"At the same time," noted the *Daily Mirror* in New York, "it was reported here that Buckner, a personable young man with international business interests, was engaged to marry Loretta Young." Buckner's luggage and briefcases were seized by authorities, and among his confiscated effects were letters and cables from Loretta.

On hearing the news of Buckner's arrest, Loretta reacted with shock and utter disbelief. Loretta told the press that, indeed, she knew Buckner "very well," but refused to comment on the report of an engagement. "Of course I will see him when—and if—he comes to Los Angeles, but I don't wish to say any more about our friendship at this time."

The initial details which emerged regarding Buckner's activities were surprising indeed. Buckner and a stockbroker,

William J. Gillespie, were both arrested and questioned for hours in the office of the United States attorney general in the Federal Building. Around midnight they were taken to Manhattan police headquarters, fingerprinted, booked, and lodged in cells.

According to newspaper reports, Buckner and his associates had created a "beauty lobby" the previous year in an effort to influence congressmen. According to New York's *Daily News,* "He flew to the capitol with five girls from a New York nightclub and registered at the Carlton. Members of the pulchritudinous lobby went through their routine for good old Philippine Bonds."

Despite her efforts to keep a low profile, from the very beginning Loretta's name and picture dominated everything written about William Buckner. Her photographs were splashed in tabloids coast to coast. It was reported Buckner phoned Loretta directly after his arrest and told her "not to worry."

Newspapers across the country were having a field day. "Loretta Young wired her love to Buckner at thirty-four cents a word" proclaimed one headline. "Loretta's Darling Buck Held in Swindle" shrieked another. One story asserted, "The film star with the melting eyes let it be known . . . that she had no notion of the extracurricular activities of her self-styled fiancé."

Almost immediately Buckner was freed on five thousand dollars bail and applied for permission from federal judge William Bondy to "visit friends in California." Permission was withheld at first, until Buckner told the court whom he wished to see, for how long, and why.

It must be noted that in the nineteen thirties most major cities had several daily newspapers (New York had eight), and most of these had several editions, so that stories were updated and repeated constantly, as is done today on television news.

The Young-Buckner story became a media blitz. Young

had unwillingly become the real-life star of a grade-B Torchy Blane script. Reporters speculated wildly as to the true nature of Young and Buckner's relationship. Was Buckner rushing to see Loretta? Would she stick by him? Were they engaged? The fact that Loretta was known to be such a lady made the situation all the more provocative.

It seemed obvious why Buckner wanted to go to California, especially when every news story carried a picture of Loretta with quotes from the "love cables" she had sent to him in London. But Buckner was told that if the California visit was granted, he would have to post an additional bond of two thousand dollars.

Over the objections of prosecutor William Maloney, Buckner obtained permission from Judge Bondy to leave New York for a two-week business trip to California. "I'm definitely opposed to granting permission," Maloney said. "I fear if he goes he won't return." Bondy countered, "Buckner could have left without permission. The fact that he asked for permission is in his favor. After all, he has not been indicted yet and he is presumed to be innocent."

The public, meanwhile, only wanted to know if he was going to see Loretta. The questions were soon answered when Buckner and Loretta were photographed attending Christmas Day Mass together, and the photo was whisked across the wire services to every hometown daily.

While Buckner was in California, he was indicted by a federal grand jury in New York. It was revealed that "federal officers would seek out the beauty in the film colony to learn what she knows about Buckner's supposed swindles."

Meanwhile, pictures of Loretta and Buckner appeared constantly in the newspapers. William Maloney was incensed. "I see by the papers that the defendant took care of his business in Los Angeles," the prosecutor observed with sarcasm.

The press speculated that "government agents fear Buckner is planning to marry Miss Young. If they should wed, Miss Young could refuse to testify against him. Investigators believe the film star may have important information, inasmuch as the Philippine bonds were mentioned in letters she wrote to Buckner while he was abroad."

John C. Walsh, a member of the United States attorney's office, went to Hollywood to question Loretta. The press was quick to point out that Walsh was known as "the Adonis of acting U.S. Attorney Maloney's staff."

Walsh brought with him the letters and cables Loretta had written Buckner. "It is not known whether the federal men will return them to her," reported the press.

Daily headlines kept the public informed of Loretta's involvement, and new incriminating information soon came to light. Not only was Buckner involved in the Philippine bond issue, but when he had been in Hollywood his associates had approached various stars with get-rich-quick schemes.

Among those subpoenaed to testify were Loretta, Miriam Hopkins, Ronald Colman, Frank Morgan, Herbert Marshall, Bing Crosby, Binnie Barnes, Cary Grant, and studio mogul Joseph Schenck.

Agents of the SEC came to Hollywood in January to interview the witnesses, and a great deal of Buckner's correspondence was read at the hearings. Newspapers reported that "throughout all the correspondence from his associates there ran a thread of bitterness at Buckner because he had failed to cash in on his love affair with Miss Young. 'Why Bill doesn't work something with Miss Young I can't tell you,' one letter complained."

Other reports noted that Buckner had "started his courtship to borrow money from Miss Young but wound up falling madly in love with her." There was no doubt that the press was painting Loretta as someone who had been set up.

Outside the hearing room, Loretta Young successfully maintained her dignity and composure. "He did not ask me to invest any money and I certainly didn't invest any," she emphatically declared.

More facts about Buckner's past began to surface. "This

isn't the first time he's been accused of failing to account for funds," Maloney asserted, and the shrewd prosecutor presented a letter dated 1937 revealing that Buckner, a lawyer, had resigned from the bar because he could not successfully defend himself against a charge of embezzlement. After the hearings Buckner had to return to New York to face trial.

Throughout this hectic period Loretta Young's image as a gullible movie star engendered headlines such as LORETTA'S HEART ENTANGLED ANEW and LOVELY FILM STAR ONCE MORE FACES TROUBLOUS ROMANCE. Each article about her listed at least a dozen men she had dated, and readers were always reminded of her relationships with Spencer Tracy and Clark Gable.

Loretta dealt with the Buckner affair as she dealt with all adverse publicity: ignore it, rise above it, and it will eventually fade. And sure enough, the incident began to disappear from the headlines. But Loretta had been badly burned—made to appear foolish—a role she was not accustomed to playing. The disillusioning experience left her hurt, vulnerable to criticism, and more cautious than ever. But professionally, Loretta still remained a risk taker.

There is an old show business axiom: even bad publicity is better than no publicity as long as they spell your name right. The recent Buckner headline splash had placed Loretta Young's name in the news more than ever.

The Fox studio had finally made her a spectacular offer: a five-year contract for two million dollars. Adjusted for inflation, that would be twenty million dollars today.

To everyone's astonishment, Loretta refused to sign. Some people, she recalled, said "You fool! You willful fool!" But as one of her brothers-in-law has observed, "With all her sweetness and gentleness, Gretchen has a mind of her own, and once she has made a decision neither snow, nor sleet, nor combined family and studio entreaties can shake her."

Myron Selznick was equally surprised, but respected her

decision. Selznick was a big-time gambler and risk taker like his brother David, and probably relished the challenge of once again taking on the lions.

At first it appeared Loretta's free-lancing career would encounter few obstacles. Producer Walter Wanger offered her the lead in *Eternally Yours,* a contemporary romantic comedy-drama he was producing for United Artists.

It was rumored that Loretta personally selected David Niven as her costar in the picture. "I hope that Walter decides to make a permanent team of Niven and Young," she said. "Nothing would make me happier." In reality, Wanger had wanted Charles Boyer, but settled for Niven. In the picture Niven played a master magician, and Loretta was cast as the Episcopal bishop's niece who falls in love with him.

The *Eternally Yours* script was, at best, ordinary, but under Tay Garnett's direction, the extraordinary cast (which included Billie Burke, C. Aubrey Smith, ZaSu Pitts, Virginia Field, and Raymond Washburn) lifted it off the ground and gave it wings. It presented Loretta with her most challenging love scene to date. "The setting was a bedroom," she recalled. "That always helps to make things difficult. The couple were having breakfast on the bed. He started to pick into her food. Then there were other lighthearted suggestions of intimacy, ending in a kiss. It was one of those borderline scenes. Done with just the right touch, it would amuse audiences. Otherwise, it would embarrass them."

Few actors had "the right touch" for such material, but this twosome did. Viewing the picture today, one is amazed at the seemingly effortless, charming performances of Young and Niven.

Virginia Field, who costarred in this (and two other films) with Loretta, is one of the few actresses with negative things to say about Miss Young. Field told author Richard Lamparski that Loretta Young was "the only actress I really disliked.

She was sickeningly sweet, a pure phony. Her two faces sent me home angry and crying several times.''

Offscreen Loretta was keeping a low profile in the romance department, but she was still dating. One of her escorts that year was Franchot Tone, ex-husband of Joan Crawford. Fan magazines had a field day, claiming that Young was dating Tone to spite Crawford. The gossip implied that Loretta didn't like Joan, and over the years the dislike became mutual, although Crawford remained good friends with Sally Blane.

Loretta had distanced herself from the embarrassment and pain of the Buckner affair. She never adopted a self-pitying attitude. "I've never been 'a tragic character.' I don't consider myself unlucky in love, either. Victim of fate, my foot!''

Nor, Loretta said, was she soured on men. "I want romance in my life. I'm not underestimating its importance. It's far more to me than acting.''

Many of Loretta's attitudes would not have been popular with today's "liberated woman." For example: "It's not brilliant to forget that we were, after all, designed to be men's mates. I don't rebel against being a woman." And yet, other statements were years ahead of liberated philosophy: "I already have a meal ticket. I *earned* it myself. And a home. And all the other material possessions I could possibly want. No, I'm afraid it will have to be love to tempt me into marriage.''

To Loretta's credit she was intelligently in control of her professional life, unlike most female stars of her generation, and she was not naive about the rough course she had chartered for herself. "I don't pay any attention to those leisurely souls who assure me everything will be all right if I merely sit tight. Experience has taught me you can't let anything slide. Things don't work out. They don't straighten themselves out until you decide exactly what you want and how you want it and then do something about it.''

Loretta had been warned by her agent that she might experience the wrath of the movie moguls for her refusal to sign with Fox. The big studio men were ruthless competitors, and they all had actors under contract who might become just as dissatisfied with long-term contracts as Loretta had. An unwritten law existed among the studio heads—hands off hiring people who defied the bosses. It was, in effect, a blacklist.

Twenty-six-year-old Loretta Young, a top star earning approximately $200,000 a year, suddenly found that no studio would hire her. Furthermore, as she had been warned, industry publicity turned biting and spiteful. Powerful radio commentator and newspaper columnist Jimmie Fidler led the attack. "Today's 'horrible lesson' in greed is Loretta Young," he wrote. "Dissatisfied with the Twentieth Century–Fox contract that paid her well and guaranteed fine roles, Miss Young looked with hungry eyes on the seeming independence of such free lancers as Carole Lombard and Janet Gaynor. She decided she, too, would free-lance. . . .

"Most contract stars fail to appreciate the 'safety' of a long-term tie-up. They don't realize that a 'free' actor can be killed dead as vaudeville by two or three poor films, while a contractee has a sure job and the chance of a comeback after baddies.

"If Miss Young's next picture is in a class with her initial free-lance venture [Eternally Yours], I fear clamor for her may hush to a whisper. Meanwhile, I don't think it's too late for peace with Twentieth Century–Fox (and I believe Zanuck would welcome her back; he needs her)."

But Loretta steadfastly defended her free-lance decision. "I refuse to sign another long-term contract because I know what being on continued studio call is like. My whole life was geared up like a streamline train. It was rush, rush, rush, and I'd have burned myself out if I'd kept it up."

What Loretta didn't divulge was that she was financially independent and didn't need the guaranteed income of a long-term contract. Like Katharine Hepburn, Cary Grant, Irene Dunne, and a very few others, Loretta could risk free-lancing. Loretta and her mother had wisely invested in real estate and sound securities, while never falling into the financial trap that ensnared many stars who lived beyond their means and went into debt to their studios. The studios found it profitable to advance money to their important stars, forcing the actors to keep re-signing for extended periods.

Although Loretta's career prospects seemed momentarily dubious, she was still a darling of the fan magazines—her fame and beauty were even known in the remote hills of Kentucky. When a girl was born to an impoverished mountain couple in Butcher Hollow in that state, the baby's mother picked up a movie magazine, saw a picture of the beautiful Loretta Young, and named her new daughter Loretta. The baby grew up to be Loretta Lynn.

By 1939 Loretta Young's fame was assured and she had an ample amount of money, but she still needed to work. "I thought I'd go stark, raving mad with all that idleness time," she recalled about the months following her departure from Fox.

Of course she now had time to enjoy Judy and the rest of her family, while seeing a great deal more of her friends, including Josie Wayne. Josie and Duke now had three children and were expecting a fourth, but Wayne's drinking had drastically altered his relationship with his wife. Loretta, of course, could empathize with Josie because of her own experiences with Grant Withers (who remained one of Wayne's drinking-hunting-poker buddies).

In 1939 the moviegoing public was deluged with Loretta Young: *Kentucky* was released in January, *Wife, Husband and Friend* in February, and *The Story of Alexander Graham Bell* in the spring.

Loretta was top-billed in *Kentucky,* but she and Richard Greene shared the movie ads with a horse: "Magnificent thoroughbreds! The sport of kings climaxing when the silks flash by at Churchill Downs in the famed Kentucky Derby! In all the splendor of Technicolor!" Loretta was escorted to the glittering premiere at the Cathay Circle Theater in Los Angeles by Greene and David Niven. ("I'm here for moral support," Niven quipped.) It rained, but the festivities weren't dampened. The governor of Kentucky and his family were special guests, and the lavish party at the Trocadero afterwards brought out most of Hollywood's elite.

For *The Story of Alexander Graham Bell* the studio pulled out all the stops with a whirlwind publicity junket to San Francisco for the film's gala opening. It was the kind of event which could never happen today, since no studio has a roster of contract stars obliged to take part in such hoopla.

Nineteen thirty-nine was a year of elaborate exploitation stunts; all the major studios were chartering trains to carry stars, executives, and members of the press hundreds of miles to movie previews. Warner Bros. previewed *Dodge City* in Dodge City, Kansas, hiring a train for Errol Flynn, Ann Sheridan, John Garfield, Gilbert Roland, Humphrey Bogart, Jane Wyman, Wayne Morris, and cowboy stars Buck Jones and Hoot Gibson. (Actor Stuart Erwin reportedly said, "I'll work for nothing, just for the trip!")

For *Alexander Graham Bell* a special train sped Loretta, Don Ameche, Sally Blane, Sonja Henie, Tyrone Power, Annabella, Cesar Romero, Nancy Kelly, Al Jolson, Constance Bennett, Douglas Fairbanks, Sr., Anita Lousie, and Lynn Bari to San Francisco.

A million dollars worth of talent was gathered together to launch the picture. Young, Ameche, Power, and Annabella— now Mrs. Tyrone Power—were a luncheon foursome on the train, and elaborate preparations had been made for everyone's comfort and amusement. It was like a scene out of a glamorous Loretta Young–Tyrone Power movie.

Upon arrival there was a parade through San Francisco, where Loretta and Don Ameche received the key to the city, followed by a reception by the mayor. Afterwards the stars were treated to an elaborate luncheon and dinner, a tour of the San Francisco Fair grounds, and the preview of *The Story of Alexander Graham Bell*.

All this heady promotion couldn't disguise the fact that Loretta Young was still without future picture commitments. The David Selznick deal hadn't materialized, and the prized role of Scarlett O'Hara had by now gone to Vivien Leigh.

Loretta had also been in the running for the second most coveted role of the year, the second Mrs. De Winter in Alfred Hitchcock's *Rebecca,* another Selznick production. "There are many people here who feel strongly that an ideal selection would be Loretta Young, whom it would be easy to deglamorize and who would have the advantage of youth, and who is a much better actress, I am sure, than most people think," Selznick wrote in early August 1939. In late August he wrote, "I feel Loretta Young is a very good bet, and that with a few good pictures she is the logical successor to Joan Crawford—but we don't think she is right for *Rebecca.*" The six finalists for the role were Vivien Leigh, Joan Fontaine, Margaret Sullavan, Anita Louise, Anne Baxter, and Loretta Young. Fontaine got the part.

In 1939 John Earle Young reappeared in the lives of his daughters. Purportedly he first made himself known to his mother, eighty-two-year-old Mrs. Laura Young, claiming he had fallen down and suffered amnesia the day he'd left home in 1916. This was difficult to believe, since he had been living under the name John Earle for years. In the twenties he had moved to Alhambra, the Los Angeles suburb where the Young girls had enrolled in a convent school.

During his twenty-three-year absence, John Earle had married a woman named Rhoda, who died childless in 1934. He had worked as a tailor and a furniture salesman, and had run a hotdog stand, a stationery store, and a music shop.

Sometime over the years John Earle had lost a leg. He gave varying accounts of the disabling accident, but one fact was clear: although only in his early fifties, he was an old man. And the story goes he was in dire need of financial help.

When John Earle Young's mother finally acknowledged

that this man was indeed her son, she had only one demand
—he must not embarrass his former wife and children. He
must continue to keep his identity a secret.

There are conflicting accounts as to how Loretta and her
family learned of John Earle Young's reappearance. Loretta
Young has been quoted as saying, "My parish priest came to
me and said that a man who called himself Jack Earle said he
was my father. He had come to him needing help. I asked the
priest what I should do, and he said that the man's story
seemed clear, so I told him to send the man to my lawyer. An
arrangement was made for me to contribute to his support."

According to another account it was Gladys Belzer who
called a family conference when Young resurfaced, telling
her children that their father had turned up and needed
money for an artificial leg. According to this same account,
Loretta's response was vehement: "No, not a dime. Not one
cent. He walked away from you and that's it." Mrs. Belzer
calmed her children, saying, "I'm sorry, but he's your father,
and whether you want to or not, we're going to take care of
him. You can afford it."

These were the publicly accepted sequence of events, as
related not only at the time but subsequently. There is still
another version of the story: according to a close relative,
only John's mother received a small stipend from Gladys
Belzer, but John Earle received nothing, either directly or
indirectly. He was, in fact, self-sufficient and self-supporting
and never asked his children for anything.

In any event, in 1939 the man remained anonymous as far
as the world was concerned—and John Earle Young remained John Earle.

Loretta's publicity, which had earlier claimed her father
was dead, now erased any such reference, becoming vague as
to whether the man was living or dead. In the minds of most
people, however, the father of the famous Young sisters was
surely dead.

Eternally Yours was released in October. The film's story

included the biggest media event of the year—the 1939 World's Fair in Flushing Meadows, New York. Wanger shot footage at the fair, including some spectacular aerial scenes, which provided the framework for the film's climax. Despite this, the movie was an also-ran in the year that produced *Wuthering Heights, The Wizard of Oz, Dark Victory, The Private Lives of Elizabeth and Essex, Goodbye, Mr. Chips, The Women, The Story of Alexander Graham Bell,* and of course, *Gone With the Wind.*

Loretta Young now faced a real career dilemma. There is a Hollywood rule that if a career doesn't maintain forward momentum, it will soon begin to move rapidly in the opposite direction. The corollary to this rule is: when a career is in difficulty, act as though nothing is wrong—dress to the nines, appear carefree, be seen with the best people at the best places, and keep your name in the papers. That is precisely what Loretta did. She went to all the important parties, including Mrs. Basil Rathbone's "A Night at St. Moritz," which brought out many of Hollywood's elite. The setting was an Alpine village reconstructed at the Beverly Hills Hotel, complete with ice-skating rink, toboggan slide, and ski jump.

Stars showed up by the sleighful: Loretta, Bette Davis, Margaret Sullavan, Ann Sothern, Cary Grant, Ann Sheridan, Binnie Barnes and Mike Frankovich, Orson Welles with Lili Damita, and Joan Crawford with Cesar Romero.

Hostesses like Ouida Rathbone were forced to re-create Europe's playgrounds in Hollywood because the continent was now off limits—although the United States was not yet involved, World War II had begun in Europe. Many of the elite international set were settling in Hollywood for the duration. Hollywood, however, remained a very insulated community. At the height of the crisis in Europe, when fascist troops invaded Albania, Louella Parsons led off her column, "The deadly dullness of the last week was lifted today when

Darryl Zanuck admitted he had bought all rights to Maurice Maeterlinck's *The Blue Bird* for Shirley Temple."

During this period, while Young's film career was in transition, she appeared on many network radio shows, including *Lux Radio Theater,* appearing in a re-creation of *A Man's Castle* with none other than Spencer Tracy. It was not a film actor, however, who now became the romantic focus of Loretta's life, but a handsome executive met through the medium of radio.

> *All I have is a sublime faith that some day*
> *it will come along, and make everything else seem*
> *trivial and unimportant. I'm not going around*
> *looking for it. Love isn't something you find.*
> *Love is something that finds you.*
>
> —*Loretta Young*

Nine

In 1938 Tom Lewis was the fair-haired boy of the radio department in the powerful Young and Rubicam advertising agency. Lewis, a graduate of Union College, had ten years broadcasting experience at NBC in Schenectady and Cleveland before joining Young and Rubicam in New York City in 1936. However, describing Tom Lewis as an important advertising executive doesn't remotely convey his status in the broadcasting industry of the day, his creative input to radio programming, or the accomplishments he had already achieved by the time he ventured to Hollywood.

In the thirties and forties sponsors owned and packaged the leading radio shows, and therefore dealt directly with the program's stars. The sponsor's advertising agency was in effect the creative packager, whereas today, talent agencies like William Morris—have assumed that function. While with Young and Rubicam, Lewis had formulated and produced many of the shows for that massive agency; he was the man who brought together all the creative elements and molded them into a weekly radio show. Robert Landry, radio editor of *Variety* in the 1930s, remembers Lewis as "a very potent man in the industry. A man of considerable influence in his time."

In New York, Lewis had been responsible for the highly successful *Kate Smith Hour.* Miss Smith had started with a fifteen-minute program, which Lewis developed into an hour show slotted opposite the immensely popular Rudy Vallee program. Soon Smith was beating Vallee in the ratings.

Lewis was innovative as well as daring. After seeing the Broadway play *What a Life,* starring Betty Field and Ezra Stone, Lewis adapted it as a segment on the Kate Smith show, and later developed it into *The Aldrich Family,* which became one of the most successful shows on radio—and later on television.

Charles "Chet" LaRoche, chairman of Young and Rubicam, was Tom Lewis's mentor. LaRoche was not happy when Lewis decided to accept the challenge of mounting *The Screen Guild Theater,* a major network radio program to be based in Hollywood. Although Lewis would also oversee other coast-based Young and Rubicam radio shows, such as *Silver Theater, The Jack Benny Program,* and *The Burns and Allen Show,* the dynamic young executive's energies would be focused on the new experimental project.

The concept for *The Screen Guild Theater* was not unique—like *Lux Radio Theater,* it would adapt popular movies for radio. But there was an important twist: all salaries would be donated to the Motion Picture Relief Fund for the building of a hospital and retirement home for people in the motion picture industry. Gulf Oil was set to sponsor the show, but there was not enough time to negotiate the many contracts and agreements with all the necessary guilds and unions. The success or failure of the project would rely on the ability of one individual to pull together all the necessary elements—and that individual was Thomas H. Lewis. "It was a challenge. Apparently I had to have challenges," he says. And he notes that *The Screen Guild Theater* "was a very pioneering effort, which always appealed to me."

Three actors who were passionately dedicated to the effort were Mary Pickford, George Murphy, and Robert Montgomery. "Mary Pickford was a great woman," Mr. Lewis says. "She would have been a great success at anything, and she had the spirit of what that proposed motion picture home was all about." Lewis also notes that Murphy and Montgomery were incredibly helpful in opening doors. "I had to meet the top performers, top producers, the studio heads. I was going ahead with just a letter of agreement. I had to know those responsible would keep that agreement. Gulf Oil Company's reputation and money—Young and Rubicam's reputation and income—were at stake."

One of the key executives Lewis met was David O. Selznick, and the men quickly became very good friends. Today Lewis remembers Selznick as "an extraordinary man, extraordinarily talented. He interested me greatly because he had such a lively and inquiring mind."

Selznick wanted Lewis to work with him, but Lewis told the studio mogul that film "was not my medium. 'I'm a big frog in my pond, David, and I've never been anyone's assistant.'" Selznick didn't give up easily; he told Lewis he would set him up with his own autonomous division in the Selznick organization, and that he would personally teach Lewis "all you have to know" about the motion picture business "in six weeks." Lewis countered that the men should remain "friends," not employer and employee, and Mr. Lewis remained in the radio business.

Lewis launched *The Screen Guild Theater* in 1938 with George Murphy as master of ceremonies, and the show was an instant hit.

There are many versions of how Loretta Young met Tom Lewis.

One is that Loretta's radio agent, Nat Wolff, telephoned

her. Loretta was contracted to do *The Screen Guild Theater* and the first rehearsal was scheduled for eleven o'clock Sunday morning. Miss Young, however, told her radio agent she was going to eleven o'clock Mass that Sunday and would miss rehearsal. Wolff called the producer of the show, Lewis, who suggested Miss Young go to an earlier Mass.

More telephone calls. She said she was attending a party the night before and would be sleeping late.

Lewis, it seemed, was also attending a party Saturday night, but he was going to an earlier Mass, at eight o'clock.

Loretta later recalled her feelings: "What made the man think I cared what he was going to do?"

The story continues—the enterprising Mr. Lewis, still through the intermediary agent, suggested he could pick up Miss Young, take her to eight o'clock Mass, and they would both get to the rehearsal in plenty of time. Loretta, tired of the phone calls, perfunctorily agreed to the arrangement.

When Lewis called for Loretta early Sunday morning, she was still asleep. Her maid woke her up to announce a visitor, which was very unusual, since the woman zealously and effectively guarded Loretta from such intrusions.

Loretta rushed to get ready, then made a very grand entrance. She would later remark that Lewis was "grinning the most attractive grin I ever saw in my whole life."

Tom Lewis's recollection of their initial meeting is considerably different from this romantic version. According to Lewis, one of the first stars the Screen Guild committee took him to see was Loretta Young. Today Lewis recalls: "The day I was brought out to Loretta's house to meet her, they were shooting stills for *Alexander Graham Bell*. They were photographing on the staircase of the house. I thought they were crazy, all those people, all those light cables. The girls were all in hoop skirts. I thought they were all mad." He laughs.

When the photo session was over, Miss Young joined Lewis in the drawing room. "I remember that she sat quietly while I outlined the general format of the show. It was when I touched on the purpose of the show that she grew restless.

" 'You can count on me and most of the people in Hollywood to help the Motion Picture Home, Mr. Lewis,' she said, 'if the scripts are good. By the way, do you have one with you?' 'No,' I said, 'it's a little premature for that.' 'Too bad,' Loretta replied. 'I asked Robert Riskin to drop by when I heard you were coming. He's such a fine writer. Would you like to meet him? And while I remove this makeup, would you like a drink? It'll take me five minutes.' "

Lewis was romantically involved with actress Glenda Farrell when he met Loretta, and almost a year elapsed before he broke up with Miss Farrell. Lewis was no longer content in Hollywood. The hub of the broadcasting world was New York City, where the power and decision making were centered.

"At first I was very restless in Hollywood," Lewis recalls today, "because the money in *my* business was in New York. It had taken me so long to get from Schenectady to New York, and I felt Hollywood was preoccupied by its own business, like a mill town. People here were interested only in pictures. After *Screen Guild*'s first very successful season, I decided I was going to return to New York and stay there. I was not going to spend so much of my time in traveling back and forth."

One day Lewis ran into Ann Sothern and her husband, Roger Pryor, at the Brown Derby. Pryor had just replaced George Murphy as master of ceremonies on *The Screen Guild Theater*.

"Roger tells me you're going back to New York," said Sothern. "For how long?"

"For good, as far as I'm concerned," Lewis said.

Later, Pryor went over to Lewis's table and said, "Annie would like to give a little dinner party for you before you leave." Lewis joined the Pryors, and Miss Sothern said, "I understand that you and Glenda are no longer going out together. Who shall I ask for you?"

"It doesn't matter."

"You know, there's a girl that you would love—she's just great. Lots of fun. Ann Sheridan, over at Warner Brothers."

"Oh, yes," Lewis said, obviously pleased. "Fine!"

But a few minutes later Lewis rejoined the Pryors. "Annie," he said, "as long as you're asking someone for me, ask Loretta Young."

"All right," said Miss Sothern. "But wait, I really don't know Loretta. Would you call her and tell her I'm going to invite her?"

"Of course," said Lewis. Back at his apartment, Lewis phoned Loretta. "I'd love to come to the dinner," Miss Young replied. "When is it?" When he told her the proposed date, she answered, "Oh, I can't. I have a family commitment and I just can't break it. But this is women's work. You forget it. I'll talk with Ann Sothern and we'll call you back."

The dinner party was rescheduled for a night Loretta was available. Lewis says, "We went out every night after that until I had to leave for New York."

Lewis, meanwhile, continued to shuttle between coasts. "It was not feasible for me to be based entirely in New York," he said, "since I was head of production for all Young and Rubicam." In late 1939 Loretta was also dating James Stewart, one of the town's leading bachelors. Once again tongues wagged: would *he* be the one for Loretta?

Not according to Miss Young: "The reason I've been rumored engaged year after year is because reporters assume we're engaged here in Hollywood after two dates in a row."

There was even gossip that actor Conrad Nagel—romantic screen star of the twenties, now primarily a character actor—was seeking "solace for a broken heart" in the company of Loretta Young. The rumor started when Nagel drove to see Loretta at Lake Arrowhead, where she was vacationing. However, it turned out that the visits were actually story conferences for the new season premiere of the *Silver Theater* radio show. Nagel directed Loretta in *Lost Yesterday,* in which she played an amnesia sufferer. That same month she did another *Lux Theater,* recreating Bette Davis's role in *The Old Maid.*

As the year drew to a close, Tom Lewis phoned Loretta from New York and asked what her plans were for New Year's Eve. She told him she was going to Myron Selznick's New Year's Eve party at his lodge in Lake Arrowhead. (Arrowhead, only about one hundred miles from Los Angeles, is high in the San Bernardino mountains, and provides a drastic change of scenery and climate.)

Lewis said he'd see her at Myron's party.

According to Loretta's account, she completely forgot about Lewis and decided to miss Selznick's party and stay home on New Year's Eve. Her evening was interrupted by a phone call—it was Lewis.

"I'm at Myron's—why aren't you here?"

Loretta rushed to get ready and drove herself to Lake Arrowhead. On the road she asked herself why she was making this dangerous late-night drive to the lodge alone. With the realization that she "wasn't driving to Lake Arrowhead! I was driving to Tom Lewis!" came the further realization that Tom Lewis was the man for her.

Loretta and Tom began dating in earnest. "We'd go out every night that I was in town," Lewis recalls. Loretta introduced him to all the members of her family—there were dinners at Polly Ann's, at Sally's, even at Josie's. Tom told Loretta, "I have the feeling they're looking me over," and Loretta replied, "What are families for?" The family—Mamma in particular—approved. Tom was a dashing, successful fellow, and also—most significantly—a good Catholic. He was obviously one of the most eligible bachelors in Hollywood, and had his choice of many of the town's glamour girls—he'd even dated Bette Davis. But Tom Lewis had obviously fallen in love with Loretta, and just as obviously, she had fallen in love with him.

Meanwhile, Loretta was still anxious to return to films. She had told Myron Selznick that she wanted to work, and that money was "only a part of what I get from my work." Loretta felt Selznick's $75,000 per picture asking price for her was the reason there were no takers.

She acknowledged, however, that she had incurred the wrath of the moguls by not signing a long-term contract. "I'm an awful rebel in their eyes for deciding not to work so strenuously, but dumb as it may seem, I want to have more time to enjoy living!"

There were five major studios at the time—M-G-M, Warner Bros., Paramount, Twentieth Century–Fox, and RKO—all of whom "built" stars and kept them under long-term contract. Only two major studios—Columbia and Universal—relied heavily on the services of free-lancers. Selznick was finally able to make a deal for Loretta, but not at his original asking price.

Harry Cohn at Columbia Pictures was already a legend in the business, firmly established as one of the town's most unscrupulous characters. Even his peers were wary of him, although his empire was not in the same league as L. B. Mayer's or Jack Warner's.

Despite the departure of the legendary Frank Capra from Columbia after ten years of providing prestige movies, the small studio's stock was still rising thanks to recent successes utilizing free-lance directors and stars. Columbia produced such pictures as Leo McCarey's *Theodora Goes Wild* (starring Irene Dunne) and *The Awful Truth* (Dunne and Cary Grant); George Cukor's *Holiday* (Grant and Katharine Hepburn); Howard Hawks's *Bringing Up Baby* (Grant and Hepburn); and *Only Angels Have Wings* (Grant and Jean Arthur).

Harry Cohn himself, however, was hell to deal with, especially for a woman. Although he was married, every woman was fair game to Cohn. In the words of Columbia writer-producer Virginia Van Upp, "He verbally raped every woman on the lot."

Bette Davis recalls Cohn materializing one day in her dressing room when she was on a loan-out to Columbia. He hadn't entered by the door—there must have been a secret entrance—but Bette, very young and naive at the time, had no idea what Cohn wanted! In retrospect, she felt her innocence had paid off; Cohn left the dressing room without pursuing his intentions.

Louise Brooks told of Cohn receiving her in his office naked from the waist up. "Harry Cohn gave me a personally conducted tour of hell with no return ticket."

Katharine Hepburn, needless to say, had no such experience with Cohn. She respected Cohn for hiring her at a time when motion picture exhibitors had voted her "box office poison."

Rosalind Russell, who worked with Cohn during the early 1940s, said in her memoirs that she found him a tough but likable businessman—and that she found him personally attractive.

Jean Arthur despised him, as did Rita Hayworth, who was under contract to Columbia. "Harry Cohn was the Gestapo at Columbia," Rita later said. Cohn and Hayworth remained adversaries for her entire twenty-year tenure as Columbia's reigning superstar.

On Loretta Young's behalf, Myron Selznick proposed a deal to Harry Cohn that the mogul could not refuse: he could secure the star's services for only $50,000 per picture on a two-picture deal.

Cohn faced a dilemma. He would be breaking ranks with Schenck and Zanuck if he accepted the deal. But Cohn could not pass up such a bargain, and the contract was soon signed. *The Doctor Takes a Wife* would be the first picture that Loretta would shoot at Columbia since she had filmed *A Man's Castle* there with Spencer Tracy. The lot must have held bittersweet memories for her.

Under Alexander Hall's direction, Loretta and her costar, Ray Milland, delivered slick, professional performances, and Loretta looked beautiful, as always. Unfortunately there was no chemistry between Young and Milland. If the picture was an indication of her career's new direction, she might soon be longing for the good old days with Zanuck. The Cohn deal, however, had broken the stalemate. Other offers now came Loretta's way.

Loretta and Tom Lewis had decided to marry. Shortly after Loretta's engagement, she became friends with Irene Dunne. Over the years Loretta had seen Miss Dunne in church as well as onscreen, and thought her an inspiration. Here was a woman of dignity and religious convictions who at the same time had maintained her position as a top-level film star. She was the quintessential lady, both on and off the screen.

Although years older than Loretta, the ever-youthful Irene had started in films much later. Her husband was a former dentist who had left his practice in New York to join Irene in Hollywood.

Helen Ferguson has given insight into Loretta's relationship with Irene Dunne. She recalled how their friendship began: "It was during a lavish party which Elsa Maxwell had given for a group of the reigning Hollywood beauties. During dinner Irene leaned across the table to say, 'I've just heard about you and Tom, and I wanted to tell you that I think it will be an ideal marriage.' Later in the evening, while applauding an extemporaneous speech by Elsa, Irene tipped over backwards in her chair and did a complete somersault. It embarrassed Irene terribly and she was quiet the rest of the evening.

"Before Loretta left the party, she made a point of talking to Irene again. 'I wanted to thank you for your very sincere congratulations on our marriage,' she said. 'And I want to compliment you on your acrobatics. There wasn't another woman at the table, myself included, who could have done what you did without losing her dignity.' " Irene and Loretta have been friends ever since.

During her engagement to Tom, Loretta finished filming *He Stayed for Breakfast* opposite Melvyn Douglas. Douglas had starred with Greta Garbo in *Ninotchka,* and his film with Loretta would prove to be *Ninotchka* in reverse: Loretta was the sophisticated westerner and Douglas the stodgy foreigner. The film was, at best, an entertaining programmer.

Young and Harry Cohn surprised cynics in the industry by establishing an excellent business relationship. Cohn respected Loretta's professionalism and he regarded her as a "hands off" lady, à la Hepburn and Russell. Years later, however, Young revealed that Cohn had had a "crush" on her and had told her so.

Loretta, meanwhile, continued with her radio commitments. In May she made *True Confessions* for Lux, costarring with Fred MacMurray, who had starred in the movie opposite Carole Lombard.

Concerning Loretta's radio career, Tom Lewis says, "She was very good at it. She had a wonderful voice, which was largely natural. It wasn't something that she had to work at and develop. It was there. She was also stimulated by radio because she was permitted to do parts that she did not get in pictures and really should have gotten."

The announcement of Loretta's engagement brought potshots from the press: "Unlucky-in-Love Loretta Plighted; Pals Wish Luck," one headline read. "Everyone in Hollywood will sigh with relief when beautiful Loretta Young becomes the bride of Tom Lewis." The stories mentioned Loretta's first marriage and divorce, noting, "For the next seven years she had numerous romances and numerous beaux but all came to naught in Loretta's life." William Buckner was frequently mentioned, but in the interim Buckner himself had married.

The Young-Lewis wedding, on July 31, 1940, was page one news. It occurred a month after the opening of *The Doctor Takes a Wife* and one month prior to the opening of *He Stayed for Breakfast.*

It was an ideal wedding—beautiful movie star bride, handsome groom, happy families, elegantly decorated church altar, gorgeous clothes, even clear weather. Loretta finally had her grand church wedding, and with considerably more fanfare than she actually desired.

Although Louella Parsons and others had reported the wedding would be held at the Church of the Good Shepherd in Beverly Hills, it was actually held at St. Paul's Church in Westwood. Perhaps misinformation had been given out to avoid a crush, but the ploy did not work. A huge crowd, reportedly in the thousands, filled the streets surrounding the church. Several zealous fans broke through restraining ropes to catch a glimpse of Loretta, while some bystanders actually fainted.

Like most people, Loretta wanted privacy on this special day, but the public wouldn't be denied its share of the romance and glamour of Loretta Young's wedding.

The Reverend Francis G. Quinan officiated at a nuptial Mass. Loretta was breathtaking in her gown of palest blue and pink with matching hat and veil. The gown, designed by top studio designer Irene, was long-sleeved and high-necked. Loretta carried a harmonizing bouquet of blue water lilies and pink hyacinths. Her sister Georgianna was her maid of honor and only attendant.

Tom Lewis was formally attired in tails. Dr. Charles Lewis of Troy, New York, was his brother's best man. Loretta's brother Jack gave the bride away, and John Engstead took the wedding pictures. It was definitely a family affair.

After years of headlines asking if Loretta would ever marry, the newspapers now announced, BACHELOR GIRL GIVES UP.

Book Two

*I learned you have to fight for yourself
in the picture business.*
—*Loretta Young*

Ten

Helen Ferguson, a woman who would prove essential in the life and career of Loretta Young, now entered the scene. Miss Ferguson, a former actress herself, was now a career counselor and high-powered personal publicist eager to sign Loretta as a client. She had been Glenda Farrell's press agent, and met Loretta through Tom soon after they were married.

Only Helen Ferguson and Margaret Ettinger, who was Louella Parsons's cousin, were in the top ranks of personal publicity agents at this time. According to Henry C. Rogers, then a budding public relations man, only these two women had achieved social acceptability among the Hollywood stars.

Miss Ferguson was expecting Loretta to be a great beauty, and she was not disappointed, but she had not expected "the firm, strong handclasp, the straightforward questions, and the competence with which she directed the interview. This was no fortune-favored dollface. This was an intelligent, trained, and disciplined professional." When the interview was over, however, Loretta "suddenly was all charming hostess." The friendship and business association between Loretta Young and Helen Ferguson would last until Miss Ferguson's death, over thirty years later.

Ferguson was candid with her employer, and in return she found Loretta to be frank and generous, a "girl with all the answers." She also saw that Loretta was a perfectionist, and that she was now determined to have the perfect marriage.

Tom Lewis was a mature, intelligent man who, while in the entertainment business, was not caught up in the glamour and mystery of Hollywood. Sources report that he brought Loretta down to earth, in a manner of speaking, and in their first year of marriage transformed her from a headstrong girl of twenty-seven to a determined woman of twenty-eight.

Loretta's social circle now broadened to include Tom's friends and business associates, who were unlike the usual Hollywood group. One of Tom's closest friends was Dr. George Gallup, a vice president of Young and Rubicam and an innovator in the field of marketing research. Tom was fascinated by research and marketing techniques, and was even a vice president of Gallup's Audience Research, Inc. Loretta liked Mrs. Gallup, but found that she had little in common with most of the other wives in the group.

"I understood she would be retiring," Tom Lewis says today. "Loretta had planned not to continue in pictures beyond her thirtieth year." According to Mr. Lewis, Loretta held to the old-fashioned notion that stars retired before lines on their faces began to show onscreen. But when the time came, retirement was not yet viable; Loretta needed to continue working, and Lewis understood. Her whole life had been geared to work and there certainly seemed no reason why she and Lewis couldn't enjoy a dual-career marriage. Signing a personal publicist was an indication that Loretta intended to continue her career.

In her next film Loretta portrayed a character whose story somewhat paralleled her own. *Ballerina,* adapted from Lady Eleanor Smith's novel of the same name, starred Loretta as

Polly Varley, the London slum child who became Varsavina, the most celebrated danseuse of her generation.

This film was a pet project of veteran actor-director Gregory Ratoff. The budget on the picture was high for the day—over eight hundred thousand dollars. The behind-the-scenes talent was top-drawer, including cameraman Harry Stradling, borrowed from Alfred Hitchcock, and ballet instructor Adolph Bolm, and Sergei Tamoff, who coached Loretta for months in New York before coming to Hollywood for the picture.

Loretta's agent next negotiated a deal at Universal for her first western, *Lady From Cheyenne.* The original title of the project had simply been *Cheyenne,* but a clause in Loretta's contract allowed her to play only title roles. At the same time, Young was never a star to insist on solo billing. "Unless it's a very unusual story," she said, "one which demands such procedure, I believe no star has the right to take solo responsibility." Of course, when a movie flopped, solo-billed stars received solo blame.

Lady From Cheyenne costarred Robert Preston, Edward Arnold, and Gladys George, and was directed by two-time Academy Award winner Frank Lloyd, whose *Berkeley Square* Loretta had so desperately wanted to star in seven years earlier.

Loretta had become almost a regular on radio, appearing on the Lux show at least twice a year. At this time, she recreated for radio audiences the movie *Jezebel,* another famous Bette Davis vehicle.

While Loretta's schedule was as hectic and demanding now as when she had been under exclusive contract to Fox, the difference was that now *she* decided which pictures she would do, and when she would do them. Her choices were not forced upon her by any studio; rather, they were strictly her decisions.

Loretta had witnessed the dramatic change of the entire motion picture industry—from silent pictures to the first crude talkies to the sophisticated art form motion pictures had now become. And although the cast of characters had radically changed over the years, Loretta still remained a part of it all. To date, Young had survived fourteen years in pictures, and there was no end to her career in sight.

It was an entirely new Loretta Young who bloomed for her fans in the forties. She was Mrs. Tom Lewis now, and if she visited the town's leading nightclubs, it was with her husband. Lewis says he was never aware of photographers before he met Loretta. But after he began appearing in public places with Loretta Young, he learned he could "sense from her" when a photographer was taking a candid shot.

Photographs from this period all reflect Loretta's happiness. To the world at large, Loretta Young was living the ideal life as a successful movie star married to a successful executive. Her life was the fan magazine reader's fantasy, combining glamour and dignity.

During the first year of their marriage, as with many beautiful women whose glamour is a key ingredient in their lives, Loretta strove to be glamorous at *all* times for the new man in her life. However, this was not the easiest of tasks, even for Loretta.

According to Miss Young's recollections, Lewis patiently explained to her that in the privacy of their home "glamour" was not necessary. He had fallen in love with *her*, not what she represented on a movie screen. "Loretta Young" was for the fans; to him she was Mrs. Tom Lewis.

It was no longer a problem if Lewis's projects had him spending months on the east coast. Loretta didn't have to make six pictures a year anymore, so she could accompany her husband to New York. Marriage was the wonderful union she had always prayed it would be.

In addition, Loretta began to develop professional interests other than show business. For years she and her mother had been investing in real estate, while Gladys had become one of the most successful of southern California's interior designers, an expert on antiques. Some sources said that Loretta and her mother owned as many as thirteen houses before Loretta's marriage.

As 1940 drew to a close, Loretta appeared to have achieved her two most important goals—to maintain a successful free-lance career and have a happy marriage.

It continued to be difficult, however, for free-lancers to get positive publicity in the fan magazines. The studios still had great influence with the press. Despite this control, one report of the day noted, "Loretta Young is picking her own parts these days and doing it very well indeed, thank you." (The account also reported, "Jean Arthur ditto and not so successfully.") Helen Ferguson was doing her job very well.

Lady From Cheyenne was released in the spring of 1941, premiering at New York's prestigious Roxy Theater, and while it was still in general release Loretta re-created her role on *The Lux Radio Theater* with costars Preston and Arnold.

Loretta's little Judy was now six and legally adopted by Tom Lewis. As an adult, Judy Lewis recalled this period: "I led a very protected, sheltered, and comfortable life, and whenever Mom wasn't there to help me, I had a wonderful English governess who taught me discipline."

Through 1941 the Lewis family bounced back and forth between New York and Hollywood. Loretta was as close as ever with her family. By now both Sally and Polly Ann seemed content staying home and being wives and mothers.

Although Polly Ann had appeared in several low-budget pictures, including *Port of Hate* and *Invisible Ghost,* and Sally and Norman had talked about doing stage work together, Loretta noted, "I guess they're definitely out of pictures. Occasionally, only Georgianna, who is seventeen and perfectly beautiful, declares, 'I'd like to get some work.' I say to her—remembering all I've gone through—'Do you really love the studio? Do you feel a great urge to act?' And she invariably answers, 'Oh, no; I want to earn some money for a new wardrobe.'"

Mrs. Belzer often took Georgianna with her on business trips to New York. On one such venture the two women met Carmel Snow, editor of *Harper's Bazaar*. Miss Snow was taken with Georgianna's beauty and arranged for the girl to be photographed. Soon after, Miss Snow signed up Georgianna for a modeling contract. "Georgie" was truly gorgeous —tall, with high cheekbones and striking features. In photographs she closely resembled her sisters, but she also had a very sensuous quality, not unlike the young Ava Gardner. Being a model provided Georgianna with a career—one which, for her, did not require the fierce ambition and concentration necessary to achieve and maintain stardom.

Ballerina, now retitled *The Men in Her Life,* was being released by Columbia and had been booked into Radio City Music Hall. The studio had great hopes for the picture, but the final product hadn't proven as impressive as hoped for. Although beautifully photographed, it was a peculiarly passionless pastiche.

A behind-the-scenes, unpublicized drama unfolded during the filming of Loretta's next picture, *Bedtime Story,* costarring Fredric March. Loretta received top billing, even though March had a "top billing" clause in his contract too. But the problem on *Bedtime Story* didn't concern billing. It concerned Loretta and Harry Cohn, in what some people would consider a ridiculously small matter—but one which finally made adversaries of the two Hollywood personalities. The designer Irene had created Loretta's gowns for the film, but there remained one costume to be sketched. Loretta told Harry Cohn that she would simply buy a dress for that scene and bill it to the studio. The mogul agreed.

A couple of weeks later Cohn phoned Loretta at home late at night. He was in a fury. The dialogue went something like this: "You're not gonna make money on me," he shouted.

"Just a minute, Harry—what's this all about?"

"You know what it's about. You pick up a dress for a hundred and a half and you try and palm it off on me for seven hundred. The price tag was still on it!"

Loretta attempted to explain; the gown had needed changes in design and alterations, and Irene's services were costly. Since the designer's going rate was between six and eight hundred dollars per gown, Loretta had merely settled on seven hundred.

But Cohn wasn't listening to anyone's explanations. "Nobody's gonna cheat me and get away with it. I'm taking away your top billing, and you're not gonna wear that dress in the picture either. You'll wear what I tell you to wear."

Loretta was now encountering the Harry Cohn that the rest of Hollywood already knew. She decided not to knuckle under. She showed up for fittings for the studio-made gown hours late, so the wardrobe staff would have to be paid overtime. This kind of sly behavior was probably not what Loretta had in mind when she had earlier said, "When I'm dissatisfied with some studio detail, I telephone whoever's responsible and complain as intelligently as I can."

Cohn was not one to respond to intelligent debate. He was sincere in his desire to punish Loretta, and gave March top billing in print ads. Although Young was still contracted for one more picture at Columbia, from this point on Loretta and Cohn were no longer on speaking terms.

At this time a new cast of characters was taking its place on the Hollywood scene. While Loretta Young was still considered one of the most beautiful women in town, a fresh crop of glamour girls had rocketed to stardom. Twenty-year-old Lana Turner was a young hopeful at M-G-M, twenty-three-year-old Rita Hayworth was being groomed for stardom at Columbia, and Gene Tierney and Linda Darnell were Zanuck's current young brunette goddesses at Twentieth Century–Fox. Each of these women was making four or more pictures a year, just as Loretta had in the beginning of her career, and their names were being linked with many of the same men Loretta had dated.

Gossip traveled fast, and Loretta could not have been unaware that Spencer Tracy and Ingrid Bergman were having an affair during the filming of *Dr. Jekyll and Mr. Hyde* at M-G-M. Furthermore, Tracy and Bergman were set to perform *A Man's Castle* on radio.

But as always Loretta Young was not concerned with the past—only the future. Studio publicity people remember that Loretta was adamant about remaining Mrs. Tom Lewis in real life and Loretta Young only onscreen. Her attitude often found its way into print, but not without being reported with a somewhat mocking tone. ". . . And here's another thing to get straight," ran one newspaper account. "Mr. Lewis is not to be thought of as Loretta Young's husband. Loretta Young is Mr. Lewis's wife. That's the way Loretta wants it. And that's the way it is."

The Men in Her Life opened in December 1941 to poor reviews, but by then even Hollywood realized that there were far more important matters going on in the world: the attack on Pearl Harbor plunged America into World War II. Tom and Loretta were both deeply affected by the Pearl Harbor tragedy—they had visited there only months before, and had been aboard the very ships which were now lying on the bottom of the harbor. They had met and dined with the officers of those ships, and Loretta had been applauded by the assembled crews.

Lewis wanted to join the navy immediately, but the government had other plans for him. Loretta and her peers swiftly became involved in various causes connected with the war effort as the Hollywood dream machine ground tirelessly on.

Top names turned out to attend Edward Arnold's defense meeting at the Beverly Wilshire Hotel. Pat O'Brien, George Burns, Ann Miller, Linda Darnell, Jack Benny, Kay Francis,

With David Niven and Richard Greene at the glittering 1938 premiere of *Kentucky,* the Technicolor big-budgeter starring Loretta and Greene. Loretta's silver fox coat was the height of style then, and today.

With Henry Fonda and Don Ameche in *The Story of Alexander Graham Bell* (1939). Loretta was nearing the end of her Twentieth Century–Fox contract.

Loretta and sisters Polly Ann Young, Sally Blane, and Georgianna Young (later to become Mrs. Ricardo Montalban) in *The Story of Alexander Graham Bell.*

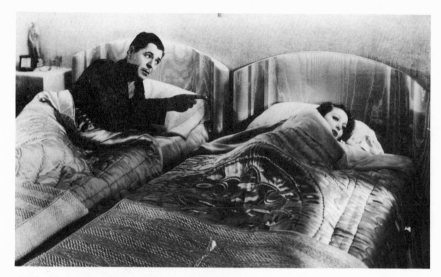

With Warner Baxter in *Wife, Husband and Friend* (1939). He had been Fox's most popular actor; now Loretta got top billing.

With David Niven in *Eternally Yours* (1939). The stars remained lifelong friends.

The real-life mob scene outside Loretta's home on her wedding day (1940). If a lady chose to become a movie star, then her private life was no longer her own.

With Fredric March in *Bedtime Story* (1941). It was the beginning of Loretta's career as a free-lance star.

As a child, Loretta had dreamed of becoming a ballerina. She portrayed one in *The Men in Her Life* (1941).

Loretta maintained her glamour-girl image during the World War II years.

She was also photographed in the kitchen, as were all other glamour girls during this period.

With best friend Irene Dunne and members of the Marine Corps at the 1942 Hollywood premiere of the patriotic *Wake Island.*

Alan Ladd was Loretta's leading man in the blockbuster *China* (1943).

Gary Cooper and Loretta teamed for *Along Came Jones* (1945).

With Orson Welles in *The Stranger* (1946). Young gave a superlative performance as a woman who discovers that the man she has married is a Nazi-in-hiding.

With Joseph Cotten, Keith Andes, James Arness, and Lex Barker in *The Farmer's Daughter* (1947). Her role as Katie won her the Academy Award as best actress.

With Cary Grant in Samuel Goldwyn's *The Bishop's Wife* (1947).

Loretta presents the Oscar to Jane Wyman for *Johnny Belinda*. Loretta had won the previous year for *The Farmer's Daughter.*

With William Holden in *Rachel and the Stranger* (1948).

Clark Gable, and Carole Lombard were a few of those who attended.

Shortly thereafter, in mid-January 1942, the country was stunned when Lombard was killed in a plane crash near Las Vegas as she returned from a bond-selling tour. The world-famous Gable-Lombard marriage had in fact been on shaky ground, and Gable was having an affair with one of M-G-M's newest blonde bombshells at the time. The shock was incredible, however, and Gable's grief was real. His friends rallied around him at the time of the tragedy, but he was inconsolable—guilt and grief stalked him for the rest of his life.

After Pearl Harbor, stars soft-pedaled their party images and began doing charity work. Hollywood's biggest names volunteered for the Red Cross, helped to sell Defense Bonds, and donated their time and talents to "every possible program that will help the cause of winning the war and keeping up the nation's morale." Although Loretta was not usually a joiner, she was active in many organizations such as China Relief and the Hollywood Victory Committee.

She also immersed herself in charity work, for which she was inexplicably derided by some in the film industry and, later on, by certain film historians. Perhaps because she had a reputation for being a diamond-hard personality in business negotiations and a stickler for what was right for Loretta on the set, she was regarded as hypocritical by attempting—successfully—to be generous in other areas.

There was talk at the time of Loretta retiring from films to raise a family. She had turned down picture offers so she could travel to New York with her husband. By now Lewis was a stockholder in Young and Rubicam and vice president of the West Coast office, and the couple led a bicoastal existence.

Young appeared on many patriotic radio programs during the war years, all of which were variations on the theme "All Out for Victory." On the Screen Guild's radio show *Liberty Is a Lady,* Loretta essayed seven different roles. Only an actress with Loretta's vocal skills could attempt such an endeavor. In 1942 she and Clark Gable won the "Best Screen Voices" award from the American Institute of Voice Teachers, the third year in a row that Loretta had won the award.

Even in discussing her voice, Loretta could not resist throwing in a bit of her life's philosophy: "Become better, not bitter, through anything unpleasant that happens in life. That's the way to grow and profit."

Loretta made recordings on enunciation and pronunciation of English for Chinese students at the request of her friend Father Charles Meeus of the Catholic Trust Society of Hong Kong. On one of the records Loretta read a chapter of *China Through Catholic Eyes* by Father Thomas Ryan, and also read the book's introduction by Madame Chiang Kai-Shek.

While the Reverend Meeus was in Los Angeles raising funds for China Relief, the Lewis family hosted a party for the priest at which over five thousand dollars was raised. Loretta devoted most of her energies to the China Relief charity during these years.

Bedtime Story opened at Radio City Music Hall in March 1942, following Spencer Tracy and Katharine Hepburn's first film together, George Stevens's *Woman of the Year.* Columbia launched an extensive advertising and promotion campaign, which included the use of Loretta's beautiful face in the latest Lux soap ads.

The booking of *Bedtime Story* into Radio City indicated Loretta's stature with film exhibitors. But *Bedtime Story* was not close in quality to the Tracy-Hepburn picture which it followed. It is still a mystery why Young didn't seek out top directors like George Stevens. However, as Douglas Fairbanks, Jr., observed, "When you free-lanced, you took your chances."

While Loretta and Tom were in New York for the *Bedtime Story* premiere, she made an appearance for Navy Relief at

Madison Square Garden, did the CBS radio program *We the People,* and attended, with Tom, the premiere of Paramount's *Wake Island.*

During much of 1942, Loretta continued to shuttle back and forth between coasts. Publicity on the star was considerable. In a Red Cross uniform, she was the cover girl for *Saturday Home Magazine.* She found time to make a four-week bond-selling tour, and sold over seven million dollars worth of bonds. She kept busy on radio with three Lux programs that spring, including *The Great Lie* with Mary Astor and George Brent, *Arise, My Love* with Ray Milland, and *Bedtime Story* with Don Ameche.

She completed her Columbia commitment with *A Night to Remember,* costarring Brian Aherne. It was a run-of-the-mill mystery story, bearing no relation to the famous property filmed years later about the sinking of the Titanic.

Loretta and Harry Cohn spoke only through intermediaries. It was reported that Loretta had earned $85,000 from Columbia in 1941, while that same year Roz Russell had earned $100,000. Other stars in town were earning much more. Tyrone Power had made over $200,000, as had Spencer Tracy, Ginger Rogers, Bing Crosby, Bob Hope, and Bette Davis. Cary Grant had grossed a whopping $351,000 that year, and Gary Cooper had earned over $300,000 as well. Claudette Colbert had topped them all with $390,000.

Loretta had paid her dues by working for well under her normal salary at a minor studio. When her agent finally negotiated a lucrative, nonexclusive contract with Paramount, Loretta Young joined the ranks of top free-lancers.

The relatively smooth course of Loretta and Tom's marriage was interrupted when Lewis entered the armed services. Although at forty he was too old for combat, Lewis possessed an expertise that the government needed.

Director Frank Capra had become a major in the army, assigned to the Morale Branch in Washington. Capra was very unhappy with what he perceived to be the army's incompetence.

One day Colonel Munson, Capra's superior officer, asked, "Do you know Tom Lewis?"

"I know *a* Tom Lewis," said Capra. "Married to Loretta Young."

"That's the man," said Munson. "We think he's the best candidate to head up our radio section. How well do you know him?"

At this early point in his army career Capra felt he was being used to recruit Hollywood talent, and the idea made him sick to his stomach. "Let me give it to you straight," Capra told Munson. "I know Tom Lewis well enough to tell him to stay the hell out of uniform unless he wants to become another 'body' to be kicked around by some jerk superior. Well enough to warn him not to get sucked into becoming head of another one-man section in a one-room Morale Branch. You see, I'm a lousy pimp, Colonel Munson."

Munson, however, explained that the film director had been commissioned into the Signal Corps and assigned to Special Services at the personal request of General George C. Marshall. The army understood that Americans looked on *propaganda* as a dirty word—that the millions of troops in uniform would need to know *why* they were in uniform and the army was simply looking for the best men from the motion picture and broadcasting industries to help explain it to them. Capra would be assigned to supervise a series of films to be entitled *Why We Fight.* Tom Lewis was eventually commissioned as a major and stationed with Capra's group headquartered in Washington.

Loretta would not be idle during Tom's absence. Paramount put her to work immediately, teaming her with their hot new male star, Alan Ladd, in *China,* a war epic. Young's casting in the film seemed inevitable, considering her activities on behalf of China Relief.

The film's director was John Farrow, who had already directed one of the classic World War II dramas, *Wake Island*. Loretta had known Farrow socially for years. When he married actress Maureen O'Sullivan, the wedding reception was held at Gladys Belzer's home. Farrow was a devout Catholic like Loretta, but he was not without a peculiar sense of humor. Years earlier he had had a snake tattooed on the inside of his left thigh. During his courtship of Miss O'Sullivan, Farrow often posed on the swimming pool diving board of the hotel where O'Sullivan was staying. Farrow wore very brief swimming trunks while posing, so that the tattooed snake appeared to be emerging from his crotch! No one seemed more adept than John Farrow at chiding Hollywood society while remaining one of its most respected members.

Loretta had no trouble working with Farrow on *China*. Paramount, however, thought the picture was going to be Ladd's last movie as a civilian, so they were giving the star a big buildup.

Maris MacCuller, who was there at the time, remembers that the job of focusing attention on Ladd wasn't easy, because "Loretta Young, who knew every angle of the film business, also knew tricks of attention getting that are learned only after years of working before movie cameras."

According to Miss MacCuller, Loretta was "sharp, full of energy and ideas, and had positive opinions about the way things should be done and sound reasons to back them up." One person on the set slyly suggested Young "be given directorial credit along with John Farrow."

Suddenly, Loretta's fans were being given information that heretofore only insiders on the set knew—notably that Loretta was a fighter. Paramount began leaking stories to influential columnists, casting Loretta in an unflattering light. "Many Hollywood stars—particularly holdovers from silent pictures—think it necessary to be trouble-makers to impress with their importance," wrote Jimmy Fidler. "Loretta Young is a case in point. For years, her presence on a set ran up

battle flags within a week. I've seldom seen a star make enemies faster than she did in her last picture."

As always, columnists such as Fidler covered all the bases
and attempted to diffuse the explosiveness of their stories. "If
Loretta were disagreeable, I wouldn't comment," Fidler
added. "But she is one of our nicest. I know how considerate,
friendly, and generous she is when she lays aside her tiara
and acts herself. She would be wise to realize times have
changed."

In *China* it was unusually difficult for Loretta to maintain
her glamorous image. Rain beat down during many key
scenes, and the synthetic rainstorms wreaked havoc on Loretta's hair and makeup. Ever-resourceful Loretta kept her hair
in place with colorless lacquer, an ancestor of today's hair-
spray, and brushed oil on her eyebrows so they wouldn't
"droop." She used a protective coating on her eyelashes instead of mascara, and a light grease foundation on her face to
keep the powder from streaking. In the finished film she not
only managed to look great but gave a strong, taut performance.

Paramount was confident they had a big winner in *China*
and the advertising and publicity department geared up to
give the film a big push.

Loretta was on Lux radio again in December 1942, playing
Hedy Lamarr's role in *Algiers*. Charles Boyer received top
billing re-creating the Pepe Le Moko role for the broadcast.
It was the first time Loretta relinquished top billing on Lux.

Loretta visited Tom in Washington and New York, then
returned to Hollywood, where she was met at Union Station
by a delegation from the Chinese community. The Chinese-
Americans presented flowers to Loretta in appreciation of her
efforts on behalf of United China Relief. Loretta had posed
for posters used by UCF in its campaign to raise funds, and
was also a member of the China Relief Legion, heading several committees for that organization.

Miss Young's involvement in China Relief was not a publicity stunt, and in fact had been going on for some time. "Actually, this war began when Japan first moved into Manchuria in 1931," she noted. "Nothing was done to stop the aggressor then—except by the Chinese themselves—and the world is paying the price now."

To promote the film *China,* the Young visage was now used to plug Royal Crown Cola. "I'm working twice as hard today," said Loretta in the cola ads, "so when I take time out to rest, give me the cola that tastes best!" In an added bit of patriotism, the copy went on to say, "When busy Loretta Young isn't making pictures, she's visiting plane plants on morale tours or working at canteens." This claim was not just hype.

Though Loretta received top billing and was paid ten times as much as her costar, the ads for *China* conspicuously featured Alan Ladd, bare-chested and brandishing a machine gun. "Alan Ladd and Twenty Girls . . . Trapped by the Rapacious Japs! . . . The hottest Ladd on the screen in his first big production!" proclaimed the ad copy.

Small head shots of Loretta and William Bendix flanked the towering torso of Alan Ladd (who in real life was only five foot five).

China opened in New York City at the Paramount Theater, with Harry James and his orchestra as the stage attraction accompanying the film. The film was a hit, and the theater grossed an impressive $105,000 during its opening week. Loretta toured army camps that spring, and during this time she obtained the rights from Margaret Bourke White, the world-famous photographer, to do a film based on her experiences. Young offered the package to Paramount, but the deal never went through.

Under the aegis of her old friend Walter Wanger, Loretta next made *When Ladies Fly* for Universal. Retitled *Ladies Courageous,* the film was Universal's entry in the women-in-war sweepstakes—M-G-M had *Cry Havoc* and Paramount *So Proudly We Hail.* Diana Barrymore and Geraldine Fitzgerald costarred with Loretta, and a young actor named Blake Edwards—later to become one of the top producer-director-writers in film—also appeared.

Frank Capra had finally convinced the army brass that his division really belonged in Hollywood. According to Capra, his superiors agreed—"especially if I could find a set-up for Tom Lewis's Armed Forces Radio, which desperately needed the broadcasting talent and facilities on the West Coast."

Capra went to Darryl Zanuck, now a commissioned colonel, and acquired space at the old Fox studios on Western Avenue. Though Lewis's Armed Forces Radio unit now worked out of Hollywood, Tom—now a lieutenant colonel—would still have to travel extensively.

"It was another pioneering effort," Lewis says of Armed Forces Radio. "The planning was not terribly difficult; the execution of the plan *was* enormously difficult. But it was the most rewarding thing I have ever done. It was a long, long fight to assure that no propaganda would be broadcast over Armed Forces Radio. *Ever.* Finally, I was able to win that fight by enlisting the aid of Dr. Milton Eisenhower."

Before going into the service, through Frank Griffin, Irene Dunne's husband, Lewis had met Hernando Courtright, a vice president of the Bank of America. Courtright was operating the Beverly Hills Hotel as an officer of his bank, which owned the hotel. Bank of America, however, wanted to sell the property, and Courtright put together a package deal for Loretta and Tom Lewis, Frank Griffin and Irene Dunne, Will Hays, Harry Warner, businessman Willard Keith, Tom Hamilton, and several others.

"Now it wasn't just staying at the Beverly Hills, where movie stars came for cocktails," writer Sandra Lee Stuart observed. "It was staying at, you know, Irene Dunne and Loretta Young's place." The Lewis couple and the Griffins subsequently made other highly profitable real estate investments together.

Ironically, while Loretta was happily married, her close friend Josie was on the verge of divorce. John Wayne had begun talking of divorce years earlier, but Josie would not consent, even though Loretta advised her friend to give Wayne the separation he wanted. The Wayne children were being affected by the tense situation. The Waynes, in fact, had lived apart for some time, and apparently Wayne had already chosen his next wife—Esperanza Baur Diaz Ceballos, an actress from Mexico City who had moved to Hollywood to be near Wayne. Josie finally granted Duke the separation, and the following year she would divorce him, with Gladys Belzer among those who testified on her behalf.

Loretta's radio work continued with *The Philadelphia Story,* in which she appeared with Robert Taylor and Robert Young, and later in the year Paramount arranged a reunion of all the *China* stars on a Lux broadcast.

By this time Ladd had been released from the service for medical reasons, and with the big grosses that had rolled in on *China* it was natural to reteam him with Loretta. The duo starred in *And Now Tomorrow,* in which Loretta once again portrayed a deaf girl. The script was coauthored by Raymond Chandler from a best-selling novel by Rachel Field, and Irving Pichel served as director. Up-and-coming Susan Hayward played Loretta's sister, and the film also featured Barry Sullivan, Beulah Bondi, and young Darryl Hickman.

As always, Loretta took her work very seriously. Since she was playing a deaf girl, Loretta researched the role by talking with several deaf people. When filming began, she put wax plugs in her ears during scenes in which she had no dialogue. She was also very concerned that the girl's eventual recovery might mislead people. "I don't want deaf people to get false hopes," she said. "You see, the cure we use doesn't exist."

As 1943 drew to a close, Loretta was thrilled by important news that had nothing to do with her career: she was pregnant.

I'm grateful to God for His bountiful gifts. . . .
He gave me courage and faith in myself, and He
must have sent me the great, understanding man
who is my husband. Without him, no matter how
brilliant my career, my life would be incomplete.
—Loretta Young

Eleven

In 1942 Loretta Young had met Sister Mary Winifred, a Franciscan nun who had taken over a tiny twelve-bed shelter for unwed mothers in Los Angeles called the St. Anne's Maternity Hospital. Loretta remembered, "It was a small, one-story stucco building almost hidden . . . in a rundown Los Angeles neighborhood."

Because of the war there were many more displaced persons and dislocated families than usual—and many more unwed young girls. "The innocent victims (the babies) all made their haunting impression on me, and I resolved to help." Loretta soon made good on her resolution, helping to raise almost fifty thousand dollars for a new building.

Over the years Loretta has been quoted as saying, "Bad girls don't have babies." In truth, these were the words of Sister Winifred when she described St. Anne's to Loretta. "The girls there are not bad girls," she said. "Bad girls don't have their babies. Abortion is too easily come by these days."

In 1944 Sister Winifred asked Loretta to become president of St. Anne's board of trustees. As Loretta recalled, "I laughed at the idea, then got panicky. I never got beyond the eighth grade in school and felt expert only in my job as an actress. And in those years it was all-important to me that I *not* look foolish."

The persuasive five-foot-two Sister Winifred candidly pointed out to Loretta that the star had name value; her fame would open doors, sell tickets to benefits, and generate direct interest from other wealthy and influential people; and it would be reassuring to the girls involved to know that someone like Loretta cared about them.

Loretta deliberated. Some contend that it was Tom Lewis who finally convinced her to say yes, pointing out that this was exactly the kind of thing she should be doing to round out her life. Undoubtedly, her husband's support was invaluable in making this decision.

Accepting the presidency of the St. Anne's Foundation would prove to be a big step for Loretta. For decades people assumed Loretta's involvement with St. Anne's and "unwed mothers" occurred on the heels of her adoption of Judy, but the facts are otherwise.

Helen Ferguson recalled that around this time St. Anne's Foundation was a possible recipient of Lockheed Aircraft's "Buck-of-the-Month Club" charity award. Numerous charities vied for the money, and St. Anne's best chance was to have a celebrity go to the Lockheed plant and speak to the club members in person.

Loretta was eager to represent her favorite charity, and a date was set for her to visit the Lockheed plant in Burbank and make a personal pitch for St. Anne's.

Helen Ferguson and a young man representing Lockheed picked up Loretta in a limousine. Loretta settled quietly into a corner of the car, which Helen thought unusual, since the star was normally gregarious. The press agent and the man from Lockheed were somewhat uncomfortable, but attributed Miss Young's silence to the dreary weather and the early hour.

At the Lockheed plant Loretta made a vigorous plea for St. Anne's, listened to other speakers, and gave scores of autographs to the workers. Finally, the whistle sounded and the employees went off to work.

Loretta immediately grabbed Helen's hand after the ceremony ended. "May we go now?" she said tensely, and Ferguson realized something was amiss. The press agent quickly maneuvered Loretta through the "essential good-byes," while the star "waved and smiled from the car until we were outside the gate."

Once outside the gate, Loretta abruptly turned silent. By now Ferguson and the chauffeur both realized that Loretta was not well. The driver pulled onto a side road and stopped the car, opening the door for Loretta as she became ill.

"Loretta is not the least bit shy about telling whatever she wants to tell," Miss Ferguson said. "I knew that whatever this was, she'd tell me in her own good time or manner, or never tell me at all." But she assumed, of course, that Loretta was suffering from morning sickness.

Ferguson's point in relating this story was to illustrate that Loretta was a person of such commitment that no matter how she might feel, she always appeared before the public as the star the public expected.

In February 1944, Young signed a contract with William Goetz's new production company, International Pictures. The prestigious independent employed many industry notables, including Nunnally Johnson, the top-flight writer-producer whom Goetz had lured away from Darryl Zanuck.

The press made a big deal over the fact that Loretta had signed an exclusive contract, her first such deal since Twentieth Century–Fox. Shortly after the announcement of her signing, however, news leaked out that Loretta was pregnant. The baby was due in August, and Loretta decided she would not make any more pictures until the following November.

"That's okay," said Bill Goetz, "we'll wait for her." International had announced that Loretta would do a film called *Home Is the Sailor* but that project never materialized as a Young vehicle.

She completed *And Now Tomorrow* at Paramount, and then kept a low profile while awaiting the birth of her child. She was seen in theaters across the country, however, when *Ladies Courageous* was released that March.

Loretta continued to devote herself to various unpublicized charity endeavors. Young, Irene Dunne, Josie Wayne, and Dolores Hope (Bob Hope's wife) were considered the city's leading benefactresses of Catholic charities.

A missionary friend approached Loretta for help in acquiring a trailer and projection machine for his new mission in Utah. Loretta didn't have the necessary five thousand dollars, but told the missionary she'd do "all I could to raise the money from my friends."

"No, we'll work on this together," he told her. "I will pray."

Loretta could earn the money easily by doing a radio show, but the studio stood in her way. International received fifty percent of her radio pay, which was the main reason she had turned down a *Lux Radio Theater* program a week earlier.

She called Bill Goetz and explained her dilemma—she wanted to donate all the radio money to the missionary's cause, and wondered if the studio would waive their fifty percent. Goetz gladly complied and even insisted on making a donation himself.

Loretta immediately contacted the Lux people. Her role in the radio play had already been cast. But the leading lady had suddenly taken ill. Producer Cornwall Jackson was thrilled to hear from Loretta, and eagerly reoffered her the part.

Because of the expected baby, Loretta and Tom decided to look for a new house. They found one they liked in posh Holmby Hills—a mansion at 250 North Delfern Drive. The owner was Benjamin "Bugsy" Siegel, a man with questionable business associates who was laughingly described in some reports as "a New York sportsman."

The Lewis couple made a down payment on the $85,000 house, but soon afterward it was discovered that the house was infested with termites. Tom and Loretta backed out of the deal and Siegel subsequently sued them, generating much publicity. In the meantime, Loretta and Lewis decided to convert a spare room of their house into a nursery.

Josie Wayne threw a baby shower for Loretta. Among the guests were Loretta's sisters and fellow actresses Jean Arthur and Ann Sothern. Loretta told friends that according to war regulations, she could spend only five hundred dollars to add a window or a partition to their house for the nursery.

She also told them that she had already picked the name of her child. If it were a girl, "she'll have Theresa somewhere in her name, after my favorite 'little flower,' " she said, referring to St. Theresa. "If it's a boy, he'll have Christopher in his name. Names only mean to me the person to whom they belong. I think any child should be given a name that belongs to someone who is in your heart, not just a pretty or fancy name."

Loretta also told her friends that she and Tom were going to "have a whole houseful of children." Irene Dunne observed, "I have never known a girl to want a baby so much."

Tom Lewis had been out of the country working with Armed Forces Radio, and Loretta was uneasy until he was back on American soil. Lewis traveled a great deal as commandant of Armed Forces Radio, and any overseas travel during the war was hazardous.

Loretta had good reason to be concerned. In January 1943 Lewis's colleague, author Eric Knight *(This Above All, Lassie Come Home)* was on a mission for Armed Forces Radio when his plane was lost in the Caribbean. It was believed the plane was shot down by German U-boats.

Like millions of other women whose husbands were in uniform, Loretta often feared for her husband's life. "I remem-

ber one night when I lay in bed sleepless," she later recounted. "I had awakened in a cold wave of fear, afraid for
my husband's safety. I began to pray. I asked God for Tom to
come home safely. 'Or if he must go,' I prayed, 'let him be
ready to meet You.' Suddenly I was warm and relaxed, no
longer afraid. I had placed Tom in His care and deep within
me was the knowledge 'Tom's safe.' Peacefully, gratefully, I
fell asleep.

"Late the next day I learned that the instant when I had
known he was safe, Tom's plane had landed in the U.S. after
a pretty frightening incident over the Arctic Sea."

Tom arrived safely back in Los Angeles, and on July 31 the
couple celebrated their fourth wedding anniversary by having a small dinner with Gladys, Polly Ann, and other family
members. In the middle of the meal, Loretta suddenly began
having labor pains. She was rushed to the Queen of Angels
Hospital, where she gave birth to her son Christopher Paul at
six A.M. The baby was christened on September 17, and
shortly afterward Loretta returned to work.

"When it became apparent that she was going to continue
making films, we talked about it," reveals Lewis. "I said, 'If
you're going to do pictures, do them to be the best. Do them
to win an Academy Award.' She told me, 'No, I will never
get an Academy Award.'

" 'Why?'

" 'Because people in pictures, if you're raised in pictures,
don't get Academy Awards. It's the people who come from
the theater, they get the Academy Awards.' "

Lewis replied, "That's not true. You should not be in any
business where you don't think you're going to reach the top.
So pick your pictures and think of yourself accordingly."

Appropriately, her new film was a prestigious project,
utilizing all the formidable talents of International Pictures.
Nunnally Johnson had written the script, Stuart Heisler was
set to direct, and Gary Cooper served as both star and producer. Costarring were William Demarest and Dan Duryea,

and William Goetz was personally overseeing the entire production.

The film was an unconventional western titled *Along Came Jones*. Johnson's screenplay, based on Alan LeMay's novel *The Useless Cowboy,* was a subtle satire on the western genre. The producers knew the dangers of spoofing the genre, and furthermore, Cooper would be playing against type. Loretta, meanwhile, would be playing the sharpshooter!

There is an amusing anecdote about the making of this picture. As producer, Gary Cooper was supposed to oversee all expenses. He complained about mounting costs, including the price of one dress in Loretta's "plain" wardrobe. When Goetz and others suggested to Cooper that, as producer, it was his job to personally speak to Young, the lanky actor hemmed and hawed and, eventually, decided to forget the whole thing rather than confront the actress.

While Loretta was filming *Jones, And Now Tomorrow* was finally released. The film had been completed months earlier, but release had been held up by the studio. Film distribution policies had changed drastically with the advent of World War II. In the thirties and again in the late forties, films were often shuttled in and out of theaters in a matter of days. But during the war, with audiences desperate for escapist entertainment, films often ran for weeks or even months. The studios suddenly found that they had a backlog of product, and began holding pictures from six months to a year after completion. *And Now Tomorrow* was a big hit—a woman's picture in which Loretta took second billing to Ladd, although hers was the starring role.

Loretta became pregnant again, and after completing *Along Came Jones* she announced her retirement from films until after the birth of her next child. Loretta was radiant—the Lewises were finally going to have the family she had always dreamt about.

Almost all of Tom's time, however, was consumed by Armed Forces Radio. He had brilliantly fulfilled the government's expectations by quickly mounting and staffing an entire operation within a matter of months. He had also brought his brother-in-law, Major Carter Hermann, into the outfit as head of the Short Wave Division. Also serving under Lewis were his friends True Boardman, Sam Fuller, and Pat Weaver.

Commandant Lewis was concerned that the Armed Forces Radio network stay intact after the war. The government assured him it would.

In 1945 Ed Sullivan was the arbiter for a special poll conducted among top male Hollywood stars to pick their all-time favorite beauties. Among the leading men participating were Van Johnson, Humphrey Bogart, Errol Flynn, Joseph Cotten, and Ray Milland.

Loretta appeared on both Flynn's and Cotten's lists, sharing honors with Hedy Lamarr, Greta Garbo, Ingrid Bergman, Marlene Dietrich, Joan Crawford, Dolores Del Rio, Virginia Bruce, Olivia De Havilland, and Danielle Darrieux. Loretta Young was a "legendary" beauty at the ripe old age of thirty-one.

Joseph Cotten also cited Sally Blane as one of his all-time favorite beauties. Although she had been out of American films for years, Blane had made a Mexican picture, *La Diligencia,* with—among others—Ricardo Montalban. The film, shot at the Azteca Studios in Mexico City, was directed by Sally's husband, Norman Foster. The couple had moved there when Foster had signed on to direct a Mexican film called *Santa,* also starring Montalban. Ricardo, whose parents had emigrated to Mexico from Spain, was a handsome young man in his early twenties who spoke English and Spanish. He had spent some time in Los Angeles, where his older brother, Carlos, was a bit player in films during the nineteen thirties. (Carlos became a businessman and much later became famous as El Exigente in the television commercials for Savarin coffee.)

The Fosters became quite friendly with Ricardo Montalban, so in 1945 when the young Mexican actor made a trip to Hollywood, Sally insisted he stay with her family. Ricardo declined, but Sally insisted: "Nonsense. My sister Polly Ann has plenty of room. Besides, my sister Georgianna will be there, and I want you to meet her!"

According to Montalban, he had been in love with Georgianna Young ever since seeing her in *Alexander Graham Bell.* When the two finally met, it was love at first sight for both of them. Montalban could only remain in California for three weeks, but before leaving he and Georgianna eloped to Tijuana and were married in a civil ceremony.

In Hollywood, Loretta and Tom were eagerly awaiting the birth of their second child. The war in Europe was over and it seemed that the war in Japan could not last much longer.

With the war coming to an end, Hollywood slowly began to reactivate its social scene. The Paris-born Claudette Colbert even threw a Bastille Day celebration party that year at her elegant Holmby Hills home. The newspapers were sure to emphasize Miss Colbert's concern that she was not going to get enough ration points to adequately feed her eighty guests. "Maybe you won't suspect it," she was quoted as saying, "but this is a practically nonrationed menu."

The public was still living on ration stamps, but the stars of Hollywood hadn't had to cut many corners to maintain their life-styles.

Louella Parsons was at Miss Colbert's party and helped the hostess keep an eye on the pregnant Loretta. Early in the evening Loretta admitted she didn't feel very well but decided to stay on anyway. Tom and Loretta weren't worried—after all, the baby wasn't due for several weeks, and there were five doctors at the party, including Claudette's husband, Joel Pressman.

Loretta stayed at the party until two in the morning, maintaining she'd never felt better in her life. Once at home, however, Loretta experienced labor pains. Lewis rushed her to the hospital, where their second son, Peter Charles, was born at 7:05 A.M.

Loretta Young was now a mother with three children—who happened to be a movie star. The public always wanted its Hollywood gods and goddesses to be special while at the same time maintaining a Middle American, folks-next-door image. Loretta and Tom filled the bill.

In the forties the press began widely publicizing Loretta's strong Catholic convictions. A few weeks after Peter's birth, Loretta met a dynamic young priest named Patrick Peyton who would help further magnify her Catholic image.

Tom Lewis first met Father Peyton during the summer of 1945, while he was still commandant of Armed Forces Radio. "A college friend of mine in New York had written me insisting I see Father," Lewis explained, "telling me little about him except that he would be unlike anyone I had ever met before. He was right on about that. Such an operation as the Armed Forces Radio Service was very difficult to penetrate during wartime. There were several checkpoints before one reached the commandant's office: the barrier beside the reception desk, the staff sergeant's office, the adjutant's office, the executive officer's office, and my secretary's office and waiting room. Father Peyton cleared all points without breaking stride, giving each person he passed a hale, hearty 'God bless ya!' in his rich Irish brogue, and confirming the blessing with his glistening Irish face."

The priest told Lewis he wanted to use Hollywood's stars and facilities to broadcast his message of strong family values during the upcoming postwar period. "Family prayer is the key to family unity," he said.

The priest was eager to meet Mrs. Lewis, so Tom took Father Peyton home. Father Peyton told Loretta that he had been invited to speak at the Church of the Good Shepherd in Beverly Hills the following morning. A great many stars would be among the congregation, and the priest wanted to try to enlist their aid. His mission was to promote daily rosary and family prayer.

"Sell them on the idea of family rosary, but don't give them any details of how you want them to help," Loretta advised him. "Have Monsignor Concannon in the front of the church as they leave to invite them to come back to the sacristy to meet you personally. Then clinch the sale."

The handsome young priest mesmerized the congregation at the Church of the Good Shepherd the following morning. He followed Loretta's advice, meeting later with Charles Boyer, Irene Dunne, Ethel Barrymore, Maureen O'Hara, and other stars.

"I really believe I am one of the first persons to know about Father Peyton's Rosary Crusade," Miss Dunne recalled. "I can see him standing in my hallway taking his leave after we had been talking over his plans. In his very confident yet humble way, he said, 'Mary will see this whole thing through. You can be sure of that.' He spoke of Mary with such—What is the word?—assurance, maybe—familiarity, perhaps. He seemed so near to her I honestly felt her presence."

The priest met with other stars in the ensuing weeks, including Ruth Hussey, Jimmy Durante, Jeanne Crain, and June Haver, all of whom wanted to help in his crusade. Even Louella Parsons joined the father's team. Now that he had corralled the stars, Father Peyton returned to New York City with high hopes of selling the networks on his idea of broadcasting the rosary. Almost a year would elapse, however, before the project started moving ahead.

In many ways *Along Came Jones* was a picture years ahead of its time. Loretta was adroit in her role, a perfect complement to Cooper's low-key style. She looked particularly youthful and beautiful in the picture. Although *Jones* was not the kind of film Gary Cooper's fans expected, he was one of the biggest box office draws of the decade and his fans were loyal.

Along Came Jones proved to be one of the top moneymakers of the year.

And Now Tomorrow also proved a box office smash. Loretta's decision to free-lance had paid off—she was playing opposite the screen's leading male stars in the industry's biggest commercial hits.

International Pictures announced that Loretta would now star in an offbeat project, *The Stranger*. The screenplay was by John Huston and Anthony Veiller, although only Veiller got screen credit.

The war was over, and many people were worried that Nazi leaders had escaped Germany and were hiding in South America—perhaps even in the United States itself. As the Nuremberg trials got under way, Hollywood began to address the theme of Nazis-in-hiding. One of the first and most successful films of this genre was *The Stranger,* the story of a Nazi intellectual living as a professor in an American college town.

Producer Sam Spiegel, who then used the name S. P. Eagle, struck a deal with Orson Welles to star in the film. Welles, married to screen goddess Rita Hayworth, was still considered Hollywood's bad boy. He had not directed a film in years, although he had starred in several, most notably *Jane Eyre*. Welles was eager to direct again, and agreed to star for Spiegel if he could also direct the film. Spiegel complied, but on the condition that Welles shoot the script without any changes. The producer was shrewd enough to have Welles sign an ironclad contract stipulating that if he ran over schedule or budget he could be replaced as director while still having to complete his role as the professor. Since Welles was anxious to prove that he could follow the rules if he wanted to, the "wonder boy" accepted.

Edward G. Robinson was cast in *The Stranger* as the war crimes commissioner in pursuit of Welles. The director had wanted his friend and colleague Agnes Moorehead, but the studio insisted on Robinson for marquee value. Welles had recently done a radio broadcast with Loretta, and one story contends that it was he who suggested she play opposite him in the film. It must be remembered, however, that she was under contract to International, and this would be her last picture for the indie company (International would later merge with Universal).

In *The Stranger* Loretta played the young woman who marries the new professor (Welles) and later discovers he is a Nazi war criminal. Loretta was fascinated with Orson Welles but a bit apprehensive about working with him: "I was so afraid I couldn't take direction from him, and not because he isn't a good director. He's brilliant, really, and whatever else you may say about Orson, he's not dull. That's important. He's never dull.

"But he looks like such a baby! A real baby, with a round, fat face and such serious eyes. Now, you can't take direction from a nice, sweet, fat baby. I did worry about it before we started. Then it was all right. He'd make suggestions quietly, and I'd take them. I think he's a brilliant director."

Orson Welles remembered, "There was a famous fight about a close-up. Spiegel wanted to cut into a scene for a close reaction of Loretta. I was opposed to this, and remarkably enough, Miss Young took my side in a heated debate involving Spiegel, her agent, and a number of other officials. Because the female star demanded that she should *not* have a close-up, we won the day."

Former Broadway star Philip Merivale, now a great Hollywood character actor, was cast as Loretta's father, a Supreme Court justice who is somewhat opposed to her hasty marriage. On their first day of shooting together, Loretta and Merivale played a scene in which she tells him she wants to marry the young stranger. Loretta looked at Merivale, and suddenly burst into tears.

"I have no idea why," she later confessed. "Of course it wasn't in the script. But he looked so sweet and so serious and maybe so worn that I just started to cry."

Everyone on the set was startled. Welles told Loretta if she wanted to play the scene that way, it was certainly an interpretation they could try. Loretta managed to stop crying, however, and they filmed the scene as written.

Merivale was ill at the time and died shortly after the film's completion.

Many actors were returning home from the service, including David Niven. Though Niven had been off the screen through the war years, Goldwyn renewed his contract upon his return. Almost instantly he was loaned to Paramount to make the comedy *The Perfect Marriage.* Producer Hal Wallis had already signed Loretta for the female lead.

Meanwhile, Georgianna Young and Ricardo Montalban confirmed their earlier civil marriage with a church wedding at St. Paul's in Westwood, where Georgianna's sisters had been married before her. Georgianna's wedding, unlike those of her sisters, was a quiet ceremony with only family and close friends in attendance.

Montalban later revealed that Georgianna was seven months pregnant when they were married. "Georgianna had explained to her family about the Tijuana wedding," Montalban recounted. Although the couple had made a vow not to consummate their civil marriage, in Montalban's words, "the flesh is weak, and we did." However, the St. Paul's wedding was a dignified affair with a small reception afterward.

Montalban has remembered that he and Georgianna often fought during the early years of their marriage. Neither of them, however, thought of separation. They each had their own methods of cooling off—he would often take a drive; she would often run to her mother.

Loretta and Tom's marriage continued to be peaceful and serene by comparison to the Montalbans. At the time, Loretta described her married life as "almost honeymoonish."

After release from the service, Tom was offered the presidency of several radio networks and major advertising agencies. But Lewis, out of loyalty to Ray Rubicam and the various sponsors he had worked with over the years, chose to rejoin Young and Rubicam for a year. He headed West Coast operations for the agency and was made vice president. In addition, Lewis was on the board of directors of the Beverly Hills Hotel, the Huntridge Development Corporation, and the Huntridge Theatre Corporation, all investment companies in which the Lewises and the Griffins were partners. Tom also remained active in civic affairs. He was radio subcommittee secretary for both the Army-Navy Commission and the Hollywood Victory Committee.

In the spring of 1946 the Lewis family traveled to Troy, New York, where Tom's family still lived. Loretta, however, soon had to return to Hollywood. She had decided to accept the exciting challenge of a new project.

*Loretta Young can do no wrong in front
of a camera.*

—*Dore Schary to Tom Lewis*

Twelve

Dore Schary had proven himself a brilliant creative executive
and writer-producer at M-G-M. David O. Selznick had lured
him away with a five-year contract as production chief of Vanguard Films, a subsidiary of Selznick International Pictures.
Schary was placed in total charge of all Vanguard films—at
least until the rough-cut stage, when Selznick would have his
say.

Schary's tastes in filmmaking traditionally ran toward material with a message, but he was able to pack plenty of show-
manship and entertainment into his projects. *Katie for Congress*
was such a "message" property. Originally based on a Finn-
ish play, for Hollywood's purposes it was turned into the tale
of an innocent Swedish-American farm girl who goes to work
as a maid for a United States congressman and his wealthy
family. She eventually becomes a congresswoman herself,
and in the process teaches one and all the true meaning of
American values.

Selznick was still personally managing the career of Ingrid
Bergman, so naturally she was the producer's first choice to
play the part of the Swedish maid. Schary went to the Para-

mount lot to discuss the property with Bergman, but got a firm turndown. In Schary's words, "She brushed me off, along with the script." Once again the star had annoyed Selznick. Bergman had already passed on many properties which later became major vehicles for other stars—including *The Spiral Staircase* (Dorothy McGuire) and *To Each His Own* (for which Olivia De Havilland won an Oscar).

Meanwhile, the rest of the film had been cast: Joseph Cotten (under contract to Selznick) was set to play the congressman; Ethel Barrymore, Charles Bickford, and superb character actors Harry Davenport, Rhys Williams, Thurston Hall, Anna Q. Nilsson, and Rose Hobart were also cast.

Selznick then suggested to Schary that Dorothy McGuire might be right for the part of the maid, but Schary didn't agree. Schary proposed Loretta Young, but Selznick didn't like that idea, and countered with Sonja Henie—after all, she *was* Scandinavian. Miss Henie was then married to Dan Topping, part owner of the New York Yankees, and while her career as a film star was essentially in eclipse, her name still had huge drawing potential demonstrated by her successful Hollywood Ice Revue.

Schary, however, didn't like the Henie casting idea at all. He sent Selznick a memo: "I honestly feel with deep conviction that Loretta Young could approximate much more of what we want, and in the company of the rest of our cast she would make a far, far better picture.

"Please, fellas, don't brush this aside as a producer's frantic fear. I am sure that if this picture was going to be a Selznick International picture we would never take Sonja Henie. Don't sell me Henie and bet on the Yankees. Sitting down here on my heinie—I am convinced that Henie won't do.

"With all good wishes, I remain, sincerely, your obedient servant."

With a touch of humor and an uncharacteristically brief retort, Selznick wired Schary, "Okay, forget Henie. But don't come around to me when you want some skating lessons."

Now that Schary had sold Selznick on the idea of casting Loretta Young, he went to work on securing the actress's participation, first sending her the script. Some reports assert she turned down the role outright. Schary, however, contended that although she loved the script and the role, "she expressed serious reservations about her ability to fashion the Swedish accent."

Schary then set up a meeting with Loretta at Lucey's, the famous restaurant across from the Paramount and RKO lots. The executive was amazed at the slim star's incredible appetite at lunch: "She astounded me. There were two tall glasses of milk, a bowl of soup, lamb chops, baked potatoes, green peas, stewed tomatoes, rolls and butter, apple pie, and ice cream." And Schary conjectured what most other people believed: "Loretta's metabolism must be perfect." He later discovered that she was famous in Hollywood circles for this appetite.

Another thing that impressed him was Loretta's directness. Schary knew that she had the beauty and talent to play the part of Katie, but he felt that this in-person quality of directness underscored her appropriateness for the role. He told her he knew it was a gamble for her to attempt the role, since it was different from what she had done before. But he also told her he believed she could win an Academy Award. Schary later commented, "It was not a ploy. I truly believed that she could win an Oscar."

Loretta was never better than when facing a challenge backed by someone who had faith in her and would encourage her. She later described how one night she sat up till dawn at the home of Schary and his wife, talking about the possibility of playing Katie. Even after her great success in the role, she would tell people: "I still don't know why he thought of me." But he had thought of her, and she finally accepted.

While Loretta was in New York, prior to the start of filming, she said, "For years cameramen have been trying to get
me to dye my hair or anyway just to lighten it a little. I've
never done it. Blond wigs, yes, lots of them. But I've never
touched my hair. Now I've got all the cameramen so discour-
aged they never mention it anymore. And all by myself, I'm
considering whether to make it a light brown, like Ingrid
Bergman's, maybe, for this Swedish part. That would startle
the cameraman if I did that, and all on my own." (One of the
reasons Loretta had never dyed her hair was because her hair
was baby-fine. Had she subjected it to harsh chemicals over
the years, she would have had a major problem by now.)

When preproduction started on *Katie* (as the film was then
called), Loretta, in Schary's words, "plunged into the role."
Selznick suggested they hire Ruth Roberts, the sister of
writer-director George Seaton, to coach Loretta with her
Swedish accent. When Selznick had brought Ingrid Bergman
over from Sweden in 1938, he needed someone to perfect
Bergman's English and work with her as a diction coach.
Selznick remembered that the Seatons were of Swedish stock
and that George's sister had taught English to Swedish immi-
grant children back in Minnesota. Ruth Roberts then began a
lifelong association with Miss Bergman, but occasionally she
did take on other assignments. Now she worked with Young
on acquiring a Swedish accent. They worked for weeks,
hours, every day. It paid off: Loretta's accent in the picture
was excellent and consistent.

Katie was a very practical, common-sense, roll-up-your-
sleeves-and-get-the-problems-solved kind of lady, not unlike
Loretta herself. Loretta, under H. C. Potter's expert direction, remained totally in character throughout the picture. In
a couple of scenes—one, traveling in a car, another, giving
Joseph Cotten a rubdown—there were wisps of hair actually
out of place. This was obviously not a typical Loretta Young
clotheshorse role. There was a naturalness and a controlled
intensity in her performance. She was very appealing and

convincing, and looked good as a blonde (she had actually bleached her hair for this role, although her hair seemed to get darker as the film progressed).

At a crucial point in the story Katie is ready to give up on her race for a seat in Congress because of the opposition's mudslinging tactics. Her father (played by Harry Shannon) tells her the easiest thing would be for Katie to quit the race —but "You must *fight!*" She does and of course wins the election. The philosophy of not giving up in the face of adversity is surely Loretta's own.

The picture was typical of Schary in its strong stance against prejudice. The villain was clear-cut and despicable, a character who espouses belonging to the "right kind of religion," "no foreign-borns," "no nonwhites." The film had simple villains and simple heroes, a formula that has served many films, including modern-day blockbusters such as *Star Wars.*

Loretta's brothers in the film were played by three newcomers: Lex Barker (who would later play "Tarzan" and marry actresses Arlene Dahl and Lana Turner), James Arness (who became, in *Gunsmoke,* television's most successful sheriff), and Keith Andes (who went on to become a popular leading man in RKO films).

During production of *Katie* Schary had a running argument with Selznick over the title. Schary wanted to call it *The Farmer's Daughter* and later noted, "David finally permitted me to use the term, which he thought was vulgar, redolent of cheap traveling salesman stories."

Schary was consistently impressed with the rushes of each day's work. He told Loretta, "Believe me, you'll get the award."

Loretta's only film in release during 1946 was *The Stranger.* It proved not to be a typical Orson Welles film. Instead it was a straightforward mystery-adventure, not requiring its audience to interpret hidden meanings or discover symbolic psychological eccentricities. Perhaps for that reason Welles himself didn't particularly like the film ("There was nothing of *me* in it," he later said). Nor is it one of the Welles cult films, although it deserves greater recognition. It is outstanding in every department and is one of the films of the 1940s that has stood the test of time.

Although Loretta was second-billed to Edward G. Robinson, she was billed above Welles and her face dominated the ads. "After what you've done to me . . . Kill me!" ran the ad line. Nowhere was there a mention that the picture was about tracking down a Nazi.

To publicize the film Loretta agreed to pose for Max Factor's Pan-Cake Makeup ads, further enhancing and maintaining the legend of Loretta's eternal beauty: "Look Beautiful Always . . . today *and* tomorrow!"

Although in private life her demeanor and attitude reflected that befitting a young matron and mother of three, Loretta Young was still concerned with beauty if not youth. She confessed, "I am unfortunate enough to have circles under my eyes and I insist on having them blocked out" (she referred to the airbrushing of still photos). "An actress must give the illusion of beauty—not age."

The beautiful Loretta Young graced the cover of *Life* magazine in August 1946 as *The Stranger* was released nationwide.

That summer Father Peyton was back in Hollywood. He had finally convinced one of the networks—Mutual—to give him free air time—but for a top-quality entertainment program, not for recitation of the rosary. He would have to bear all production costs, and any religious message had to be nonsectarian. Although it was not what he had prayed for, Father Peyton accepted the challenge.

Many of the stars reaffirmed their faith in his crusade and their willingness to participate, but he still needed other talent—as well as a great deal of money. One night he visited with Loretta and told her his problems. A friend of the period recalls that although Loretta had continued supporting

Father Peyton, Tom had remained aloof. That night, however, Loretta said, "I've got an idea. I'm going to get Tom to come down and talk. They pay him fifty or sixty thousand dollars a year to do the kind of thing you're talking about. Let's draft him."

Lewis agreed to help, but he said to the priest, "I'll get you on the air . . . after that, you're on your own." In Lewis's words, "It was no small matter to get, free of charge, a half hour in evening prime time on a major radio network. . . . I asked for volunteers among my staff at Young and Rubicam to get the program started, notably Al Scalpone. . . .

"Several times when I was on the verge of making a deal and had called Father for a consultation, I discovered he was away giving a 'triduum.' A triduum is a three-day period of prayer.

"When I finally reached him I said, 'Father, do you want a local pulpit from which to direct a series of three days of prayer? Or do you want a national pulpit?'

" 'Why Tom, that's why I came out here.'

" 'Well, then, Father—let's forget the "triduum," or whatever, and stay in town until I get a deal—will you?'

" 'I will,' said he, with that contagious brogue."

With Lewis's help, Father Peyton lined up Roz Russell, Bing Crosby, and other top stars as well as ace radio drama writer True Boardman, who had served under Lewis in Armed Forces Radio.

Ruth Hussey's husband, Bob Longenecker, was brought on as a full-time producer. Al Scalpone came up with the show's slogan, "The Family That Prays Together Stays Together," and it was decided that it would be used to conclude each program. Boardman would write the first script.

Loretta signed with Sam Goldwyn for a picture with a theme that was close to her heart, an inspirational story of divine intervention in mortal lives based on *The Bishop's Wife*, a novel by Robert Nathan, who had also written the immensely popular *A Portrait of Jenny.* An added factor in her decision was Goldwyn's reputation for sparing no expense and hiring the very best and most commercial talent for his productions.

Robert E. Sherwood and Leonardo Bercovici had written the screenplay, a story concerning an angel who is sent down to earth to aid an Episcopal bishop in raising money to build a new church and, coincidentally, to straighten out the deteriorating relationship between the bishop and his wife. Loretta, playing the wife, would be flanked by two of the screen's top leading men: Cary Grant as the bishop and David Niven as the angel. On Grant's insistence the actors exchanged roles. Then he decided he didn't want to make the picture at all and attempted to get out of the commitment. But Goldwyn prevailed, and Grant played the angel.

An incredible supporting cast had been assembled, including Monty Woolley, Gladys Cooper, Elsa Lanchester, Regis Toomey, James Gleason, Isabel Jewell, and Sara Haden. Henry Koster eventually took over as director.

Some thought Loretta, in the title role, had been typecast. She disagreed. "I thought of the wife as a frustrated little thing, rather lonely and rather thwarted." Loretta felt the role offered her an acting challenge—the part was a decidedly unself-assured woman, the total opposite of Loretta Young.

Despite a long shooting schedule, Henry Koster later said that Loretta Young was one of the "easiest actresses to direct." During shooting Koster utilized an old radio technique. A performer who flubbed a line had to donate a dollar to a kitty. At the end of each scene the performer who in the opinion of Koster had done the best job received the lump sum. Invariably it was Loretta who pocketed the cash.

Many people relate stories about Cary Grant and his insistence on perfectionism, and there is one concerning *The Bishop's Wife.* Loretta and Cary were shooting a scene when Grant stopped abruptly, declaring, "If it's supposed to be cold outside, and the house is nice and warm inside, why isn't there any frost on the windows?" This was the kind of detail that was rarely overlooked at the Goldwyn studio, and everything stopped until the proper frost effect was accomplished by the propmen.

This incident irritated Loretta, and she indirectly explained why, years later, when discussing Ronald Colman. She called Colman "a delicate perfectionist, whereas other stars I've worked with tend to be trying perfectionists." Without naming Grant she said, "Before going into a scene, for instance, they'll say something like, 'Just a minute—if it's hot inside this room and frosty outside, why is there no frost on the window?' And it would throw me completely. I would go into the scene wondering why there was no frost on the windows instead of thinking about the contents of the scene itself." She observed that if Colman "had anything to say like this, he would do it alone with the director and never disturb anybody else's concentration."

Even in 1947 Loretta didn't contain her annoyance. She politely asked Grant if he would not do that sort of thing, at least in front of her. Grant, of course, graciously complied. A decade later, discussing Loretta's star temperament, an associate noted, "I'd hate to see her and Cary Grant on the same set today!"

David Niven was going through a personal crisis during the making of The Bishop's Wife. Only a few months before, his beloved twenty-five-year-old wife, Primmie, had died in a freak accident at Tyrone Power's house. While playing sardines, a hide-and-seek game played in the dark, Mrs. Niven had opened what she thought was a closet door and had fallen down a flight of stairs into the cellar. A few days later she was dead.

Niven went into a deep depression which lasted for many months. People on the set of The Bishop's Wife recall that although his personal life was in turmoil, Niven was such a consummate professional that none of his suffering carried over into his work.

Loretta was more diligent than ever on this film. "This was the hardest part I'd ever played," she has remembered. "If I'd ever showed in that picture, the whole thing would have gone to pieces. If I'd showed—if I'd ever taken hold of one of those scenes . . . That was why it was so hard—I had to avoid doing anything with a scene. It would have been so easy. They were such lovely scenes, so well written. I was so tempted, really, to play one for all it was worth. You know, to show." (Obviously Miss Young had learned her lesson well from George Arliss—the play was the thing, not an individual scene.)

Loretta later said that during production she and Henry Koster "used to talk it over all the time—how delicately each scene must be played. There mustn't be any fireworks, any emotional acting. Did you notice that I never cried? Not once. I never tried to get anyone to feel sorry for me, and it would have been so easy in that part. I was terribly tempted sometimes."

On February 13, 1947, Father Peyton's dream became a reality when the premiere broadcast of *The Family Theater* was aired over the Mutual network. Loretta starred with Don Ameche in "Flight From Home"; James Stewart narrated; Meredith Willson did the music. The program was broadcast live at eight-thirty P.M. in Los Angeles, an eleven-thirty broadcast on the East Coast.

Although the show received mediocre to outright dreadful reviews, it was a hit with audiences and would remain on the air for an astonishing ten years. Later, it was broadcast at six-thirty P.M. in Hollywood for nine-thirty P.M. airing in the East, and then repeated at eight-thirty P.M. for Pacific Coast listeners. "The Family That Prays Together Stays Together" became part of the nation's language.

This show, along with her continuous involvement with

religious activities, further intensified the image of Loretta Young as the perfect wife-mother Catholic.

Professionally speaking, 1947 was a banner year for Loretta Young. It was the first year since the old Fox days that she had three films in release.

The Perfect Marriage—released in 1946 but still in distribution in 1947—was a pleasant but run-of-the-mill sophisticated comedy. *The Farmer's Daughter,* however, released in March, was well received by critics and was a hit at the box office. Even James Agee liked it: "Patricians, politicians, even peasants are portrayed with unusual perception and wit." *The New Republic* said of Loretta, "She gives an appealing sustained performance that should mean for her, in comedy, a new lease on life." Other critics found her "convincing," "striking," "charming," and said that she had given a performance of "dramatic force" and "finesse."

Heretofore, Loretta had never been a hit with the critics. Perhaps Schary was right: she might be nominated for an Oscar. Actually, the word was that she would have two chances for a nomination, since *The Bishop's Wife* was slated for release in December, in time to qualify for the Oscars. Talk in the industry was that the picture was sure to be another Goldwyn critical and box office success. It had been chosen for the 1947 Royal Command Performance in London.

Loretta began work on a new film for Dore Schary. With David Selznick's blessing, Schary had left the mogul's independent company to assume production control of the RKO studios. One of the properties that Schary inherited was *Rachel and the Stranger,* Waldo Salt's screenplay of Howard Fast's story about a bondswoman in the 1790s. Once again he wanted to star Loretta Young.

In a sense, this part was typecasting—Rachel was a strong-willed woman who overcomes all obstacles while maintaining her femininity and winning the man at the fadeout.

RKO had Robert Mitchum for one male lead and borrowed rising young star William Holden for the other. Holden, who even then had a drinking problem, was still a young man and could handle it. He always behaved as an ultra gentleman in the presence of ladies. Mitchum, on the other hand, was Mitchum—no airs, no attempts to be anything other than what he was. His sleepy-eyed exterior masked a highly intelligent and hedonistic person.

Mitchum was a shrewd professional when he had to be. He was not happy that Norman Foster had been brought in as director, noticing that Loretta and her brother-in-law would have quiet conferences about scenes which Mitchum felt would subsequently be directed to her advantage. Some on the set remember that Mitchum did many bits of business that would subtly catch the camera's eye. However, Loretta sweetly called him on this ploy, pointing out, in so many words, that the only one to suffer would be the movie. Mitchum, it is said, understood—as most people did when Loretta talked turkey—and the picture stayed on track.

One of the earliest references to Loretta's famous "swear box" was on the set of *Rachel and the Stranger*. No one seems to remember it before this picture, but there is no doubt that the swear box—a box used to hold fines levied against anyone who swore in the star's presence—was present on all succeeding Young pictures.

There are many versions of how the swear box originated and what the penalties were. Some say it dates from Loretta's involvement with the St. Anne's Foundation. Loretta was always vocal about St. Anne's, always anxious to help Sister Winifred. So Loretta came up with a new idea to help raise money—the swear box. One story claims that she at first only used it in social situations, when playing charades or the like at her house. Another version asserts she brought it onto the set and announced, "Cussing is the one thing I dislike about making pictures. Every time I hear a cuss word it jars me. I just decided to do something about it."

It has been reported that on the set of *Rachel* Robert

Mitchum stuck a couple of bills in the box each morning and said, "This should cover me for the day."

Through the years stories about the swear box have become legion, with the reported fines varying from ten cents to five dollars. The most widely related tale is that somebody slipped Loretta a large-denomination bill and said something to the effect of "Now can I tell you to go ——— yourself?" The tale has been attributed over the years to many people, including most of her costars and many of the female stars noted for their colorful vocabularies, such as Tallulah Bankhead and Ethel Merman.

Years later, when asked about the famous swear box, Loretta said, "Yes, it's true, I had a swear box, but it wasn't swearing that bothered me, only blasphemy." But she denied the story about Ethel Merman. "She supposedly came up to me at a party and gave me a dollar. I don't ever recall meeting Ethel Merman."

Meanwhile, *Rachel and the Stranger* had a long shooting schedule. A former RKO employee claims that memos, sent back to the studio from location shooting in Oregon, assert that Loretta was "no end of trouble" during this picture. This same employee says that Loretta only got the part because everyone else turned it down, and that Loretta was ill during the shooting and production was delayed for a time. However, others working on the film recall Loretta as being most cooperative.

According to Virginia Lane, then a publicist for RKO, Loretta was popular with the crew on this picture and was always concerned for their safety. Back at the studio, the actress had even offered to personally pay for extra safety guards for lighting technicians who had to work dangerously high above the sound stage.

Certainly Dore Schary was pleased with his choice of star. He told Tom Lewis, "Loretta can do no wrong in front of a camera." And everyone agreed that in *Rachel* Loretta delivered one of her most convincing performances.

The first preview in Hollywood of *The Bishop's Wife* was a special occasion for Loretta. Danny Kaye was in attendance and Loretta was familiar with Kaye's unorthodox behavior at previews. "He's just a cut-up. He's always the comedian, and very funny too," recalled Loretta. "Even when he's looking at a picture. I warned him I couldn't stand any jokes during *The Bishop's Wife*—not the first time I saw it, anyway. Danny promised to keep quiet. Afterward, he said very earnestly that the picture was so beautiful that he didn't even want to talk. And that from Danny Kaye!"

There was enormous enthusiasm about this picture, and Loretta, Tom, and Judy, now twelve, were going to London for the Royal Command Performance, where Loretta Young, the little girl who grew up in a boardinghouse and hadn't even gone to high school, was going to be presented to the king and queen of England. Tom Lewis had already been decorated by the king, having been awarded the Excellent Order of the British Empire and the Degree of Honorary Officer for his wartime efforts.

Loretta, Tom, and Judy sailed on the *Queen Mary*. Among their fellow passengers was Noël Coward, of whom an anxious Loretta asked, "When I curtsy to the queen how low shall I bow?" To which Coward replied, "To the floor, ducky."

England was still feeling the aftereffects of the war. London was being rebuilt, the people were still on rations, and inflation was rampant. There was strong anti-American feeling, especially toward film stars who seemed to epitomize everything the British resented about America. In addition, the British public was being denied American films owing to the exorbitant taxes levied on those movies by the English, who were attempting to restore their own movie industry.

The Bishop's Wife was to be shown at the Command Performance and at one other benefit performance, but the masses would not have the opportunity to see the much heralded film.

However, unlike sex symbols Lana Turner and Rita Hayworth, recent visitors to England, Loretta Young did not engender hostility from the British press. She was there not to vacation and party—although Noël Coward did throw a party in her honor. She was traveling with her distinguished husband and their daughter, and their unofficial hosts were Vivien Leigh and Laurence Olivier. The film Loretta was in England to publicize was wholesome family fare which happened to costar two British leading men. Furthermore, the Lewises were to be presented to the king and queen.

Loretta was not disappointed upon meeting the royal family. She later recalled, "As the big moment approached, I kept running around trying to find out whether I should wear my long white gloves. Everybody was so excited, and I was no exception. Although we had been well rehearsed for the event, we all just plain forgot. I was frantic, for suddenly the line began to move and my turn was coming. At the last minute I got a peek at the others and saw they had their gloves on. I never got gloves on so fast in my life."

However, Loretta wasn't in the best of health on this trip, and was briefly hospitalized for a minor operation, the nature of which was undisclosed. The Lewises then headed back to America, stopped off in New York, where Loretta gave two rather unfortunate interviews.

She told columnist Earl Wilson, "Those English people are starving. We took seventy-five pounds of food with us, and when we found out how bad conditions were, we couldn't swallow it.

"I took the food down to a London Catholic priest, the Reverend Maurice Ryan. He seemed so quiet and reserved about it that I thought, 'He must think I'm rude. But he can think it, because I'm going to satisfy my conscience.' Since then I have had a letter from him saying I prolonged the lives of ten people for approximately six months."

This comment made even Earl sit up. "You mean to say people are really that close to starving?" he asked.

"Well," Loretta continued, "if there are six of you and you have one ration card each, you can pool your stuff, but if you're alone with one ration card, you can't live on that." Loretta said that she had sent out to a fruit wagon for some grapes and two apples. "And they cost me $8.50. We sit here and crab if this room is a little too hot or too cold. I saw many blue hands, no gloves on, and it's *really* cold there." She noted, "People will say I'm wrong to talk this way and maybe they're right. But over there people are starving. When people of forty-five to fifty get sick, a lot of them die. They haven't the resistance to fight off the sickness, because, well, they just haven't been eating."

Loretta then saw Associated Press feature writer Gene Handsaker, and his interview with her reflected much of what she had told Wilson, plus a few additional comments in the same vein.

When these interviews appeared in London there was a hue and cry from the British public. Sir Alexander Maxwell, who was the head of Britain's tourist office, said, "I trust Miss Young will have the good sense to retract. There is not an item of truth in any of her statements." *The Daily Mirror* snidely observed, "The contrast between Hollywood opulence and our own modest state may have made the film star ultrasensitive."

The London papers then ran snickering accounts of what Miss Young was supposed to have said, under titles such as, "Life in Britain by Loretta Young," and comments like, "We don't generally print fiction, but we thought our readers might be entertained." They quoted Loretta as saying British factory workers faint around eleven o'clock for lack of food . . . Englishmen have beards because there are no razor blades available. . . . People walk on cardboard-patched shoes.

In Hollywood, Loretta issued an official statement: "I have

no apologies to make for any accurately interpreted statement I have made of conditions I saw in England, but I do refuse to accept responsibility for authorship of inaccurate or garbled quotations attributed to me or quotations emotionally interpreted. Specific replies to such garbled, generalized statements as have been reportedly attributed to me in the London papers will be made as soon as I am fully informed as to what I am supposed to have said in the first place."

Eventually Loretta did admit that much of her information on conditions in England had come secondhand. But in all fairness to Miss Young, it must be remembered that the people in postwar Britain did not have unlimited food supplies. They were kept on rationing coupons until the early 1950s.

The Bishop's Wife had opened in the states and was on almost every critic's list of the top ten films of the year. It would prove to be a box office hit, but not quite the blockbuster that Cary Grant's other recent releases were.

In many minds Grant had been miscast as the angel, since it was obvious from the beginning of the story that he could never get the girl. In retrospect, Goldwyn's original casting —Niven as the angel, Grant as the bishop—was much more apropos. For Loretta the picture capped a fine year.

But even better was the stunning news Loretta learned one Sunday while Irene Dunne and her husband, Frank Griffin, were having brunch with her and Tom at the Lewis home. The phone rang. It was Dore Schary with the news that Loretta had been nominated as best actress for *The Farmer's Daughter*.

"I was completely dumbfounded, then wildly elated," Loretta later recalled. She went running back into the dining room yelling, "I've been nominated! I've been nominated!"

Tom and the Griffins were equally excited. As Loretta danced around the room, she suddenly realized that Irene had already received four nominations. (She would receive a fifth the following year for *I Remember Mama*. She never re-

ceived the award.) In later telling the story, Loretta noted
that Irene must have known what she was thinking, because
she graciously told her, "You'll be even more excited the
next time, Loretta."

Loretta's competition was formidable: Rosalind Russell for
Mourning Becomes Electra, Joan Crawford for *Possessed,* Susan
Hayward for *Smash-Up,* and Dorothy McGuire for *Gentle-
man's Agreement.*

Loretta was happy with the nomination because it meant
that for the first time in twenty years, and after more than
eighty pictures, she had finally received official recognition of
her ability from her peers. She did not hold out much hope
for actually winning.

Charles Bickford had been nominated for best supporting
actor for *The Farmer's Daughter. The Bishop's Wife* had been
nominated in the best picture category, and Henry Koster
had been nominated as best director. Most of the critical
hosannas, however, had gone to Darryl F. Zanuck's production, *Gentleman's Agreement.*

A *Daily Variety* poll predicted that *Gentleman's Agreement*
was going to win as best picture, that Ronald Colman *(A
Double Life)* would beat Gregory Peck *(Gentleman's Agreement)*
as best actor, that Edmund Gwenn *(Miracle on 34th Street)* and
Celeste Holm *(Gentleman's Agreement)* would walk away with
the best supporting actor and actress Oscars, and that Roz
Russell was a shoo-in for best actress. According to *Daily
Variety,* the odds favored Roz, Dorothy, Joan, Susan, and Loretta—in that order. Roz Russell and Celeste Holm had already won the Golden Globe awards that year, signaling
their probable victory for the Oscar.

Russell and Young were very close friends, a friendship
that went beyond being colleagues. Roz's older sister,
"Duchess," was married to "Chet" LaRoche, Tom's friend
and former boss. All sources indicate that Loretta truly expected Roz to win the award, especially since she had been
expected to win the previous year for *Sister Kenny.* Surely this

year the Academy would vote her the winner—many Oscars have been regarded as "consolation prizes" for performances that went unrewarded in previous years.

Besides, Rosalind Russell's picture, *Mourning Becomes Electra,* was heavy drama, and Russell had played Lavinia to the hilt. Crawford and Hayward had also played tour-de-force roles, and McGuire had the advantage of starring in the odds-on favorite for best picture. *The Farmer's Daughter* was a much lighter vehicle, and Loretta's performance was subtle in its power—not the hammer-over-the-head job that usually wins Oscars.

Even though Loretta saw little chance of winning, she was, of course, excited about attending the ceremonies. For her gown she chose an elaborate frilly green taffeta creation by Adrian, definitely not designed for climbing stairs—another indication, some speculated, that Young had no thought of winning.

Loretta subsequently reported that on the day of the Oscar awards Russell had phoned her and said, "Only God and me knows who's going to win. So when you get it, unscrew it, if you can, and send me a little piece of it."

That Saturday night—March 20, 1948—the Shrine Auditorium was packed with over six thousand people. Dick Powell and Agnes Moorehead hosted the ceremonies, and as the evening progressed it appeared that *Daily Variety*'s poll would prove to be accurate: Gwenn and Holm won the supporting actor and actress awards as predicted.

Rosalind Russell was seated in the thirty-ninth row. Henry Rogers, her publicity agent, was seated nearby. In his mind, he had engineered the win for her. He recalled, "The Price, Waterhouse representative walked onstage with an envelope grasped in his hand. He gave it to Olivia de Havilland. She started to open it. Roz Russell began to stand up. Olivia read, loud and clear, 'Loretta Young for *Farmer's Daughter!*' Roz Russell's beads broke and scattered all over the floor. The audience gasped in surprise." However she may have felt,

Miss Russell immediately composed herself, stood fully erect, and led the applause, which became a standing ovation.

For several seconds Loretta didn't seem to respond. One account reported that Tom Lewis nudged her and said, "Get up, dear, it's you!" Loretta herself said, "I thought it must be a mistake when they called my name. But Tom kept saying, 'Get up, dear, get up! Go get your Oscar.' And then I knew it wasn't a mistake."

She slowly made her way up to the stage, and when she was handed the gleaming statuette, she grasped it and said, with characteristic directness and honesty, "At long last!" She had been so certain that she was not going to win that she had rejected suggestions that she prepare a speech, but Tom had insisted and reluctantly she had memorized one he had composed for her. After the applause died down, and as she clutched her Oscar, she managed to remember the words of the speech.

As always, the winners were gathered in a room backstage after the awards for publicity shots with their Oscars and the other winners. People there recall Loretta saying to Tom Lewis, "What about Roz? What will I say to Roz?" Even to the photographers and reporters, Loretta admitted, "To be perfectly honest, I never expected this in my life. I thought Rosalind would get it."

And Miss Young later said, "My only regret about the whole thing is Roz Russell. And don't say 'Poor Roz,' because she will go on to win an Academy Award and then some. But it was cruel for the poll to come out and say that she was going to win. I hope that will discourage them from taking polls next year."

After the press conference, the stars were off to the Academy celebration party at the Mocambo. The Hollywood press corps, who normally ignore the losers, were still curious as to Miss Russell's reaction.

(The tale of the embarrassing moment of an actor starting to stand before his name was called and discovering another has won the award, became so much a part of Hollywood legend that twenty years later this incident was incorporated into the novel and subsequent movie *The Oscar.*)

According to a Louella Parsons informant who was on the scene with Rosalind Russell that fateful night, "She was all right until we actually got home. She held her head high and joked with the sidewalk crowds about not carrying the Oscar home. But the minute she was inside her own walls, she broke down and sobbed. She was so ashamed. She kept telling Freddie [her husband, Fredric Brisson] and me, 'I'll be all right. It's just an emotional reaction. Just let me sit here a minute. I'll be all right.'"

In a little while, Miss Russell was completely in possession of herself. She changed into a bright red ensemble and headed for the party at the Mocambo, where she electrified the guests by making a grand entrance and rushing over to Loretta to kiss and congratulate her. Roz hugged Loretta, burying her head in Loretta's shoulder. The two women huddled. Roz whispered, "I'm not going to say I'm happy I lost, but I will say that if someone else had to win, I'm glad it was you." Miss Russell added, "Now, when we look up, smile. The photographers are right here!"

Loretta Young had at last reached the pinnacle of movie stardom. Before going to the Academy celebration party, Loretta had rushed to the nearest phone and called Gladys, who was at home asleep. "Mamma," she shouted excitedly, "I won! I won!" "That's nice, Gretchen," her mother said. "What did you win, dear?"

*I believe that prayer is our powerful contact
with the greatest force in the universe.*
　　　　　　　　　　　　　　—Loretta Young

Thirteen

She had actually won an Academy Award! Loretta was ecstatic, and nothing could dampen her spirits, not even her
mother's nonchalance.

Tom Lewis reveals that after the Oscar night rounds of
parties and activities they got home very, very late and finally
went to bed. In the darkness Loretta was restless. Tom asked,
"What's wrong?"

Loretta answered, "I can't sleep. I'm too excited. I don't
want to go to sleep. I don't want this night to end."

Lewis turned on the lights and said, "You're right. Let's
not go to sleep. Let's stay up and talk." And they did.

The day after the Academy Awards, both Loretta and best
actor Ronald Colman appeared on Louella Parsons's network
radio program. Later, Louella was happy to report in her
column that "in spite of all the excitement of the Awards,
Loretta went into the retreat which she had planned before
she won her Oscar. She's consistent on all things—her religion, her home life, and her career."

There are numerous varieties of religious retreats. A retreat is a program whereby people renew and deepen their

faith by gathering together to pray, meditate, observe periods of silence, discuss their religious experiences, and participate, if the retreat is a Catholic one, in attending Mass and receiving the sacraments. A retreat may last anywhere from one day to several weeks.

Loretta has always joined in retreats, but because this particular retreat came so soon after the award, it was given notice by the press. It was the first time her public was made aware that she was so deeply religious. Although some in Hollywood scoffed at what they perceived to be religious posturing, Loretta's beliefs were sincere, and she took quite seriously her position—due to her high visibility—as "an example" to others, an especially difficult path considering her profession.

Following the retreat, Loretta returned to work on *The Accused,* a Hal Wallis production dealing with a psychology professor (Young) who accidentally kills one of her students while fending off his advances. It was another nonglamour role, an acting challenge. The director was William Dieterle, and her costars were Robert Cummings and Wendell Corey.

Then Loretta had the pleasure of signing—on her own terms—a multipicture contract with Darryl Zanuck. She would return to Twentieth in triumph. In her words, she ended "a silly feud with the man I thought was my one big enemy." However, in the midst of all this good fortune in her professional life, Loretta's personal life was jolted.

Only three months after her Oscar win, the public learned that Loretta Young's father was alive—by virtue of the fact that he had just died. The secret was out: John Earle Young had been living quietly in California, allegedly supported by his famous daughters.

Headlines screamed: LORETTA YOUNG'S DAD DIES A PAUPER, UNKNOWN TO STAR.

Earle had been living in a rooming house in Alhambra, California, and had suffered several strokes. After he died in the county hospital, his body was claimed by a lady friend,

Laura Lund. Miss Lund contacted Earle's mother, who was by this time herself bedridden, requesting money for funeral arrangements. All Mrs. Young could offer was a grave in her family plot. Mrs. Young then wrote her granddaughter Gretchen a brief note:

"I am obliged to tell you, you should know, that a person who called himself John Earle died in the county hospital of a stroke or heart attack yesterday, June 6, 1948, and is to be buried in Woodlawn Cemetery in Santa Monica at one-thirty Thursday. Please notify your mother and others who should know.

"Everything has been taken care of as the monthly check I receive from the Good Samaritan [Loretta] has not been used for provisions and I could save some of it. So again, dear, you pay.

"I am just back from the Queen of Angels Hospital due to a bad fall I received trying to get up and into the wheelchair. Tricky thing, when one can't stand or take a step or stop them when they start to roll away from you. That bill was also paid. I am so glad to be able to do so without having to call on you all for everything, though always so gallantly and generously given. Thank you so much again. You have paid for everything. All my love, Grandma."

However, some facts were not made public. An indisputable source has now disclosed that it was Tom Lewis who had in fact taken over sending Mrs. Young money, and had been doing so since his marriage to Loretta. The actress had little contact with the woman.

The "Pauper" headlines were highly misleading. John Earle may not have left an inheritance, but he had earned his own living up to the end. The "revelatory" letter from Grandma Young to Loretta undoubtedly found its way into print via Miss Young's highly dedicated press agent, whose concern for her client and her client's image was always paramount.

There was family controversy about attending John Earle

An atypical shot of Young: her hair is disheveled and she is casually costumed. It was between takes on *Rachel and the Stranger.* Loretta was thirty-five.

Loretta and close pal Rosalind Russell caused a sensation when they arrived as the Toni twins at the 1948 Hollywood Photographers' Costume Ball.

Tom Lewis (far right) and his wife chatting with Monsignor Frank Kerr and producer Bryan Foy. The occasion was a screening of a picture Loretta didn't appear in but in which she was interested, *The Miracle of Our Lady of Fatima.*

In *Come to the Stable* (1949). She received a second Oscar nomination, but didn't win the award.

John Forsythe (thirty years before *Dynasty)* was Loretta Young's leading man in *It Happens Every Thursday,* a 1953 programmer for Universal.

Fans across the country responded when Loretta made her television debut in 1953. The perennially youthful star was forty. She became the first Oscar winner to receive an Emmy.

Tom Lewis and Loretta on the set of her TV show.

Loretta Young, flanked by Ralph *(This Is Your Life)* Edwards and Robert *(Father Knows Best)* Young, proudly receiving an Emmy.

Loretta (right) was unforgettable portraying an Oriental woman in several of the episodes of her TV show. Her versatility was one reason for her three Emmys.

With Mae Clarke on *The Loretta Young Show.* Loretta always hired the best in the business.

The New Loretta Young Show (1962). The public wasn't interested in Loretta as an "ordinary" housewife and mother. This show failed.

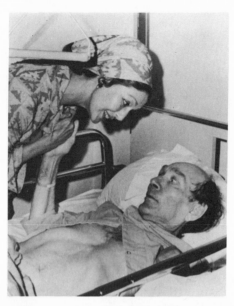

After her "retirement," Loretta devoted herself to charitable activities.

Young became involved in launching a youth project in Phoenix in 1971.

Loretta Young, flanked by Ralph *(This Is Your Life)* Edwards and Robert *(Father Knows Best)* Young, proudly receiving an Emmy.

Loretta (right) was unforgettable portraying an Oriental woman in several of the episodes of her TV show. Her versatility was one reason for her three Emmys.

With Mae Clarke on *The Loretta Young Show.* Loretta always hired the best in the business.

The New Loretta Young Show (1962). The public wasn't interested in Loretta as an "ordinary" housewife and mother. This show failed.

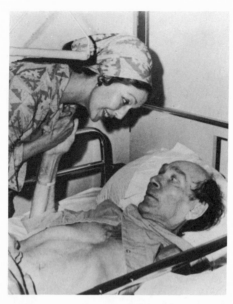

After her "retirement," Loretta devoted herself to charitable activities.

Young became involved in launching a youth project in Phoenix in 1971.

Loretta in 1976, attending an opening. The star was sixty-three.

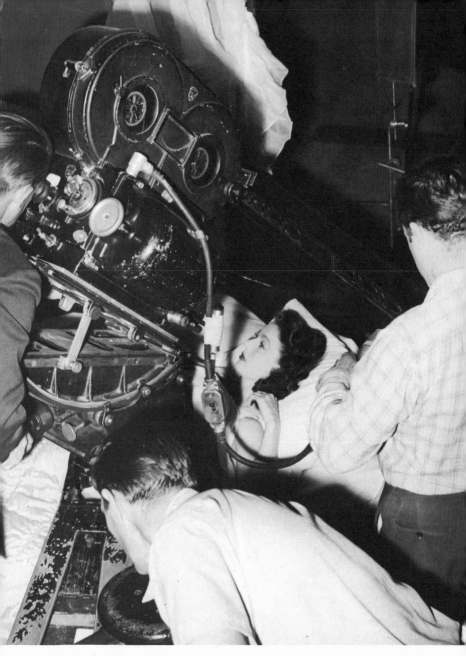

A symbolic photograph: some people contend that Loretta Young was happiest just as the camera was ready to roll.

Young's funeral. Polly Ann and Sally went to the simple Christian Science service; Loretta did not, and a statement was given out that a film assignment prevented her from attending.

Gladys Belzer issued a brief statement: "If the man who died under the name of John Earle was really he, I respect his desire to die in the identity he chose and maintained in his life."

Many years later, Loretta Young conceded, "I'm sorry now that I sat in judgment on him. This was one of those things I wish I could do over again. Frankly, I brushed him off and I think this was unforgivable of all of us."

The film Loretta had completed following work on *The Farmer's Daughter* had yet to be released, but when it was shown it was accompanied by a great deal of publicity.

A month before *Rachel and the Stranger* premiered, Loretta's costar, Robert Mitchum, made worldwide news when he was arrested and jailed for possession of marijuana. (He subsequently served a two-month jail term.) This kind of attention, coupled with Loretta's Oscar, ensured *Rachel* ample coverage in the press. Loretta's performance in the picture was well received, and there was talk that she would receive a second Oscar nomination.

On her first day back on the Fox lot Loretta walked into a dressing room filled with flowers—apparently Zanuck hadn't forgotten Loretta's complaint ten years earlier that in all the years she had worked for him he had never sent her flowers.

Loretta was now thirty-five but looked years younger. Nevertheless, in her first film at Fox, *Mother Is a Freshman,* she took on the challenge of playing the young mother of a teenager who goes back to college and vies with her own daughter for the affection of a college professor, played by Van Johnson. Rudy Vallee portrayed the "other man." The script was written by Richard Sale and Mary Loos (niece of Anita

Loos). Sale recalls that there was a swear box on the set, but that "Rudy Vallee did all the cussin', I didn't."

With *Freshman,* Loretta proved that she hadn't lost her flair for comedy. Her next film was also a comedy, but one of a different sort, providing her with her favorite role of all—that of a nun—a characterization peculiarly appropriate, but something she had never attempted before.

The film was *Come to the Stable,* based on a story by Catholic convert Clare Booth Luce. Sam Engel, veteran Fox producer and Zanuck's buddy, was producing, and Henry Koster, who had gotten such a great performance from Loretta in *The Bishop's Wife,* was set to direct. Also in the cast were Celeste Holm, Hugh Marlowe, Elsa Lanchester, Regis Toomey, Thomas Gomez, and Dooley Wilson.

Concerning the experience of working with Loretta, Sam Engel later complained, "I would go each morning to her house and we would have some good knock-down-drag-outs over certain things. Invariably, we surmounted every roadblock she put up. Roadblocks that at times appeared to me to be selfish. Sometimes I was incapable of understanding what the hell she was getting at, because she was not articulate enough to tell me."

Engel's complaint was unique; no one else has ever labeled Loretta inarticulate. She, herself, however, has admitted that there were difficulties during the shooting of this picture. Neither Engel nor Koster were Catholics, and Loretta obviously felt it her duty to oversee the project to make sure it was technically correct. As she has said, "I was the star, I had certain prerogatives, I knew what they were, and I used them." Even though Loretta knew others thought her difficult, she felt justified in her demands because in her heart she knew she wasn't doing this for herself but for the good of the picture.

Father Keller, the priest who had established the Christophers and who was a friend of Tom Lewis's, visited Loretta on the set. He listened quietly to Loretta's discourse on how she had seen to it that the picture would be technically correct. As Father Keller was about to leave, he told the star, "You must not—you cannot—deprive others of their responsibilities nor of their triumphs."

Loretta was puzzled and perturbed by the priest's comments. She hadn't exactly been reproached, but she certainly hadn't received the praise she anticipated. Then, after pondering Father Keller's remarks, she realized that what he was saying, with great subtlety, was that no one had asked her to take upon herself the role of being the final word on the technical aspects of Catholicism. With what must have been some embarrassment, she realized that the studio had consulted with the Church on these points in the script, and that she had allowed herself to become preoccupied with matters that were really none of her concern.

From this point on Loretta was generous in her praise of both Engel and Koster, and the film turned out to be a product of which all concerned could be proud. *Come to the Stable* is the story of two nuns who come to the little town of Bethlehem, Connecticut, and through wit, charm, intelligence, and faith overcome all obstacles and raise the necessary money to build a children's hospital.

Sister Winifred of St. Anne's was obviously Loretta's role model. Loretta was still president of St. Anne's, but she noted, "I'll exploit Loretta Young to the hilt for the benefit of St. Anne's—but we *never* exploit St. Anne's for Loretta Young's benefit." Once again, the swear box (proceeds to St. Anne's) was on the *Stable* set.

Loretta's old beau, Joseph Mankiewicz, was currently the top writer-producer-director at the Fox studio, working on *A Letter to Three Wives.* Supposedly, in the midst of conversation in the commissary one day, Loretta suddenly said, "That'll be fifty cents."

"What will cost me fifty cents?" Mankiewicz asked.

"You took the name of the Lord in vain."

According to Mankiewicz, he gave her the money and then

said to Loretta the much-quoted line, "How much will it cost me to tell you to go ---- yourself?"

If *all* reports such as this are to be believed, Miss Young must have heard this line at least once a week.

Loretta meanwhile continued to prove herself a good and generous friend. At the 1948 Hollywood Press Photographers' Costume Ball, one of the town's leading social events, Loretta and Rosalind Russell scotched rumors that their friendship had cooled by appearing together, identically gowned and wigged, and carrying identical foot-long cigarette holders. They were costumed as the "Toni Twins." They were spoofing the then popular home permanent ad with the slogan Which Twin Has the Toni?

The highlight of the evening was Robert Mitchum's first public appearance since the scandal of his arrest on drug charges. He and his wife were cleverly dressed in checkered suits—with monkey masks. Many of the guests at the party— including Loretta—made their way to the Mitchums' table to welcome him back to the fold.

Early 1949 saw two Loretta Young pictures in release. *The Accused* opened in January, followed by *Mother Is a Freshman* in March. Loretta next signed a deal with M-G-M, where Dore Schary was now head of production. After fourteen years she would be working again with Clark Gable.

Before reporting to Metro, Loretta fulfilled radio commitments. She appeared on Father Peyton's annual "Triumphant Hour" in April, and in May she appeared on his annual Mother's Day broadcast. This year the priest had decided to do "The Story of Our Lady of Fatima," and Loretta, along with Charles Boyer and Ann Jamison, narrated.

Young next immersed herself in a major charity function for St. Anne's Foundation. The goal was to raise thirty thousand dollars, and to achieve this, Loretta and her committee had decided on an auction to be held at the Goldenberg Galleries in Los Angeles. Merchants and jewelers contributed expensive merchandise, including such items as fur coats and diamond bracelets.

Thanks to Loretta, many of the major stars in Hollywood had personally contributed something for the auction, the key to the ultimate success of the event. For example, Frank Sinatra donated a gold pen and pencil set; John Garfield, a pearl-handled letter opener; Ann Blyth, silver candlesticks; Clark Gable, an antique chest; and Robert Mitchum, a silver cigarette case with matching lighter. Cary Grant donated two antique mirrors; Claudette Colbert gave an expensive French chair; Humphrey Bogart, a liquor set; Gary Cooper, a jeweled snuff box and a set of antique china dogs. The auction raised almost forty-two thousand dollars, far exceeding the original goal.

Tom Lewis was also involved with raising money for St. Anne's. In fact, the Lewises were almost single-handedly responsible for turning St. Anne's and its subsequent companion foundation, the Holy Name Adoption Foundation, into one of Los Angeles's leading Catholic charities. By now Lewis was devoting his full time to private business endeavors and civic activities.

The Lewises, it appeared, had devised a workable schedule for Loretta which seemed to suit her need to work as well as leaving her the time for family activities. The formula was three pictures every two years. "I have reached a point where I no longer have to work for a living," Loretta observed. "I don't have to support myself and my children; my husband does that. Therefore I can be independent and take the acting jobs I want. For that reason, I have always been thankful that I wasn't a man."

Production was set to start on *Key to the City,* the M-G-M vehicle which was to reteam Loretta with Clark Gable. Produced by Z. Wayne Griffin, a good friend of Tom's, the film boasted a topnotch director, George Sidney, and an excellent supporting cast headed by Frank Morgan, Marilyn Maxwell, and Raymond Burr. There were problems, however—the script was mediocre, and Gable looked haggard. The King was now forty-eight, and although the recent re-release of *Gone With the Wind* had revitalized his career somewhat, he was really on a downhill slide, both physically and commercially. His voice, however, was still potent, and helped to keep the romantic illusion alive.

Key to the City centered around an innocuous story about mayors meeting at a convention. Nonetheless there were high hopes that the film would be a winner. Loretta was at her commercial peak, as shown by the July release of *Come to the Stable*, which was an immediate hit with many critics and public alike. Loretta Young as a nun—now this, in the minds of many, was perfect casting. The film remains a television staple to this day, especially around Christmas, and is generally considered one of Loretta's best.

While filming *Key* at M-G-M, Loretta was for the first time in years on Gable and Tracy's home lot. The story goes that one day in the commissary a particularly cheeky photographer had the bad taste to ask Miss Young to pose with both Gable and Tracy. She didn't, of course, but she did pose with her brother-in-law, Ricardo Montalban, whose career at the studio was going exceptionally well.

Georgianna had had another child, and had retired completely, as had her two eldest sisters, to become a full-time wife and mother. It's ironic that Ricardo Montalban's screen image as the ultimate Latin lover belied the reality of his home-and-hearth, devoutly Catholic existence.

Production on *Key to the City* rolled along smoothly until one day on the set, while shooting a sequence that called for fog, Loretta complained of not feeling well. At first she blamed it on the fog-producing material and continued working. Then she blacked out, and Gable had to carry her to her dressing room. An ambulance was quickly summoned, and she was raced to Queen of Angels Hospital.

In Loretta's words, "There, examination proved that I was nearly three months pregnant. I was weak and ill but I was delighted. And I thanked God that Tom and I were to be parents again." She planned to return to work the following day, but then complications set in. Her confinement to bed lengthened into two weeks. She knew something was wrong: "The doctors did everything to save the life within me. I prayed and Tom prayed constantly. And so did all of our dear ones." In her prayers, Loretta added, as she always did, "Thy will be done." But then came sorrowful news: "I was incredulous, bitter with unbelief, when they told me my baby would never be born alive.

" 'Why? Why?' I cried, and turned my face to the wall when Tom tried to comfort me. My sorrow, my feeling of loss, was so great that I did not give one thought to Tom. He comforted me and smiled, though his own heart was as heavily burdened as mine.

" 'God wanted this baby,' Tom kept repeating. 'But it was mine, mine,' I said over and over, and Tom would just look at me and start his prayers."

For days Loretta lay in her hospital bed with no desire to get up, growing weaker. But somehow, somewhere, she found the faith, the strength, to continue. As she later revealed, "I started counting my blessings and they were legion. Aware of them now, I was able to say in my heart, 'Thank You, God, for having taken Your own shortcut to salvation for my little baby. He will be happy with You in eternity. It is awfully hard for me to understand, but, Father, Thy will be done.' "

During that same year, Loretta's faith was once again tested. The incident was one she would never forget, and she has told the story many times. She was out walking with five-year-old Christopher and four-year-old Peter when the younger boy, for no apparent reason, began running toward the road. It all happened in seconds. Loretta ran after him but realized she would never catch him in time—a car was hurtling down the road. Loretta could even hear the vehicle braking. "Peter, come back!" she screamed in terror.

In Loretta's words: "It was too late to stop him. I threw myself at God. 'Please, God!' As though by a miracle, Peter suddenly stood stock-still and the speeding station wagon swooshed past—missing him by inches." When Loretta asked the boy why he had stopped, he could not answer her. Loretta has said, "Some will say it was just by chance. I know better."

Come to the Stable was an enormous success, both commercially and critically. It must have given Loretta Young great satisfaction to know that wholesome movies such as this could reach a wide audience. It was the first film with a Catholic theme to have scored such a hit since *Going My Way* and *The Bells of St. Mary's.* The initial release of *Stable* grossed over three million dollars—comparable today to over thirty million—in a year in which the top picture, *Jolson Sings Again,* grossed five and a half million.

As 1950 began, Loretta Young, now in the twenty-third year of her career, was playing to a second-generation audience. As one writer of the day noted, "They seem every bit as smitten with her as the jazz age boys and girls when her fresh beauty first flashed on the silent screen."

Loretta was again nominated for a best actress Academy Award, for *Come to the Stable.* Competition was once again keen: Olivia De Havilland for *The Heiress,* Jeanne Crain for *Pinky,* Deborah Kerr for *Edward, My Son,* and Susan Hayward for *My Foolish Heart.* Both *Pinky* and *Come to the Stable* were Twentieth Century–Fox pictures, and the voting might very well have been split, since it is always presumed that studio personnel will vote for their company's films. In any event, De Havilland was the favorite to win, especially since she had not won the previous year for her compelling performance in *The Snake Pit.*

Come to the Stable had received other key nominations. Celeste Holm and Elsa Lanchester were both nominated for best supporting actress. Joseph LaShelle was nominated for his cinematography, and Clare Booth Luce was nominated for best story. The film even received a nomination for best song, "Through a Long and Sleepless Night," by Alfred Newman and Mack Gordon.

The song lost to "Baby It's Cold Outside" from *Neptune's Daughter* (ironically, the song had been sung in the film by Ricardo Montalban); Holm and Lanchester lost to Mercedes McCambridge *(All the King's Men)*; Mrs. Luce lost to Douglas Morrow *(The Stratton Story)*; cinematographer LaShelle lost to Paul C. Vogel *(Battleground)*. By the time it came to the best actress award, it seemed certain that the favorite, De Havilland, would win—and she did.

Award or not, Loretta's portrayal of the nun has nonetheless remained her favorite role. The success of the film was undoubtedly instrumental, along with Loretta's work for St. Anne's, in her being named one of the year's most outstanding Catholic women and being awarded the Sienna medal by the Theta Phi Alpha fraternity.

Come to the Stable had been a moneymaker in a year when film revenues had dropped alarmingly. Box office receipts on Loretta's subsequent movie, *Key to the City,* were disappointing, as they were on almost all films at this time. The problem was that new phenomenon—television.

It really shouldn't have come as such a surprise to the industry—but it did. The stars and top motion picture executives had adopted a head-in-the-sand attitude toward television. As far as the motion picture community was concerned, TV was an inferior form of entertainment. However, there was one motion picture star who was a great fan of the new medium, who from the start recognized its limitless potential —Loretta Young.

Book Three

Fourteen

It was 1950 and television had a strong hold on the public's attention. Milton Berle's Tuesday night program (launched in 1948) was a weekly ritual in many of the nation's households. Ed Sullivan's *Toast of the Town* was also highly popular. Radio personality Arthur Godfrey had made the transition to television, becoming one of the medium's first superstars. Sid Caesar and Imogene Coca were just beginning their highly successful collaboration. The CBS-TV live dramatic show *Studio One* was luring established film stars such as Margaret Sullavan to appear in its productions, while at the same time introducing actors who would become stars of the future. Most of television's earliest stars, however, were either carryovers from radio—Perry Como, Gertrude Berg, Dave Garroway, and the aforementioned Godfrey, for example—or those who had never made it big in films, such as Berle, Gleason, Faye Emerson, and Peggy Wood. Other top radio programs already repackaged for TV were *Voice of Firestone* (which would stay on the air for fourteen years), *The Aldrich Family,* and *Kay Kyser's Kollege of Musical Knowledge.*

According to Loretta Young, she was already eager to

enter television as early as 1950. For the moment, however, it was not possible—she was under contract for several motion pictures.

Tom was now working as a producer for M-G-M, and he had found a property he liked, *Cause for Alarm.* He had even cowritten the screenplay with Mel Dinelli. The leading role was that of a woman whose husband was a psychopath. Metro at the time had an impressive roster of contract stars—the females included Barbara Stanwyck, Ava Gardner, Lana Turner, Janet Leigh, Elizabeth Taylor, Greer Garson, Arlene Dahl, and June Allyson, to mention a few. Other talents on the lot—like Judy Garland—were primarily musical stars, but had successfully ventured into drama.

Loretta's agent, Jimmy Townsend, of the Bert Allenberg Agency, suggested to Tom that Loretta would be perfect for the lead in *Cause for Alarm.* It would be territory heretofore uncharted by the couple—working together in Loretta's milieu, film. Loretta wanted very much to do the picture, and her husband acquiesced.

The role of the husband in *Cause for Alarm* was originally offered to John Hodiak, who declined; it ultimately went to Barry Sullivan. The supporting cast included Margalo Gillmore, Regis Toomey, Art Baker, and Kathleen Freeman. The music was composed by young André Previn, nephew of the famed conductor Charles Previn. To direct the picture, Tom and Loretta chose her old friend Tay Garnett.

Garnett has remembered that he was about to leave on a trip when the Lewises called him to direct this film. He happily accepted the assignment and postponed his vacation for what he thought would be the usual eight-week shooting schedule. Loretta sat in on all production meetings, and it was she, according to Garnett, who suggested that the cast rehearse the film like a play, for two weeks, before shooting.

In the last couple of days of these rehearsals Garnett called in the technical crew to observe. Then shooting began, and to the director's astonishment the ensemble was able to complete the picture in only fourteen days! Of course, the script called for no elaborate sets and no location shooting, but even so, the average M-G-M picture shooting schedule was twenty-eight to forty days.

Cause for Alarm had the usual M-G-M polish, and was graced by a top star; because of its low production cost it was a guaranteed winner.

When filming was completed, M-G-M's publicity department disseminated puff articles with Tom Lewis's byline about the experience of working with Loretta Young. As one of them proclaimed, "Until very recently, I did not know 'Loretta Young.' Of course, I had seen her on the screen. I knew how closely she was related to that person who means more to me than anything else in the world—Gretchen Young Lewis—but I did not know the actress or the star." Lewis was quoted as saying that Loretta Young was "sensitive to others—to the director, to the nuances of the story she's portraying, to the reactions of the cast and the crew."

Insiders knew that everything had not been quite so rosy on the set. Tom and Loretta had experienced enough problems working together in this brief time to make him wary of trying the experiment again. Eventually the couple's problems in working together were revealed to the public so as to derive maximum publicity value. An article bylined by Lewis said, "For more than ten years Gretchen and I have carefully avoided the usual hazards of Hollywood marriages by keeping our personal lives and our careers clearly distinguished." He noted in the piece that when the *Cause for Alarm* package was put together, "We made it clear to one another that we would not bring our work home—that it would end as soon as we stepped through the front door. 'Otherwise, once we start working on this picture,' I told her, 'we won't have any fun. If you have any problems about the picture, take them up with me at the studio over lunch.' "

In the article Lewis confided that there were, however,

lapses in this agreement. One night when Loretta came home, she was tired and began complaining that a particular scene needed to be reworked, that she just couldn't play it the way it was written. Lewis put his fingers in his ears as a subtle reminder of their agreement. "And Gretch understood immediately."

Discussing the continuation of a husband-and-wife collaboration, Lewis was quoted: "The answer is no, unless circumstances just happen to bring us together in our work. We both feel that husband-and-wife teams are unnatural and tend to place an undue stress upon career and the details of your work. Gretchen loves Hollywood and her work, and I certainly enjoy mine, but we are also very fond of our family, our personal life, and one another. After ten years of happy marriage, we are convinced that we are right about this."

Today, Tom Lewis does not recall this article at all. He says that he never called his wife Gretchen—always Loretta. Undoubtedly Helen Ferguson, who boasted she could give a better Loretta Young interview than Loretta herself, was responsible for the article.

Loretta followed *Cause for Alarm* at M-G-M with a Fox film, *Half Angel,* costarring Joseph Cotten. This picture was the last in her commitment to Fox, and in it she got to play a role that remains one of her personal favorites, that of a woman with a split personality.

Despite Loretta's fondness for the project, problems soon developed on the set—and were reported in the press. Harold Heffernan disclosed, "Loretta's girlish face and extreme femininity of manner conceal a strong will, which comes as quite a surprise to those who attempt to cross her. When she and director Jules Dassin disagreed on her interpretation of the role in *Half Angel,* Loretta smilingly had him yanked off the picture. She'd do the same to anyone whose method of working didn't coincide with her own. . . . Some think her a little ruthless."

There was a lot of buzzing on the Fox lot after Loretta exercised her "star prerogatives." Writer-director Richard Sale remembers today, "I was having lunch in the commissary with my wife, Mary Loos. We knew Dassin had been taken off the picture. Mary surprised me by saying, 'You're going to take over. She's picked you out.' Mary and Gretchen were old friends and she had guessed what was about to happen."

Sure enough, his wife's intuition was correct—he got the assignment. Sale recalls Loretta as "an old pro," and admits that she was a clotheshorse and would do innumerable wardrobe tests. "She was very concerned about how her clothes moved and worked." Loretta did not photograph as well from her left as from her right, but unlike some other stars, she did not insist that she be photographed from any one side or angle. He also notes, "She was damned sure of her talent and her performance, and we got along fine."

On December 27, 1950, Loretta starred in the radio production of "The Littlest Angel" on *The Family Theater*. The script had been brought to her by its author, Charles Tazewell. She had admired Tazewell's work on a radio program they had done some years earlier, and had complimented him; he later sent her a script of "The Littlest Angel" along with a note that her kind words had encouraged him: "I wrote this. I think you'll like it. Do with it what you want." Not only did she perform the script on radio, but she recorded it for Decca Records and it was an enormous hit of its genre.

Television continued to grow, and so did Loretta's desire to try her wings in the new medium. Loretta was *serious* about entering television, despite the opinions of her agents and professional advisers. Both Tom and Loretta recognized the great potential of the medium, but Lewis told his wife that she had to have patience. It took time to create "a show," he explained. She countered with arguments such as, "Who wants a show?'' Loretta contended that all she wanted to do was to ''visit,'' be herself, go into people's living rooms. Her husband patiently pointed out to her that it wasn't quite that simple, that they needed a concept for the show. What they wanted had to coincide with what the network wanted, what a sponsor wanted, and eventually what would ''sell.'' Loretta's response was typically frank and revealing: ''So this wasn't going to be easy either?''

Tom's career in advertising and broadcasting was a major asset in assisting Loretta in this new endeavor. Men like Lewis knew how to formulate a program, how to sell it to a network and to a sponsor. Lewis reveals, ''I was not going to work with Loretta. I was going to do another project. I believed we should not work together and I believed that that had been proven—but then again, there is that feeling, 'nothing is impossible.' ''

In the autumn of 1951 the coaxial cable was in place, linking ninety-four stations in over fifty cities across the country. It was that fall that Lucille Ball and Desi Arnaz launched their immediately successful sitcom, *I Love Lucy.*

By 1951 most of the major variety, situation comedy, and adventure radio programs had made the changeover to television. Bob Hope, Fred Allen, Jimmy Durante, Abbott and Costello, Eddie Cantor, and Dinah Shore were all on television with spectacular results. The advertising agencies and network offices were humming with plans to transfer other shows from radio to television.

But just as sound movies did not replace silent movies overnight, television did not immediately supplant radio drama and variety shows. Some diehards claimed that big-time dramatic radio would always be on the scene. *Lux Radio Theater* was still on the air. In May 1951, Loretta was given a special award by Lux when she made her twenty-fifth appearance on the program, the only star ever to achieve this record. But even *Lux Radio Theater* was on its way out—*Lux Video Theatre* had already made its debut.

Loretta still had three more film commitments left to complete before she could try her talents on television. The first was to be a programmer at Columbia. Young had long since ended her "feud" with Harry Cohn over the dress episode which occurred back in the early forties. The reconciliation had taken place at a party at Mervyn LeRoy's home. For some time Loretta had endured Cohn's hostile attitude toward her at social gatherings, but at this particular party she decided to do something about it. She went over to Cohn, whose back was toward her, and said, "Harry, don't turn around. It's Loretta, and I want to say something. It's been a long time, but I finally want to tell you that I was wrong and you were right. I'm sorry we had a misunderstanding. Now if you forgive me, turn around. If you don't, stay the way you are and I'll go away."

Cohn hesitated at first, but then turned around. "That's the nicest thing I ever heard," he is reported to have said; subsequently he let it be known that he would like to have Loretta Young in a Columbia picture again.

Columbia's *Paula* costarred Loretta with Kent Smith, Alexander Knox, and a young child named Tommy Rettig, who would go on to star on TV's *Lassie.* The film's story was about a barren wife who causes a youngster's deafness and eventually adopts him. Deafness and adoption were often dealt with in the scripts Miss Young chose, and they were subjects which mattered greatly to her. But *Paula,* only an eighty-minute film, was a programmer and as such would be given limited exposure and short runs and thus would not reach many people. Loretta wanted her films and their stories to reach the masses; in order to do that, she had to be on television.

She still had commitments on two more pictures but she had already informed her agents, "When these are finished, no more pictures. I'm going into television."

Finding the right TV format for Loretta, however, seemed an interminable process. As negotiations continued, Loretta, as always, remained active. She made two appearances on radio that year on *Family Theater,* one on Valentine's Day, the second in November on a program entitled "Just for Tonight," scripted by True Boardman and costarring Gigi Perreau and Mala Powers. She also made her annual appearance on Father Peyton's annual Easter program, "The Triumphant Hour."

During the year she completed the first film under her two-picture deal at Universal. Originally titled *Magic Lady*—since Loretta portrayed a magician's assistant—the title was later changed to *Because of You,* primarily to capitalize on Tony Bennett's hit record of that name. The picture, costarring Jeff Chandler and directed by Joseph Pevney, was a soap opera about a woman who is separated from her child because of her criminal past.

Actress Mae Clarke—the actress who had a grapefruit squashed into her face by James Cagney in *The Public Enemy* —worked in *Because of You.* Miss Clarke knew Loretta and Tom through "semisocial" gatherings sponsored by Father Peyton, of which there were many. "I remember one special one at Pickfair," Miss Clarke recalls. "It was Loretta who really spearheaded all the big names of Hollywood into Father Peyton's camp." Miss Clarke, a convert to Catholicism, had offered her services to Father Peyton as a receptionist at the Family Theater offices. "That's how I came to Loretta's attention. Both Loretta and Tom are very sweet and very dear to me," Miss Clarke declares.

Because of You is best remembered today as the film in which Loretta Young, in costume as the magician's assistant, displayed her shapely legs in mesh stockings. Publicity photos of her in the getup were widely circulated. Her swear box on the set also got a lot of publicity. "Loretta demanded five dollars from the chief electrician for her charity fund for unwed mothers because he uttered a four-letter word out loud on the set," wrote Erskine Johnson.

By autumn 1952, plans for Loretta's television series were falling into place. As Tom Lewis recalls, "So I said, all right, if we are going to do this show, we are going to make it the best. We'll have the best quality yet known on television. We'll have the best cinematographer, we'll have real sets, we'll do it well. . . . I did what I was trained to do at Young and Rubicam. I was very much interested in Gallup and the proper use of research. I approached the show as I had been trained."

Tom set about seeing how other shows were operating. He visited Lucille Ball and Desi Arnaz and conferred with Desi. He spent time with his old friend Jim Backus, who was doing a series with Joan Davis. Lewis knew that these situation comedy formats were not right for Loretta.

In formulating Loretta's show, Lewis first asked himself, as he had learned to do while at Young and Rubicam, "What do we have to sell here? Mostly the star. We have to sell beauty —a woman's beauty, a woman noted for wearing clothes. Setting styles. And we have something more. We have a substantial woman. A mother. A civic-minded woman. A major motion picture star and a versatile actress." Lewis concluded that all these elements had to be incorporated into the presentation in order to maximize on the star's potential.

Loretta and Tom were aware that by switching from films to television Loretta could easily be labeled a defector. At a dinner party at Jack Benny's home, several motion picture producers upbraided Loretta, telling her, "You'll ruin your career"; "You're turning your back on the industry." Later, according to Loretta, two of these same men wanted to produce her series.

To dispel the possibly strong current of unfavorable publicity she might be subjected to by going into TV, a decision was made for Young to meet with Louella Parsons to discuss her decision. Helen Ferguson wanted to be present during the sessions. (Columnist Shirley Eder has recalled that Ferguson guarded her clients "with FBI-like secrecy; no one could pry from her anything she didn't want them to know." Miss Eder reiterated what many people on the press corps discovered through the years—that Ferguson "made it a point never to leave the room while one of her stars was being interviewed.")

But the wily Louella had her own ideas. "I asked that Loretta come to my house alone," Miss Parsons said, so that she and Loretta could have "a completely uninhibited talk.

"Loretta marched into the kitchen and we opened a bottle of champagne and let down our hair."

Parsons was nobody's fool. She knew how to get facts, and she knew why Loretta was there. "Are you going to abandon pictures for TV?" she asked bluntly.

Loretta countered, "I intend to stay in pictures too. I love them, and my venture into TV is just a sideline." She told Louella the TV series would be called *Loretta Young and Your Life*—and it would be a dramatization of real-life stories. "Some will be the problems written to me by fans. Others will be the lives of Hollywood people—maybe yours, Louella." The women laughed, and Loretta continued, "But seriously, we plan to point up the courage of individuals, the obstacles they have to overcome, the heartbreak and the comedy that really live in Hollywood, and which, as you know, is seldom pictured correctly."

The format of Loretta's show was obviously shaping up, but it was still far from set. The concept of doing stories about Hollywood people was later dropped, and the title of the show was changed many times before *A Letter to Loretta* was decided on. It was to be an anthology series, with Loretta playing a different character each week. Loretta, as herself, would "visit" as she so desired with the viewer for a few moments at the beginning and end of each program. She would read a letter in the introduction, and each story would make a point that would be reiterated at the end of the show through the reading of an appropriate quotation (from Loretta's massive personal collection) from the Bible, Shakespeare, or some other appropriate source.

The people at William Morris, Loretta's representatives,

didn't agree with Lewis on the sort of pilot film he had in mind.

"For the pilot show, the one shown to the buyers, the advertising agencies, I wanted to do not the best show we could, but a *typical* show," states Lewis. "I wanted to demonstrate that Loretta was versatile and could do the things that I said she could." In the pilot film Loretta portrayed a perfume salesgirl. A young man in love with her fantasizes her as different personalities, allowing for three distinct segments in which to display Loretta's versatility as an actress.

Knowing how to thoroughly package a pilot, Lewis even included "dummy" commercials, for which he hired announcer George Fennemann (the "product" was gyroscopes for guided missiles, an enterprise Lewis and Carter Hermann had backed—"a nice, neutral thing to sell," recalls Lewis with a smile).

Loretta completed her last film commitment at the beginning of 1953, an innocuous little tale about a couple who run a small-town newspaper. The title was *It Happens Every Thursday,* and it costarred Loretta with a promising young actor named John Forsythe.

On a personal level, the Lewises were incredibly busy. Although they had a reputation for moving often, they actually lived at 280 Carolwood Drive, in Holmby Hills, for many years, from the birth of their children through 1951. They then lived briefly at Doheny Road in Beverly Hills, followed by a move to a palatial estate on Oceanfront Avenue in Santa Monica. Gladys naturally decorated each of Loretta and Tom's new houses. Loretta delighted in telling how she would instruct her mother, "Be careful where you place objects, because that's where they'll remain," indicating that she was too busy to involve herself in decorating.

The Lewises were planning to build a house in Ojai, California, adjacent to the Ojai Valley Inn, in which they had invested. Lewis loved Ojai, a resort town in the hills between Los Angeles and Santa Barbara, and wanted to live where his children could lead more normal lives. "I wanted them to be able to ride their bicycles into town and make friends," he says.

Actually, the youngsters didn't have much contact with the outside world except under close supervision. Early in 1953, while Loretta, Tom, and Judy were away and Chris and Peter were staying with their governess, an incident occurred that heightened the Lewises' fear of kidnapping attempts. In the early dawn hours an intruder broke into the house but was frightened off by the governess. Although it was not determined whether the person was a potential kidnapper or just a burglar, the Lewises made certain that additional precautions were taken from that point on.

On one of the couple's frequent trips to New York to meet with network and agency executives, Loretta sought relaxation by shopping. One of her favorite stores was the chic Giselle's on West 57th Street, whose wealthy and demanding clientele were usually condescending and often nasty in their attitude toward the staff.

An exception: Loretta Young. Irene Barany recalls: "She came in one afternoon and I admired the dress she was wearing and told her so." Loretta appreciated the compliment, and the women had a long and pleasant person-to-person conversation. "A few days later, when she came to the shop again, her daughter was with her," recalls Miss Barany. "She introduced us, and then I realized Loretta had brought a present for me!" The gift-wrapped box contained the dress Irene had admired. She didn't accept the gift, but the gesture was certainly character-revealing as far as Irene Barany was concerned. She also recalls how the other customers stared at the actress. "She was so lovely and elegant. She was like a breath of fresh air." The boys at the agency and network might not have agreed with that appraisal.

Tom Lewis had told Abe Lastfogel at the William Morris Agency that in offering his wife's new show to advertising agencies he did not want to play favorites, not even to his own alma mater. He felt that the honorable thing to do would be to let all the potential sponsors vie for it. However, shortly after the pilot film was ready to be seen, Lewis got a call from Walter Craig, head of the TV department at Benton and Bowles. He had known Craig for many years, and their careers had paralleled. Craig said to Lewis, "Don't argue with Abe—I *made* him show me the pilot. I'm in trouble with a client. I'm sure you've been in trouble with a client. I want to recommend this to Procter and Gamble."

Procter and Gamble, one of Benton and Bowles's most important clients, had been sponsoring Red Skelton on television, but the comic's ratings had dropped. Moreover, Skelton and the advertiser did not get along. Craig said to Lewis, "I'm going down on the Benton and Bowles plane tomorrow to make my presentation. I'd like to write it up to a certain point, at which time I'd like you to cap it in the form of a night letter—the longest night letter ever written in the history of Western Union—to complete my presentation and say how this series will sustain itself. How you are going to personally produce this show."

Lewis recalls, "Walter called me the next day and said, 'It's sold.'" Tom Lewis concedes it was exciting to have sold the show, but everything had happened so fast that, as he recalls, "I didn't have the company to produce it! I went to Desi Arnaz, and Desilu did the bookkeeping below-the-line production for a year. Desi was a great help."

Tom and Loretta threw themselves wholeheartedly into the new course they had set. They formed a new corporation, Lewislor, to produce the television series, which was a commitment to thirty-nine episodes per season—a grueling work schedule, the equivalent to shooting thirteen full-length motion pictures a year. For Loretta it was an actress's dream—now she would have the opportunity to pick *all* the roles she wanted to play. She could do comedy, drama, anything she felt like to explore new facets of her talent. And what was

perhaps most important to her, the program would be a plat-
form to communicate directly with millions of people.

Loretta was now forty; Tom was fifty-one. At an age, and in
an era when many successful couples were beginning to take
life easy and look forward to retirement, the Lewises were
embarking on a venture that would require more intense
commitment and energy than ever.

*Are the Tom Lewises acting silly after
fourteen years?*
—*Walter Winchell, 1954*

Fifteen

Loretta and Tom could not have been unaware that by working together again—especially on so grueling a project—they
were risking their personal relationship. With *Cause for Alarm*
there had been a specific, short-term shooting schedule. The
number of weeks that they were actually working in close
contact were limited and there had been a definite end in
sight. With the television series, this was not the case.

As with the movie, Lewis was the producer and Loretta the
star. Loretta was the kind of star, however, who concerned
herself with every aspect of the product—writing, casting,
directing, photography, editing—and she demanded perfec-
tion. In addition, Tom Lewis was not a "line" producer (one
who concerns himself with business matters and delegates
artistic decisions to others), but a creative producer, much
like Selznick, who—although he never took directorial credit
—had the final word on artistic decisions.

They hired veteran cameraman Norbert ("Brodie")
Brodine. An informal repertory company was assembled, actors and actresses who would portray different roles each

week, but all of whom worked well with Loretta. Robert
Florey was set to direct.

Lewislor signed Mae Clarke for the first season. Newcomer
George Nader, a handsome young actor, was signed to be
developed into a leading man. Actor William Campbell was
also contracted. Today, Campbell fondly remembers, "I was
one of Loretta's 'boys' on the opening season, but I never
played her love interest." Others in the first season were
Richard Travis, Jock Mahoney, and Alex Nicol. For several
episodes Lewislor also signed established actors Eddie Albert,
Bruce Bennett, and Dick Foran.

For the first three weeks of shooting, the atmosphere on
the set was like old home week, with visits from many
friends. Suddenly, however, production was behind schedule
and over budget; the No Visitors sign went up, and things
quickly settled down to a normal routine.

The Lewises celebrated their thirteenth wedding anniversary in the midst of the first season's shooting schedule, but
this hectic programming afforded little time for family togetherness. Many were astonished to learn that Loretta later
lived in her dressing room at the studio where she shot her
series. "It wasn't just a dressing room," remembers Mae
Clarke. "It was a complete apartment, and it was furnished
beautifully. She was smart. She was at the studio all day, and
this saved her a lot of commuting time."

The situation was a far cry from Loretta's "only three pictures every two years" regimen, in effect since Tom had returned from the service. In addition, it was now impossible
for the Lewises not to take their work home with them.

In September Loretta went to New York to meet with
NBC executives and to promote the show's launching. The
public was given a great deal to read about Loretta Young
during this period leading up to her television debut—including, it's amusing to note, publicity to cloud the issue of
Loretta's age (Helen Ferguson's "fact sheet" on her client
said that Loretta's Hollywood career had had its beginning in

1919 instead of 1917—a bit of misinformation that eventually found its way into official press material from both NBC and Benton and Bowles). All bases were covered in getting the show off to a strong start—all concerned knew that in the entertainment industry there is no such thing as a sure thing.

Finally, on Sunday evening, September 20, 1953, at ten P.M., *A Letter to Loretta* premiered on NBC. Loretta walked through the formal doorway of her "living room" (it was a set, of course) and into the homes of millions. It was an auspicious entrance—she would remain a welcome guest, week after week, for many years.

Loretta was not the first top-level Hollywood star—or even the first Academy Award winning star—to have a series on television. Ray Milland, Douglas Fairbanks, Jr., and Robert Cummings, among others, had preceded her. But to almost everyone's amazement, Loretta did not disassociate herself from the commercials.

After seeing the show's first three episodes, TV critic John Lester wrote, "Oddly enough, the best part of Miss Young's shows to date has been the commercials. She sells boxes of soap with such class that the viewer can't resist buying the product." Although Lester was not fond of the shows, he noted, "Loved her and her soap."

It was the kind of "money review" sponsors responded to. Although through the years it was perceived that Miss Young "sold soap," in actuality she never really did the commercials herself. Yes, the product, Tide, was always visible in her living room set, but for the actual pitch she always smiled radiantly and turned the podium over to her announcer. Even today, people who watched Loretta's show can recall her lilting voice as she said, "John?"

By the third or fourth show, her twirling entrance had captured the imagination of the country and become her trademark. People were told that the famed entrance started by accident. "Just like Dinah Shore's big kiss at the end of her show," said Loretta. "On our first program the director thought my dress was so pretty I should show off the back of it as well as the front." But Loretta was being coy. The truth was that she and her husband had devised the introduction because they knew showing off her clothes was an integral part of what people expected from Loretta Young, the fashion plate.

From the onset, Lewis was determined: "We'll do the shortest fashion show on record. Loretta will enter in a beautiful dress, she will turn around the women can see the back—see how it's made. I know my research. Women want to see the back of the dress . . . feel they can make it . . . feel they can look like the model."

The problem of how Loretta could turn around without seeming pretentious was solved one Sunday night as the Lewises were driving from Ojai to Los Angeles. They were discussing the dilemma of how she could display the gowns in a natural, non-modellike fashion, when suddenly Loretta said, "Monsignor Sheen!" Tom knew the way Loretta's mind worked—she had latched onto some concept. She remembered how Fulton J. Sheen made his entrance on his television show attired in long, flowing vestments, and how, when he entered his study, he turned to close the door behind him. Lewis got the picture—and that is how Loretta's "entrance" was born.

Another aspect of Loretta's show, one that the public was unaware of, was that Tom Lewis continued to use sophisticated research methods to build the show even after it was on the air. For example, he had originally commissioned the designer Marusia to design elaborate ball gowns for Miss Young's entrance. But when Lewis's research indicated that because of the fancy gowns people were resenting Loretta in their living rooms instead of loving her, he scrapped thousands of dollars of footage and reshot many of the entrances. Through Helen Ferguson he arranged for Dan Werle to design outfits specifically for Loretta, but geared also for "the ordinary woman," dresses that looked spectacular but could be "copied." The "ordinary woman" felt, "I could, if I wanted to, make that dress."

The season continued, and while the critics were not overwhelmed with the story lines of Loretta's programs, the plots were powerful and memorable. The scenarios of the first season's episodes set the tone for what Loretta Young's fans would come to expect and favor. In each half-hour story someone would learn a lesson that would enable him or her to lead a better life.

George Nader starred with Loretta in five episodes that year, Bill Campbell in three. Campbell recalls his favorite, "Thanksgiving at Beaver Run," with Loretta and Dick Foran. "When Loretta wanted a rest, she would take a smaller part in the script," says Campbell. "In 'Beaver Run,' a couple of other guys and I steal her car without realizing her little boy is in the back seat." Campbell's character refuses to abandon the boy in the woods, so his buddies kick him out of the car along with the youngster. In the process of getting back to civilization, the Campbell character is rehabilitated and ready to accept his punishment.

Campbell recalls, "Loretta was great to work with, she really cared for me." The actor remembers, "Loretta said to me one day, 'Isn't your brother a writer?' They were looking for someone to rewrite a script, and my brother, R. Wright Campbell, got the job." (R. W. Campbell subsequently became a noted screenwriter.)

Loretta was loyal to friends and coworkers and believed in hiring them when she could. Mae Clarke recollects, "I did three shows that first season, but it was the third, 'The Judgment,' that I remember vividly."

The plot of "The Judgment" bears repeating because it contained all the elements of a successful Loretta Young script. Miss Clarke was cast as a mother superior of an orphanage and Loretta portrayed a mother who has been separated from her child after a plane crash in South America. By the time Loretta locates the little girl the youngster has been taken back to the States and adopted. Loretta's character wants the child back—"I'm her natural mother!"

The nun explains to Loretta that the little girl has a heart condition and any shock may prove fatal. Besides, the child has been legally adopted by another couple. When Loretta meets the little girl and her new mother, she gives the child a necklace. The girl, excited by the present, has an attack and calls out, "Mommy, mommy!" Loretta rushes to help her, but the adopted mother intercedes and it is obvious that the child wants *her*.

Loretta returns to the orphanage and tells the mother superior she now knows the girl belongs with her new mother. Then, leaving the nun's office, the woman spots a group of little orphans marching to class. One adorable girl wearing a leg brace runs to catch up and falls, and Loretta rushes to help her. The child says, "I've lost a screw." Together they find the screw for the leg brace and repair it. Then Loretta asks, "May I walk with you?" The little girl offers her hand and the two walk off as the mother superior watches. The implication is strong that Loretta's character will now adopt another woman's child.

Miss Clarke had several scenes with Loretta in the episode. "I remember those gorgeous eyes. Such intensity. It was difficult playing opposite them. She projected such sympathy I wanted to stop acting and cry."

Mae Clarke also recalls that shortly after the show was completed she received a call from Helen Ferguson. "I had known Helen since the late thirties, when she was my press agent. But now getting a call from Helen was like getting a call from on high. Helen told me, 'Loretta said, *call Mae*. Tell her her performance was so right, she made me look good.' "

Narratives like "The Judgment" struck a chord in the American heartland. Needless to say, they were expertly played, directed, and produced, and while critics were unkind, it didn't matter—the public was the final judge. The letters poured in, and Loretta's show was a big popular hit.

What little time Loretta now had for herself was spent with her family. The boys were eight and nine and the Lewises continued to make it a point to keep them out of the public eye. There were no photographs released to the press of the children with their famous parents. As far as children of movie stars go, Christopher and Peter Lewis had the lowest profile. Around this time, however, there was talk that Judy, now eighteen, was undertaking a modeling career, and was thinking of entering the acting profession. There was also mention that Loretta was not happy with this prospect.

In February 1954 Loretta Young completed the last of the first season's promised thirty-nine episodes. Now the sponsor wanted to change the title of the show. A six-hour meeting ensued with Lewislor executives, agents from the William Morris Agency, and attorneys. Loretta was adamant about one point: her name had to be in the title. "I've spent 180 years building up that name," she declared. Loretta later told friends, "When I walked out of that meeting I was exhausted and felt terrible," but she had won her point. In mid-season of the first year the program was retitled *The Loretta Young Show*, and it was decided that the reading of the letter at the beginning of each program was to be retained, at least for one more season.

Loretta retired to her new house in Ojai to rest. She had never before taken on such a workload, and her friends implored her to take it easy. She was totally exhausted, so much so that for the first time in years she did not attend annual charity functions for St. Anne's.

In her first year in the medium, Loretta was nominated by the Television Academy of Arts and Sciences for "Best Female Star of a Regular Series." Lucille Ball, Imogene Coca, and Dinah Shore were also nominated, but it was Eve Arden who won (for *Our Miss Brooks*). The other nominees had all been on television one or two seasons more than Loretta.

Shooting began in June on Loretta's second season. The

days were completely filled with story conferences, legal meetings, screenings, rehearsals, sessions with agency people, portrait sittings for publicity, and of course the actual shooting of the programs. There were scores of minute details to be tended to and Loretta wanted to be involved in all of them.

Although acting was what really mattered to her, she found that she could not ignore the problems of producing. Costs seemed to mount no matter how carefully budgets were prepared. Meanwhile, she wanted quality, and got annoyed when production problems interfered. As an example, one day she complained about the stopping and re-setting up of shots.

"Why do we have to do this?" she asked. "Why can't we just play out the scene?"

It was explained they did not have a particular boom mike they needed.

"Rent one," she said.

"It's a hundred dollars a day and the budget can't afford it."

"Then buy one," the ever-practical Loretta suggested. "Charge it off our budget and then rent it out to other shows. That'll not only pay for it, it'll bring in money. Meanwhile, take the cost out of my salary."

Lewislor bought the boom, and the company, with a sense of humor and a degree of affection, had a legend stenciled on it: I BELONG TO LORETTA.

Within a short time Lewislor had burgeoned from a company set up to make a pilot film to a mini-industry with Loretta not only as its product but as its overseer.

The "Take it out of my salary" line was used by the star many times when the budget could not accommodate something she wanted. Loretta's salary was budgeted at $5,000 per week, but the money was of little importance to her. According to her, she personally received twenty dollars a week spending money and rarely had time to spend it. While five thousand a week does not compare to leading TV salaries today, these were 1954 dollars, equivalent to at least $35,000 per week today. And of course, as a partner in the production company, Loretta owned the films.

For the second season there was a new crop of leading men, notably Hugh O'Brian, Gene Barry, Craig Stevens, Charles Drake, and Chuck Connors. Again Loretta would appear in all thirty-nine episodes, usually in the lead. Child and teenage actors including Elinor Donahue, Bobby Driscoll, Dennis Hopper, Beverly Washburn, and Kevin Corcoran were also cast on the series in these early years.

The workload of the second season eventually began to take its toll, and soon there were rumors of trouble in the Lewis-Young marriage. Just as with any couple working together in a highly charged environment, it was inevitable that Tom and Loretta would have clashes. Someone on the scene at the time recalls an incident which illustrates their creative differences: "In one episode, Loretta was portraying a woman meeting her grown son for the first time. Her character was waiting on a street corner and was supposed to project nervousness. In real life, Loretta had the habit of breaking a piece of gum in two and only chewing half a stick. Tom decided to use this bit of business and to keep the camera on her hands and pocketbook as she fumbled with the gum. Loretta insisted the camera be on her face—that she could show the apprehension in her eyes and facial movements. Tom insisted the scene would play better if the camera focused on her hands fidgeting, opening the purse, tearing the gum in half. It was a real battle, but Tom eventually won out."

In a column item on August 11, 1954, Walter Winchell hinted that Tom and Loretta were splitting up. Two days later, however, the Winchell column carried a blurb, "Loretta Young and Tom Lewis celebrating fourteen years of marriage." It was obvious that Helen Ferguson had called Winchell and instantly squelched the rift rumors (actually the Lewises' anniversary had been two weeks earlier).

When Loretta's second season premiered, NBC discovered that they had formidable competition in the new CBS entry: a series with Robert Young and Jane Wyatt called *Father Knows Best*. It was pure family fare, like Loretta's show, but unlike Loretta's it was a sitcom. CBS received a deluge of mail, mostly to the effect that the show was wonderful but the late hour prohibited youngsters from seeing it. Although CBS had found a strong entry in the ratings race against Loretta, the network relented and rescheduled the series at an earlier hour for the following season.

Loretta's work schedule continued unabated. A statement was released: "Being forced to relinquish her cherished activities on behalf of St. Anne's Maternity Hospital for Unmarried Mothers, and The Holy Family Adoption Service, is the only restriction imposed by her heavy TV production schedule, which Loretta deeply deplores."

By October Miss Young had been warned by her doctors to slow down. Some sources reported that Loretta was ill, and not merely exhausted as those close to her claimed. Nonetheless she was determined to finish out the season.

That year she played one of her favorite roles, a soft-hearted floozy in "Big Blonde." It was definitely casting against type, but it was one of her perquisites as producer to choose any role she wanted. Through the years she had the TV program she was able to play nuns, shopgirls, waitresses, alcoholics, Orientals, housewives, old and young alike. It was obvious that Loretta Young wanted to experiment in character roles, but the introductory segments of the show remained very important to her. "After the audience has seen me well groomed," she reasoned, "I can wear horrible clothes, wigs, ugly makeup, and false noses during the show without having people wonder whether I've aged overnight or something."

Loretta and Tom knew her audience. At least half the viewers tuned in to see the star rather than the drama. Over seventy-five percent of the fan mail was concerned with her clothes. Therefore her gowns had to be particularly eye-catching, and without relying on color, since television still was black-and-white. The design of Loretta's clothes was paramount, as well as how the fabrics moved and flowed. Her trademark entrances were the highlight of her show, and she was rapidly coming to prominence as one of the country's leading women of fashion. As much preparation was taken with shooting the brief prologues and epilogues of her shows as was taken with filming the dramas themselves.

In one of Loretta's best-remembered episodes she was cast in the role of the Egyptian queen Nefertiti. She was able to mount an expensive-looking production for this story and still keep within her limited television budget because the spectacular costumes and sets had become available at a reasonable rental rate. They had been designed for Twentieth Century–Fox's expensive epic *The Egyptian,* and Fox was renting them out in order to recoup production costs. Loretta was superb as Nefertiti. She seemed to resemble her, and actually succeeded in capturing a quality that evoked the majesty and mystery of the fabled queen.

Years later she observed, "I could cast myself in parts no other producer would dare give me. If I wanted to be Nefertiti—and I felt identification because of the length of my neck, the shape of my head, the set of my eyes—I put on the wig and for a few seconds—I remember the camera caught me as I snapped around in anger—and the look was absolutely right—I was."

Another show had Loretta portraying a widowed maharani of a small impoverished state in India who was involved in a hopeless romance with a British journalist. (Norbert Brodine won an Emmy nomination for his photography of this show.) Episodes such as this, containing the elements of standard tearjerkers, yet always concluding on a positive note, continued the standard set for the series.

"Dateline Korea" presented yet another facet of the

Young sensibility—in this episode she played a tough female correspondent covering the Korean War.

In virtually every review of Miss Young's programs, although the critics would invariably say that the shows were "sentimental" and "sticky sweet," they would also note that the programs were nonetheless "refreshing," or that the scripts "worked," or that the shows were "a welcome change from the usual TV fare."

Whatever the formula, the fans kept watching and the sponsor's products were selling briskly. It was no surprise that Procter and Gamble eagerly picked up Young's option for another season. Loretta was riding the crest of the greatest popularity she had yet known. She was still a symbol of glamour and an example for American women that a productive and fulfilling life was still achievable at age forty. She seemed to have discovered the fountain of youth. In truth, while the characters Loretta portrayed were young, she was clever enough to avoid ingenue roles, and often she portrayed women with children (tots to teenagers). Amazingly, the younger leading men on the show never seemed too young for her.

Once again she was nominated for an Emmy. During these early years, the Academy of Television Arts and Sciences kept changing categories. This year, instead of "Best Female Star of a Regular Series," the category was tagged "Best Actress Starring in a Regular Series." No matter the name, it was essentially the same group of women who were nominated again this year—Loretta, Lucille Ball, and Eve Arden, along with Ann Sothern (for *Private Secretary),* and Gracie Allen.

At the awards dinner on March 7, 1955, there was elation among the Lewislor family when Loretta won. She was now the first star to have won both an Oscar and an Emmy.

Amidst all this success, the rift between Loretta and Tom was widening. In an obvious attempt to salvage their relationship, they decided not to continue working together so closely. Loretta told friends that she would take over sole chores as producer the following season while Tom would concentrate on developing new properties for Lewislor. It seemed to be a reasonable explanation, since the company had already announced that they had signed actors such as George Nader to develop into stars of their own series. Perhaps the Lewises were following the pattern of Lucy and Desi Arnaz in setting up a miniproduction empire.

However, a frightening development suddenly made both business matters and personal disagreements seem inconsequential.

I'm not at liberty to discuss Miss Young's illness. I can't tell you anything about her. I can't even say how long she'll be confined to the hospital.

—Nurse, St. John's Hospital,
Ojai, California, 1955

Sixteen

Her weight loss was sudden and dramatic, and those close to her were afraid for her life. The public, however, was not informed of the gravity of Loretta Young's condition, primarily because Helen Ferguson kept the press at arm's length behind a smokescreen of innocuous statements. Only one fact was publicly known to be certain: on April 10, 1955, Loretta was admitted to St. John's Hospital in Ojai.

Reports were confused and contradictory. "Loretta was running a temperature, but her condition was essentially unchanged and not serious," said one. "She is suffering from anemia," said another. "Loretta's mysterious ailment is diagnosed as localized peritonitis," wrote Dorothy Kilgallen. "Fortunately, Loretta is on vacation and won't have to return to her TV show until the end of June," reported Louella. According to *Variety* Loretta Young had lost ten pounds. According to Jack O'Brian she'd lost twenty.

Weeks went by and her illness remained a puzzle in Hollywood. One persistent reporter tracked down the nurse assigned to Loretta's room, but got no information. "Still hospitalized," continued the accounts. "Responding to treatment after six-week bout with peritonitis." "Friends concerned."

"Gaining weight," Winchell wrote. "She'll be okay soon."

Then, in mid-June, Jack O'Brian stated, "Loretta is down to eighty-four pounds and can't start her new fall TV series until she beats the anemia rap." Sheilah Graham commented, "Loretta is still in the hospital, but has gained six pounds."

Tom Lewis countered all reports that Loretta was to be flown to the Mayo Clinic. "Loretta is coming along well at the hospital in Ojai," he said, "and she'll remain there, getting her strength back, plus some poundage, toward an operation if the doctors believe one is necessary."

After Lewis's statement the rumors began to fly. What kind of operation would a person require if she were suffering from anemia or peritonitis? The word that was spoken in whispers now came to the minds of many.

Loretta, a woman who had, by her own admission, been afraid of no person and no situation, was intensely fearful of physical pain. She later revealed that a small hospital room "was the arena in which pain and I held combat," and some were shocked when she admitted, "At first I was afraid I'd die of it. Then I was afraid I wouldn't."

For over two months Loretta was permitted no visitors other than family. Her television crew, greatly concerned, kept in close touch. She had required several blood transfusions, so the crew members went to the Blood Bank and "replaced every ounce of the blood my several transfusions had required, and put themselves on a stand-by call for further donations if I needed any more transfusions!"

It never came to light that Tom Lewis now canceled Loretta's show. His wife was fighting for her life—it seemed inconceivable that she would be concerned with continuing her career. However, even in her dismal physical state her career meant *everything* to her. With the help of Helen Ferguson and agent Abe Lastfogel, Procter and Gamble was persuaded *not* to cancel the show. The program would continue. They ar-

ranged for some of Loretta's friends—Hollywood's top stars
—to fill in for her until she was able to return. Some would
star in the dramas, others would host, a few would follow
Loretta's example and both host and star. None, however,
she was reassured, would come through Loretta's doorway.
The famed entrance was sacrosanct.

During the months Loretta was fighting the pain, she was
buoyed up by thousands of letters pouring in from well-wish-
ers across the country, offering prayers for a speedy recovery.

On June 29, 1955, Loretta underwent several hours of surgery. Statements followed proclaiming that the star had come
through the surgery in good condition and was resting com-
fortably. It was announced that "inflammation of the abdomi-
nal lining had caused adhesions and necessitated the surgery," and that Loretta would have a "disciplined
convalescence and have to remain in the hospital for three
more weeks, then be confined at home for an undetermined
period."

Even when Loretta was out of intensive care and back in
her private room, the strict No Visitors rule, except for immediate family, remained in effect. And her recovery was not
quite as "quick and simple" as first accounts promised.

Her friends, however, thought it an encouraging sign that
a week after the operation Tom left on a business trip to New
York. They assumed that Loretta was improving rapidly. A
further sign that she was returning to normal came two weeks
after the operation, when Louella Parsons told her readers
that Judy Lewis, who had "wanted a career for a long, long
time," had finally obtained permission from Loretta to sign
with an agent.

Judy had been working as an assistant story editor on her
mother's show. "It was her idea," Judy said years later. "I
never used her name to open doors." The young woman was
studying acting with Agnes Moorehead and she had decided
she wanted to be an actress, ". . . just like Mommy. It was a

natural decision." One which, according to Judy, Loretta supported but never encouraged.

Reports on Loretta's recovery were often as conflicting as reports had been prior to her surgery. Some said "her friends are worried"; others said she checked out of the hospital four weeks, not three, after the surgery and was planning a three-month convalescence in Honolulu. In truth she stayed at her house in Ojai in relative seclusion.

On Sunday evening, August 28, 1955, Loretta, along with millions across the nation, tuned to NBC and watched *The Loretta Young Show* go on without Loretta Young. Rosalind Russell was the guest hostess and Phyllis Thaxter starred in the drama "Fear Me Not."

Miss Russell was also the hostess on the next week's program. The following week, Joseph Cotten hosted, introducing "Reunion," starring Nina Foch and Donald Curtis. Then Van Johnson hosted two episodes. In ensuing weeks, Barbara Stanwyck introduced a show starring Teresa Wright. Ricardo Montalban hosted and starred in an episode, as did Merle Oberon. The press and public alike were impressed with the fact that stars who had heretofore shunned television were appearing as a tribute to Loretta. Irene Dunne hosted two episodes of the show, and other guest hostesses included Claudette Colbert, Ann Sothern, and Joan Fontaine.

Loretta made her first public appearance following the surgery in mid-September, at the dedication of the new wing of the St. Anne's Maternity Hospital. She told her friends that letters and prayers had gotten her through the incredible ordeal, but that doctors had not yet given her the okay to return to work. She had gained weight and was back up to 115 pounds, the most she'd weighed in years. Loretta Young was a very determined woman, and her awesome desire to resume the career she loved would not be denied. Her return to the sound stages was preceded, however, by a carefully orchestrated return to the public eye.

She held press conferences and was seen nightclubbing

with Tom. Obviously the Lewises were trying to scotch the rumors that there was discord in their marriage. The press wasn't buying the act, however. "Close friends don't hesitate to report that Loretta and husband Tom Lewis have had a difference of views on some very major matters," ran one account.

There were other speculations that found their way into print, one of which claimed, "Although Loretta Young played hostess to the press to disprove the cancer rumors, the fact remains that she won't be well enough for full-time work in her Loretta Young TV series until after the first of the year."

Even though, for months, terms such as peritonitis, anemia, and adhesions had been bandied about, the press wasn't convinced, and persisted in writing such accounts as, "No one will give out a statement as to the nature of Loretta's illness." In fact, the nature of Loretta's illness and subsequent condition was then—and still is—considered a strictly personal matter. Her family and close friends didn't then, and won't now, discuss it. Certain illnesses can mark a performer as "uninsurable," and certain conditions can arouse pity and sympathy that the individual might not want.

However, one individual who was close to her in those years agreed to discuss certain aspects of her illness now—because "it *wasn't* cancer. All the rumors were *wrong*. It was peritonitis. She had a tubular pregnancy. It burst and almost cost her her life." The peritonitis was very serious and damaging, but the surgeons were able to save her.

Since it is thirty years after the fact, there is no reason to doubt the veracity of this disclosure. One can speculate that back in 1955, because statements regarding the Lewis marriage seemed blatant denials of the facts, *all* statements having to do with Miss Young's personal life were "suspect."

Regarding her illness, Loretta had indeed beaten her serious problem and time would indeed prove she had beaten it for good. She maintained her "no comment" attitude, and eventually the allusions in the press to her "mysterious illness" petered out and disappeared.

By October Loretta was sufficiently recovered, and after a brief vacation in Las Vegas she edged back into work, although her return was two weeks later than originally planned. It was the fall of 1955, and after an absence of seven months, Loretta Young was finally back in greasepaint. As the cameras rolled for the shooting of her traditional entrance, and Loretta swirled through the door, the crew applauded wildly and howled its joyous "Welcome home!" Everyone was sobbing, including Loretta.

That year, Christmas Eve happened to fall on a Sunday and it seemed particularly apt that Loretta should make her eagerly awaited return to television that night.

Loretta resumed her work schedule, but for this season Bert Granet was brought on as producer-writer for Lewislor. (Granet's writing credits included the Irene Dunne film *My Favorite Wife,* and he had produced Judy Holliday's recent film *The Marrying Kind.*) There were twenty episodes to go to complete the season, and while Loretta would hostess all of them, she would appear in only seven. One of the first stories Loretta filmed—and one of her personal favorites—was "But for God's Grace." In it Loretta played two parts, one the lead, a suburban housewife and mother, and the other a "bit" as an alcoholic. For the latter role she was filmed with no makeup and under very harsh lighting. Surprisingly—according to those involved with the show—she received no letters from her fans commenting on her appearance as the dipsomaniac. She had gone completely unrecognized! Episodes such as this one continued to give Loretta the opportunity to play parts for which she would never have been cast in movies. This was one of the reasons she was continuing with the series—she wanted to challenge herself as an actress.

In "The Pearl," another of her favorite stories, she portrayed, with astonishing believability and poignancy, a poor

Japanese wife. It was a remarkable makeup job by Otis Malcolm. Richard Morris, who wrote and directed the episode, was nominated for an Emmy for the script. Malcolm won the annual makeup artists award.

There was a twinge of nostalgia when sister Sally Blane starred in an episode, "Oh, My Aching Heart," a repeat of a script that had been produced in the first season. It would become a practice for the series to repeat scripts—recast and reshot—that were particularly popular with the fans.

Sally Blane had appeared on a couple of television shows in the fifties, notably *The Pepsi-Cola Playhouse* and *Star Stage,* an anthology series. She had done a bit in a feature film, *A Bullet for Joey.* But she wasn't serious about resuming her career—it was just fun to do an occasional role. She was still happily married to Norman Foster, whose career was humming along. Foster was currently with the Disney organization, where he was cowriting and directing an enterprise which was one of the most successful ever presented on television: the immensely popular *Davy Crockett* series.

Sally and Norman enjoyed a traditional and non-Hollywood marriage. Foster often joked with friends, "I guess I'm the worst kind of husband. I can't fix a darn thing. I've always told Sally she should work for Lockheed. She's handy around the house. Give her a screwdriver or a pair of pliers and away she goes."

Miss Blane is recalled by all, from her earliest days in films to the present, as a woman with a remarkable personality and warmth. Actress Virginia Sale, who knew the Fosters, says, "Norman always said, 'I got the cream of the crop.' " The Fosters had a son, Robert, in the late forties. Their daughter, Gretchen, was now a nineteen-year-old beauty who had recently been one of the finalists in the *Miss Rheingold* contest.

Loretta's other sisters stayed in permanent retirement. Polly Ann had a second child in the late forties, Betty Jane.

Georgianna had remained happily married to Ricardo Montalban. The couple now had four children. Ricardo was free-lancing and doing a great deal of television. Over the next few years he would appear on *The Loretta Young Show* more frequently than almost any other actor.

The Young family remained as close as ever. Jack was a successful lawyer and the father of four. Gladys, the matriarch of the brood, was at the very height of her interior decorating career, with clients including Bogart and Bacall, the Ray Millands, the John Waynes, the Bing Crosbys, the Bob Hopes, Joan Caulfield, agent Irving "Swifty" Lazar, and other top stars and executives. In fact, Gladys had become quite a colorful character on the Hollywood scene, and it was not an unusual sight to see her riding through Beverly Hills in a pickup truck filled with antiques. She has been described by many as delightfully eccentric, a sort of real-life Billie Burke character. Perhaps Ricardo Montalban once best captured Mrs. Belzer's persona: "Georgianna's mother is a brilliant decorator with the forgetfulness of an artist."

In the winter of 1956, CBS, which had been losing consistently in the ratings to *The Loretta Young Show*, threw in a new midseason entry, *The $64,000 Challenge*, a spinoff of their highly successful *$64,000 Question*. Big money quiz shows had swept the country, and Loretta faced her stiffest ratings competition to date.

As the season wound to a close, Loretta was acknowledged once again by the Television Academy, this time through a nomination as "Best Actress in a Single Performance." The recognition came for her characterization of "Sadie" in an episode entitled "Christmas Stopover." Her competition for the award was formidable indeed: stage actresses Julie Harris, Jessica Tandy, Eva Marie Saint, and Mary Martin, who had made television history as Peter Pan. No one was surprised when Miss Martin walked away with the Emmy.

That spring Loretta was off to New York "to choose eight new leading men for the next season." Some of Loretta's former leading men by now had gone on to fulfill the potential she'd seen in them: notably George Nader, Jock Mahoney, and Hugh O'Brian, who was currently a big hit as TV's *Wyatt Earp*. Among the actors signed for the new season were Hugh Beaumont (who a year later would star in his own series, *Leave It to Beaver*) and John Newland (who would subsequently appear in more episodes than any other actor and would direct many of the shows).

When Loretta returned to Hollywood in June to begin shooting the fourth season, there was one major change: Tom Lewis was no longer executive producer of the show. Without any fanfare, Lewis had not only left Lewislor but had taken their sons and left California. In New York, Tom joined old pal "Chet" LaRoche's advertising agency. Loretta told friends that Tom would divide his time between Hollywood and New York, but insiders knew this was not the case. Lewis understood Loretta's motives in maintaining her career —after all, it had taken her decades to get to this position of total creative control—but he had obviously made a wrenching decision when confronted with the fact that even when her life was at stake Loretta had chosen career over all else.

There were disturbing reports about Loretta's loss of weight and fainting spells as filming on the fourth year of the series progressed. Undoubtedly Loretta's health was a consideration, for she decided she would not work as hard as she had in previous years. It was announced that she would appear in only twenty-six of this season's thirty-nine episodes, still a formidable workload, since it must be remembered that this was an anthology series and that Loretta had to portray different characters each week in minidramas, not a continuing character in a one-set situation comedy. Furthermore, the star-producer continued to be involved in almost every aspect of the show, whether she starred or not.

Mae Clarke, who appeared in another episode of the program—playing another mother superior—says today that Miss Young "did everything and did it all so ably! She has not been given enough credit for being the 'everything person.' She knew story values, cutting, she certainly knew camera, and she had good taste, not only for herself but for everybody. She was an expert on beauty—of line, color, contrast."

Loretta's expertise did not always engender such a positive reaction from others in the industry. The star herself later claimed that she didn't really like "story conferences, and picking clothes, and the rest of it. I like it when the cameras roll. And in television the cameras roll all the time." There was no doubt that Loretta selected scripts carefully and even spent spare time reading magazines and newspapers, scanning the periodicals for stories. "After all, it is *The Loretta Young Show* and I'm presenting it, so the scripts have to be on —shall I say—my wavelength. We try not just to present a problem and leave the viewer depressed, worried, and irritated. Each show gives an answer to the individual problem."

Ruth Roberts, still a close professional associate of Ingrid Bergman, was story consultant and assistant producer. Miss Roberts observed, "Loretta will do anything for a good story."

Not everyone thought Loretta's scripts good, however. Murray Bolen, an executive with the Benton and Bowles advertising agency which handled the sponsoring Procter and Gamble account, noted, "If you saw her scripts on some other show, you'd throw them out. My boys read these scripts and they'd say, 'Where is this junk coming from? It's awful.' But when Loretta did these stories, she always bailed them out. Loretta kept plowing along and frankly we were amazed."

Despite the ad men's disdain of *The Loretta Young Show*'s content, the program had a large and loyal following. Erudite columnist Harriet Van Horne spoke for millions at the beginning of the fourth season when she wrote: "As usual, her joyous entrance was in itself a fanfare for a new season. With her swirling skirts and wood-nymph grace, Miss Young

makes the most arresting entrance since Peter Pan floated
into Wendy's room from Never-Never Land. . . .

"Her greeting is always eager and shy and breathless. All
terribly spur-of-the-moment and won't you come into my par-
lor? . . ."

But, Miss Horne noted: "Yes, there's the box of soap chips
on the breakfront. And, no matter how many yards of tulle
lovely Loretta may be shipping, you know she's delighted to
pause for the message that tells you how to get the grease out
of your overalls. She's got a practical streak, this airy sprite.
She wouldn't have survived twenty-five years in pictures if
she hadn't. When she tells you to pay attention to the men
with the cheery advice about your dirty laundry, you pay
attention."

Miss Horne reviewed the season's premiere: "We saw
lovely Loretta as a lady lawyer of keen wit and incorruptible
virtue. She was the more appealing because these qualities
functioned under a heart-rending handicap. Lovely Loretta
was stone deaf. She read lips. Read them from great distances
through binoculars, if necessary . . .

"Anyway, a man with an accent was murdered in Loretta's
office. Because of the accent she couldn't read his dying
words. But she solved the murder anyhow. She also pulled
her husband off the shady side of the street with a gentle
reminder that principles were more important than anything
—even clean overalls, I guess. It was a good script, despite its
melodramatic finish. And I, for one, am delighted to have
lovely Loretta back again."

"You really never know if you're on top," Loretta once
said. "Others do. You know your drawbacks—if you're
smart, you do." Loretta, of course, had nothing to worry
about; she was most assuredly "on top."

People commonly perceived the life of a star as being one
of glamour, partying, and wearing beautiful clothes, but for
television's leading stars like Loretta Young and Lucille Ball,

such was hardly the case. Quite the contrary; they spent every waking moment at the studio, working hard. The show was rehearsed on Monday and Tuesday, then shot on Wednesday, Thursday, and Friday. Loretta typically slept in her dressing room Tuesday, Wednesday, and Thursday nights, with no time for socializing. The No Visitors sign was still posted on the set, and Loretta stated, "You have to wear blinders if you want to get any work done."

She was so preoccupied with work that Loretta was getting a reputation as being someone difficult to get through to, of being a woman constantly surrounded and insulated by her "people." In reality the banning of visitors was necessary partially because Loretta was and is a talker. "She was a friendly, chatty person who loved to talk to anyone who showed up," said an associate. (Even today Young surprises people with her easy, chatty manner. Unlike most celebrities in her league she is open and friendly.)

The move to the studio had begun in part during the show's first season, and now it seemed logical and in the best interests of maintaining her health, for certainly her health was still a consideration. In early 1957 she argued with Procter and Gamble that for the fall season she wanted to do only half of the thirty-nine episodes. "I've got my health back and I intend to keep it," she declared.

Loretta was certainly in a strong position to make demands, having won her second Emmy that spring. Once again the category titles had changed; now it was "Best Continuing Performance by an Actress in a Continuing Series." Loretta's competition had been Jan Clayton (*Lassie*), Peggy Wood (*I Remember Mama*), Ida Lupino (*Four Star Playhouse*), and Jane Wyman (*The Jane Wyman Theater*).

The Loretta Young Show had climbed back in the ratings to overtake *The $64,000 Challenge*, but Procter and Gamble knew that in the fall CBS was planning to throw *The $64,000 Question* into the time slot opposite Loretta. After much haggling, the sponsor signed Loretta for a fifth season. They had compromised—Loretta would appear in twenty-four of the thirty-nine episodes—not the eighteen she wanted, and not the full thirty-nine they wanted. Procter and Gamble had made it clear that twenty-four was the minimum they would accept, and that they would cancel if she wasn't amenable. (Subsequently, however, Loretta appeared in fewer than twenty-four.)

By now Loretta could not avoid questions about her marriage. Although she insisted that she and Tom were separated only by geography, few believed her. Theirs was no Bohemian, European, or "arrangement" marriage. For fifteen years Young and Lewis had been espoused as the ideal American Catholic couple. They had been separated by the war, as had many couples, and they had been separated by an occasional business trip, but voluntarily living in different cities was not exactly a casual separation, at least not in the 1950s. These were the Eisenhower years—the Ozzie and Harriet era —togetherness in family living was paramount, and any deviation from this norm was news. Loretta could protest all she liked that distance was all that came between them, but the official proclamations that "her career is in Hollywood, his in New York" just didn't wash.

Judy, too, was living in New York, and Loretta would of course occasionally visit. Chris and Peter were in school, and later the boys would be split—Chris in New York with Tom, and Peter in Hollywood with Loretta.

In the spring of 1957 Loretta went to New York, then on to Rome for a private audience with Pope Pius XII. This was a momentous occasion for Loretta Young, undoubtedly marred for her when it was alleged in print that the reason for her visit was to ask for an annulment. She vehemently denied this allegation and upon her return to New York that May was seen a great deal with Tom. They went to see Rosalind Russell on Broadway in *Auntie Mame*. Although the two actresses remained friends until Miss Russell's death, Tom

Lewis gave insight into "star" friendships when he once noted, "It is a lonely road, being a star. Great stars have to be unique. It's a way of life. It's even hard for two great stars to be friends. They want to be friends, they try to be, but it's tough on them."

It seemed to the public, for the time being at least, that what Loretta said might be true—the marriage *was* continuing on a long-distance basis. The family knew, however, that Tom's decision had been difficult but decisive.

Since Loretta was appearing in fewer episodes of her program, she signed bigger-name stars to play in the weekly dramas. Laraine Day, Hume Cronyn, Wally Cox, Viveca Lindfors, Herbert Marshall, Anita Louise, Frank Lovejoy, Mark Stevens, James Daly, Keefe Brasselle, Jan Sterling, and Mercedes McCambridge all appeared on the show during this season.

And beginning this year and continuing right through to the end of her tenure on NBC, Loretta had the advantage of having *The Dinah Shore Chevy Show* as her lead-in. It was a double dose of glamour for TV viewers. Dinah was as magnificently gowned as Loretta and appealed to the same audience.

A fascinating sidelight on these two shows is that many of Miss Shore's exquisite gowns were designed strictly to be worn while she was onstage—they were either too fragile or too uncomfortable to be used in any other circumstances. Loretta's gowns on the other hand were functional. As far as her ensembles were concerned, some were on loan from designers, while she bought others for the program and kept them. Loretta knew her audience, and said, "They like my show because I'm able to appear in something spectacular every week."

Meanwhile, Judy Lewis began to have some professional success, although it had been a struggle for her. "I left southern California to work in New York, where I could get away from the hometown aspects of Hollywood." She noted in retrospect, "Hollywood is a company town. There are few secrets and everybody knows everybody else's business. Even though I had a different last name from my mother, there wasn't a person in movies or television who didn't know whose daughter I was. In New York it was a different matter. Very few people in the theater knew that Loretta Young was my mother. I had some marvelous years there working in theater and TV."

In the spring of 1958 Loretta was once again in the running for an Emmy. This year the Academy outdid itself with the categorizations. Loretta was competing with Lucille Ball, Gracie Allen, Dinah Shore, and Dody Goodman in a category so absurd that the presenters could not keep a straight face when announcing it: "Best Continuing Performance Female in a Series by a Comedian, Singer, Hostess, Dancer, Master of Ceremonies, Announcer, Narrator, Panelist or Any Other Person Who Essentially Plays Herself." Dinah Shore won.

Loretta's five-year contract with NBC was now over, and her new production company (Toreto Productions) signed directly with the sponsor. The show would remain on NBC, in its usual time slot, but the new three-year deal was unique in that it had a mutual option clause. The sponsor could drop the show at the end of each season—but so could Loretta. One of the most important issues under negotiation had been the number of episodes Loretta would be required to star in. "I have signed to do a minimum of thirteen shows myself," she said, "but actually I can star in as many more as I want to. It's purely a psychological thing. If I committed myself to doing twenty-six, I'd be in a constant state of worry. But doing only thirteen is a breeze. Once they're out of the way, I can go ahead and do more without the pressure of actually having to do them—and for all I know, I may wind up doing twenty-six, though twenty seems more like it."

In March, Tom Lewis shocked Hollywood—and television

fans across the country—by suing his wife. The suit was against Loretta, their partner, Robert F. Shewalter, and Lewislor Films, Incorporated. According to the complaint, Lewis had resigned from Lewislor in April 1956 at the request of Loretta and Shewalter. Lewis charged them with "dishonesty, mismanagement and unfairness." Although Lewis was in New York, the complaint was filed in Los Angeles by his California attorney, Nathan J. Neilson.

Lewis claimed that after he resigned from Lewislor, Loretta and Shewalter promptly doubled their own salaries and that the company declared no dividends, although it had a profit in both 1956 and 1957. One of Lewis's former business associates said that Lewis instituted the suit at this time because he knew the Loretta Young shows would be going into re-release soon, and under the current arrangement he would have been excluded from the residuals.

In Hollywood, Loretta's attorney, Wilson Copes, issued a statement: "Nobody has been served. All we know is what we have read in the papers. In due course, when we have been served, we will take such legal steps as are indicated." (The following month, Lewislor countersued Tom Lewis.)

Since Loretta was currently one of the biggest female stars on television, the news of the suit was splashed across every paper in America. Lewis's statement that there was "no personal implication in this action" made no difference to the press. It was finally out in the open: Lewis and Young were estranged. Since Loretta had spent almost fifteen years gushing about the happiness of her perfect marriage, and the last two years denying there were any problems, she was now fair game. But Loretta, Tom, the Young family, and everyone else connected with the matter, including Shewalter, closed ranks and denied that the suit was anything more than a legal business issue. Shewalter said, "There's no personal friction between Miss Young and Lewis as far as I know."

No one could have been more shocked by the suit than Louella Parsons, since the columnist felt she knew Loretta and Tom so well. Parsons was unable to reach Loretta by telephone—Helen Ferguson told her, "Loretta won't discuss the situation." Louella pressed further, however, and Helen had to admit that Loretta was "a bit surprised by the actual nature of the suit."

The wily columnist was not about to give up so easily on the story of the year. She got Tom Lewis on the phone in New York. He tried parrying: "The suit is just as much a protection for Loretta as it is for me." Louella, however, would not be deterred. "But, Tom," she insisted, "that was a pretty strong statement—to accuse Loretta of being dishonest." According to Miss Parsons, Mr. Lewis replied, "Just legal phraseology."

Whether Miss Parsons believed that statement or not, she felt it her obligation to note that "close friends of Loretta say she found it difficult to work with him as her producer," adding that, "one thing Loretta's friends have noticed—when she dines with them or sees them, she has managed to keep her husband's name out of the conversation."

I do hope she gives me lots of grandchildren.
—*Loretta Young, 1958*

Seventeen

The Church of the Good Shepherd in Beverly Hills was packed with family and friends. For once Loretta Young did not have star billing, and for this occasion she willingly took a back seat. Today she was merely mother of the bride.

Judy Lewis married Joseph Lewis Tinney, Jr., on a beautiful summer day that June 21st. Tinney Senior (who owned a Philadelphia television station) was best man at the wedding, and Gretchen Foster was maid of honor. B. J. Hermann, Polly Ann's daughter, was a bridesmaid. Monsignor John Devlin performed the ceremony. It did not go unnoticed that it was godfather and uncle, Carter Hermann, who gave the bride away.

After Judy's marriage, Loretta let it be known she would be pleased if her daughter decided to give up her acting career and be a full-time housewife and mother. But she added, "It's her decision, of course. Joe is a darling boy and I love him. They say they're going to have ten children and I hope they do. I want all these children to call me grandma; none of these fancy little substitute names for grandma."

Although Miss Young was urging Judy to abandon her ca-

reer and concentrate on marriage and motherhood, Loretta
was more career-oriented than ever. As the fall television
season began, Loretta—who hadn't made a feature film in
five years—stated what everyone knew: "All my interest now
is in television. It is the current medium. At this moment this
is the way you reach the people. Not only is it the medium of
today. It's the medium of tomorrow."

The Loretta Young Show was one of the few surviving anthology series. *Kraft Television Theatre, Studio One, Climax, Schlitz
Playhouse of Stars,* and *Robert Montgomery Presents* had all disappeared from the little screen. Loretta Young, in television as
in films, had started early and outlasted many of those who
had come after.

The star credited the longevity of her show to its upbeat
quality. For years critics had been lambasting her for being
"corny" and "sentimental." Loretta's retort: "What, for the
record, is wrong with sentiment? I love it. I couldn't live
without it. When people say our shows are sentimental, we
feel complimented."

She was honest enough, however, to admit that she had
lost some of her original enthusiasm. "You can't stick to a job
for five years and still feel like a Girl Scout about it," she said.
"We've settled down now. We know what we're doing, or at
least we feel we know what we're doing."

That autumn *The $64,000 Question* momentarily gave the
Young show stiff competition in the ratings, but a few months
after the season had begun, television's biggest scandal hit: it
was charged that some of the game shows were fixed and
after publicized investigations, several of them, including *The
$64,000 Question,* were yanked off the air. CBS moved the
popular *Richard Diamond, Private Detective* into the time slot
opposite Loretta.

The 1958–59 season of *The Loretta Young Show* was one of
its best. For the first and only time the series itself would be
nominated for an Emmy in its category: Best Continuing Dramatic Series.

For one of the episodes, "Most Honorable Day," Loretta again portrayed an Oriental. Several people from her company relate that Loretta loved getting into the elaborate Japanese makeup, and they recall that during the week this episode was being filmed—in November 1958—Loretta's old friend Tyrone Power, who had died of a heart attack while working in Spain, was brought back to Hollywood for burial. In the midst of filming "Honorable Day," Loretta attended the funeral services. She wore full Japanese costume and makeup, a startling stand-out from the other solemnly garbed mourners. Criticism was leveled at her for not appearing as "herself." However, her show was on such a tight production schedule that there simply had been no time to remove the complicated makeup, wig, and costume. By now the entire world knew that the studio had literally become Loretta Young's home.

Other well-remembered episodes she filmed that season were "The Woman Between" and "The Twenty-Cent Tip," in which she played a waitress. Both teleplays won awards for their "inspirational" contents. In fact, Loretta Young and her show were literally deluged with awards. For the third consecutive year she won the National Education Association award for distinguished service in the interpretation of education. For the sixth consecutive year she was voted favorite dramatic actress on television by the readers of *Radio-TV Mirror* magazine, and she had garnered six Gold Medal Awards.

To an entire new generation, Loretta Young was not a movie star—many hadn't even seen her movies (which were just now beginning to appear on television)—but a beautiful woman who entertained them on television each week. However, there were frequent reminders to the world that Loretta Young had indeed, at one time, led another life.

Reporters wanted a comment from Loretta. They tracked her down. They knew where to find her—after all, it was Good Friday—and they waited outside the church. A man from her past, the golden boy of the 1920s—the man she had married when she was seventeen—was dead, an apparent suicide.

Grant Withers shocked his Hollywood friends when he took an overdose of sleeping pills and was found dead on March 27, 1959. While mostly forgotten by the public, Withers still had famous friends among the Hollywood community, notably John Wayne and John Ford. In fact, Withers had been part of Ford's unofficial stock company, and had worked as a character actor until the end.

"I am shocked," said a distraught John Wayne. "What else can I say? He was such a great guy—I can't talk anymore, it was just too much." Wayne had been best man for Withers at Grant's last (fifth) marriage, when he had married Cuban singer-dancer Estelita, a union which had already ended in divorce.

The fifty-five-year-old actor was found propped up in bed, wearing glasses. Withers's left hand was clutching the telephone receiver, and nearby was a note which read, "Please forgive me, my family. I was so unhappy. It's better this way. Thanks to all my friends. I'm sorry I let them down." He owed back rent, he was behind on his car payments, and this had not been his first suicide attempt.

"I am so sorry," Loretta said when told of Grant Withers's suicide. She said she had not seen him for years, and her only comment was, "He was the most bewildered man I ever met." Loretta sent a wreath to Withers's funeral with a card which read simply "Loretta Young Lewis."

Negotiations had gone on for some time, but finally Loretta Young's company struck a deal with NBC. The network purchased one hundred and seventy-six of her half-hour shows for daytime network programming for a price reported to be four million dollars. What is not generally known, however, is that in order to accomplish this deal, Loretta and Tom—although still in the midst of their litigation against each other—had made a secret agreement whereby he would share half the profits of part of the sale.

Now Loretta would be seen on television five times a week during the day, as well as weekly in prime time. *The Loretta Young Show* had become a national institution.

For the sixth year in a row, Loretta was nominated for an Emmy. This year there were two opportunities to win. The show itself was a contender against *Peter Gunn, Alfred Hitchcock Presents, The GE Theater* (hosted by Ronald Reagan), *Naked City,* and *Alcoa-Goodyear Theater.*

There was disappointment among Loretta's crew and production company personnel when the show lost to Alcoa-Goodyear, but they were elated when Loretta personally won her third Emmy, beating out Jane Wyman *(The Jane Wyman Theater),* Phyllis Kirk *(The Thin Man),* and June Lockhart *(Lassie).* The category this year was called "Best Actress in a Leading Role (Continuing Character) in a Dramatic Series." Apparently, while indirectly acknowledging their acting ability, this category nominated Miss Young and Miss Wyman as hostesses, which was, after all, their only continuing character in their respective shows.

On her own show Loretta was continuing not only as hostess, star, and producer, but some said as benevolent despot. Her fierce Catholicism and tough professionalism had by now become legend. In addition to "The Steel Butterfly," she was now dubbed "The Iron Madonna." She ruled her TV domain as absolute monarch, although she denied that she had to have final approval on *everything.* "Let's just say it's a meeting of minds," she said. Concerning reports that the company and crew either deferred to her wishes or were "banished," writer-director Richard Morris conceded, "It's simply that Loretta is in absolute control. The fact that she's both star and owner doesn't make for the usual director-actress relationship. But you're aware of this when you take the job." Morris, who was associated with the show for many years, once admitted: "She's difficult when she's tired, but that happens only when personal problems sap her strength, and then her eyes fill with tears of exhaustion. I don't think she's aware the crew spoils her or that there's a reason no one crosses her."

Loretta's "decrees" sometimes caused controversy. In the late fifties, Dave Kaufman, a salesman from *Variety,* found himself barred from the set for no apparent reason. It turned out that *Variety* had carried an ad featuring stripper Lily St. Cyr posed, seemingly nude, in a bathtub. Loretta had apparently decided that the ad was offensive to public morals, and had taken her punitive action. Of course, the ban against Kaufman was later lifted.

Throughout her television years the swear box got a lot of publicity, for it was ever-present on the set, and many a time the jangle of coins would be heard as the pressures of turning out a weekly television show touched one and all. On the last day of his seven-year association with *The Loretta Young Show,* Murray Bolen, who had vowed he would never have to contribute to the swear box, was heard calling someone a goddamn fool. "Ah-ha!" said Loretta. "I finally got you." It was incidents such as these that earned Young the reputation of being holier than thou.

That spring, "The Accused," an episode of the show which had originally been broadcast the previous year, was repeated. The story concerned itself with an important issue of the day, the sale of pornography to minors. The original showing had struck a chord with citizens' groups across the country, and now this repeat telecast was eagerly awaited and supported by civic organizations. A group in upstate New York actually took out a half-page ad in local newspapers proclaiming, "Watch the Loretta Young Show tonight!"

After the second showing of the episode, mention of the program was read into the Congressional Record on May 27, 1959, by Representative John P. Saylor of Pennsylvania. He said the program was "an outstanding moral, social and civic contribution," and noted that "the general public as well as the television industry is indebted to Miss Young for her superb performance in behalf of decency."

It was with programs such as this that Loretta realized the goal she had originally set—that of making her shows not just entertainment but a valid contribution toward upholding moral standards. And with recognition such as this the star's image as a crusader for good was further cemented.

Loretta went to Europe to film two upcoming episodes and the background for others. One teleplay filmed there, centering on a woman who journeys to Lourdes, would be one of Young's most memorable shows.

Meanwhile, back in New York, her sponsor was faced with a decision. In the fall of 1959, ABC was launching a new series called *The Alaskans,* which it hoped would topple Loretta's domination of the time period. CBS, in an effort to gain dominance in the time slot, had decided to alternate the Jack Benny and George Gobel comedy programs.

The Benton and Bowles agency panicked, urging Loretta to switch time slots because the Benny competition might prove too strong. She wouldn't hear of it. A representative from the William Morris Agency was dispatched to Europe to implore her to change from her Sunday night slot to one on Wednesday night. Loretta did not argue; she simply smiled sweetly and said no.

She later emphatically told the people at Benton and Bowles, "I'm not afraid of Jack Benny and I won't give up my Sunday night time slot." She made it clear she would rather retire than move to another night. The agency and sponsor were not happy, but they went along for another season. By July, Loretta was back in Hollywood and the program was in full production, with a weekly budget that had increased to $78,000.

While a composed, relaxed, carefree Loretta Young swept into living rooms every Sunday night, the woman behind the facade was indeed troubled. Few of her fans realized that Loretta was so tense that she had been ordered by her doctors to take a drink or two before dinner in order to relax. One of her physicians had told her, "Your stomach is in a knot before you have dinner and you just don't relax. You should have at least one drink before dinner whether you like it or not."

Unknown to her fans, Loretta was also a chain smoker and had been for years (she had started smoking as a young teenager and wouldn't quit smoking until the mid-1970s). She also occasionally suffered from nightmares. She confided that she had a recurring dream in which she saw an enormous sphere floating down as if to crush her. She would stretch out her arms to keep it at bay. Loretta said the dream "never gets me down and yet I never quite get rid of it. It is a constant weight and it is terribly heavy." She added that she never tried to interpret the dream, nor had she gone through psychoanalysis. Of course it does not take a trained analyst to see the probable meaning of this dream: Loretta did have the weight of the world—her world at least—bearing down on her.

Then, in November of 1959, forty-six-year-old Loretta had reason to rejoice—she joined the ranks of Hollywood's glamorous grandmas. Judy Lewis Tinney gave birth to a six-pound twelve-ounce girl, whom the proud parents named Maria. Shortly after the baby's birth, however, Judy returned to her acting career, pursuing it more ardently than ever.

The glamorous grandma was given her seventh consecutive nomination for an Emmy. The Academy had *finally* decided on categories that suited everyone, and the categories have remained fixed since then. Loretta's category was "Outstanding Performance by an Actress in a Series." Jane Wyatt won that year for *Father Knows Best,* beating out Loretta and Donna Reed.

At the end of the seventh season, and a year before their contract was up, Procter and Gamble decided not to renew. There had been many problems. In addition to haggling over the number of episodes Loretta would star in, the sponsor and the production company had argued over the placement of a toothpaste commercial which utilized a cute animated film featuring bacteria in the mouth. Procter and Gamble wanted the commercial slotted after Loretta's opening of the show. "Gentlemen," she informed them, "I won't have the bugs in that spot." "Why not?" P&G asked. "Because it isn't dignified. It isn't me," Loretta replied, and she patiently explained to them, "You buy me because I'm a glamour kid to hang your commercials on. Why destroy me with bugs?" The commercial was placed elsewhere.

In canceling their sponsorship, Procter and Gamble claimed that because Loretta was now on daytime network television Monday through Friday, her drawing power as a Sunday night attraction was considerably diminished.

Some assert the company and agency used another excuse as well. According to Loretta, who wouldn't discuss this until years later, "I once lost a sponsor because of my convictions. I was told that a lot of people were writing and saying, 'Get rid of that religious fanatic.' "

If indeed this was true, it was a subject which could not be publicized at the time, because there would definitely have been a hue and cry. Besides, it is highly unlikely that Procter and Gamble got more than a few crank letters. Loretta's shows had moral themes, but never overtly religious ones.

It is more likely the sponsor used this ploy because the agents and TV executives could not persuade Miss Young to change her focus to compete with the current hit shows— action melodramas like *The Untouchables, The Detectives,* and *Naked City.*

Her response to their entreaties was simple. "It's none of my business what the others do on *their* shows," she said. "I won't glamorize depravity. I will not make a virtue out of vice. There is an unhealthy trend today to turn morality upside down, but not on *my* show. I will not contribute to it."

Years later Miss Young maintained, "I was called Miss Goody Two-Shoes and The Prude of All Seasons. But none of that should bother you if you strongly believe in what you're doing." And indeed it did not bother Loretta Young. She not only had the courage of her convictions—she had a strong, loyal following as well. Through the years her fans had remained steadfast and *vocal,* sending her at least eight hundred letters a week. When viewers particularly liked a show, she was deluged with compliments.

Loretta was fully aware that television fame was something completely different from movie stardom. "It's more personal," she remarked. "There's a closer, perhaps a more affectionate—even more possessive—quality about the friendliness of viewers. And a sort of 'member of the family' quality when they don't like something. They don't keep you guessing—either way!"

New sponsors were lined up immediately (Warner-Lambert Pharmaceutical Company and Gillette), and without missing a beat *The Loretta Young Show* entered its eighth season. By now the production staff and crew had become a true family. Loretta noted at the time, "All but six of us have been with the show since the pilot film." And in true family fashion there was a pecking order, a camaraderie, and there was a collective sense of humor, even in dealing with Loretta.

There is one fascinating account which helps to illustrate Loretta's sense of humor about herself. One of Miss Young's friends had told her that another famous actress had referred to Loretta as "a chocolate-covered black widow spider." When Loretta arrived on the set the following day, she told the story to the crew, since she said it had amused her. Loretta then retired to her dressing room. When the cameras were ready, the producer, John London, shouted, "Okay— we're ready for the chocolate-covered black widow spider!"

It's revealing that the cast, crew, and star could joke together about stories such as this. Loretta later said that although her friends had told her the story, "no one seems willing to tell me the name of the woman who was supposed to have made the remark, but I think I know who might have said it. And what's more, she may be right."

It was statements such as this last one that made Loretta's somewhat inflexible attitudes palpable. She has always been the first to admit that she is not perfect. She sees life for everyone as a constant battle to overcome the sin of pride.

The Jack Benny Program, which the agency men feared would be CBS's trump card in the ratings game, was transferred to another time slot after only one season *(The Alaskans* and *The George Gobel Show* went off the air). Loretta's new competition was *Candid Camera* on CBS and alternating episodes of *The Islanders* and *The Asphalt Jungle* on ABC.

Loretta chose stories for her eighth season as carefully as she had chosen stories for all other years. Always concerned with the welfare of children, she gravitated toward scripts about the young. One show, "Nobody's Boy," cast her in a story about a Boys' Club in Chicago attempting to rehabilitate a youngster on the verge of entering a life of crime.

No one could accuse her of not attacking problems of the day. In "The Choice," Loretta starred with Richard Ney and George Nader in a moving story about a woman's attempt to rehabilitate her alcoholic husband. That season also presented "A Day at the Beach." Discussing the concept of "living for today," and spending time constructively, Loretta had said, "If a woman spent a whole day staring at the sky, and found spiritual peace that way, she'd be spending that time very well. I'd call that 'living for today.' Anne Lindbergh wasn't wasting time when she went down to the seashore and spent those days alone, studying the seashells and trying to grow in understanding the real purpose of her life."

Loretta was referring to Anne Morrow Lindbergh's memoir, *A Gift From the Sea,* published in 1955. *A Gift From the Sea* still has a wide following among women, especially those seeking to combine lives of housewife-mother with personal-professional fulfillment.

The book was obviously the inspiration for "A Day at the Beach," which provided Loretta with one of her best roles. The script called for no dramatics, but rather a sensitive underplaying. With Loretta's artistry in giving dimension to a role with her eyes and subtle facial expressions, she delivered one of her most outstanding performances. "A Day at the Beach"—like the previous season's story about Lourdes—was filmed in several parts, which were later combined and released overseas as a feature film.

Loretta was once again nominated for an Emmy, her record-breaking eighth consecutive year. Barbara Stanwyck and Donna Reed were also nominated. Miss Stanwyck won.

The public usually tired of its TV stars after three, four, or five years. Few shows on television—*Make Room for Daddy, Father Knows Best, Lassie, Gunsmoke,* among them—lasted several years without making major changes of format. Loretta Young had accomplished an amazing feat—she had lasted eight successive seasons on network TV, following the same format, and in the same time slot. There was no doubt that the scripts and production values had made the eighth year of *The Loretta Young Show* one of its best. Therefore it was a shock when it was learned that it would be the last. A new deal for a ninth season could not be agreed upon by sponsor, network, and star—and Loretta Young would no longer "visit" every Sunday night.

*I don't believe anyone can sit back and wish
for the things they want. You have to go after
them deliberately.*

—*Loretta Young*

Eighteen

At first the cancellation of her television series provided a
welcome respite for Loretta. "Going off the air came at just
the right moment for me," she later said. "It's been a luxury,
and absolutely lovely, being able to sleep in the morning
ever since the series stopped."

A great deal had happened in Hollywood during the eight
years Loretta had been working so feverishly on her show.
The face of Hollywood had changed drastically. No longer
was it the film capital of the world—now only TV production
kept the town's sound stages open and the technicians employed. As a result, most of the major studios were in dire
financial trouble. The star era—at least as Loretta had known
it—was finished, and many of the big stars who had been
Loretta's contemporaries, Hollywood's first line of royalty,
were living in quiet retirement.

In addition, many of her beloved friends had passed away.
Ronald Colman and Tyrone Power had died in 1958. Even
the King was gone—Clark Gable had died late in 1960, the
day after completing filming of *The Misfits* with Marilyn
Monroe. Gable's fifth wife, Kay Williams Spreckels Gable,

gave birth to their son, John Clark, on March 20, 1961, four months later. The newspapers made much of the fact that Gable had not lived to see the birth of his only child.

Until the end, Gable had continued to portray leading men. It seemed Hollywood's male stars were ageless, that they could be cast successfully and believably opposite much younger leading women. Cary Grant, James Stewart, and John Wayne were still top box office draws, as was Spencer Tracy, although he had aged into character roles.

The women stars, however, had had a much rougher time. A few, like Barbara Stanwyck, successfully made the transition into television, while others, like Rosalind Russell and Claudette Colbert, had been able to revitalize their careers by returning to the stage. They were the exceptions, however— most stars of Loretta's era had faded away. Even those such as Bette Davis, Joan Crawford, and Myrna Loy, who were still working, were playing roles that were not exactly commensurate with their past eminence.

Loretta Young was younger than those who were considered her contemporaries, but an attempt to return to films seemed impractical; she had made her home in television, and that's where she would stay. Just weeks after the cancellation of her show, Loretta was busily discussing new projects with the networks. It was announced that she would star in three hour-long anthology shows in the 1961–62 season on NBC. She said, "No contract has been signed yet, but if present discussions materialize I'll be back in production."

There was no doubt in anyone's mind that Loretta could return to TV any time she wanted, and after a four-month rest she announced herself "ready, willing, and able" to go ahead with another project.

In any event she was not idle. A special testimonial reception was held in her honor by the St. Anne's Foundation board of trustees, and Loretta Young Lewis was given a citation expressing "the Deep Regard in which she is held for

her Noble Contributions to the Unknown World of the Unwed Mother and Her Baby."

Throughout the year she continued working, though not
on sound stages. There were endless meetings concerning a
proposed new series, and in the meantime she made her entry into a new field. In 1961 a project on which she had
worked for years finally came to fruition. To the surprise and
delight of her fans, a book by Loretta Young was now published, written in collaboration with long-time friend and associate Helen Ferguson: *The Things I Had to Learn.* In it Loretta explained how the idea for the publication had been
born.

The experience of being confined to the hospital in 1955,
for a while on the brink of death, had caused the actress to do
a great deal of soul searching. When she realized that her
show could go on without her, she said to Helen Ferguson,
"That ought to teach me something. There's a lesson in it."
Then she added, "The things I've had to learn would fill a
book," and the idea of writing a book had taken hold.

The Things I Had to Learn was not an autobiography but a
potpourri of philosophy backed up by examples from Loretta's life. The book had a strong strain of her religious beliefs
and also covered subjects such as fashion, charm, glamour,
and "How to Budget Your Emotions." The most intriguing
aspect of the book was the manner in which Loretta dealt
with estranged husband Tom Lewis. Although they had been
living apart for five years, she spoke of him lovingly and in
every way implied that they were still in the midst of a happy
marriage. Insiders, of course, knew this was not the case, and
some say that this was Loretta's attempt to prove to Tom that
she still thought there was ample room for reconciliation.

Loretta publicized the book extensively, keeping her name
and photograph in the news as prominently as ever. The
book was popular with her fans, but the critics were un-
moved. The homilies in the text led one wag to comment,
"Loretta's life story could be embroidered on a sampler."

Although Loretta was not on television in prime time in the fall season of 1961, her daughter was. Judy Lewis had joined the cast of *The Outlaws,* a successful western in its second season on NBC, playing the part of Connie Masters, love interest to the lead, Bruce Yarnell. Westerns were enjoying huge popularity among television viewers, as were doctor-hospital dramas.

When a deal could not be reached with NBC for a new Loretta Young show, she and her new sponsor, Lever Brothers, moved over to CBS. Loretta was abandoning the hour-long anthology series concept to try a sitcom. Attempts to dissuade her were unsuccessful. *The New Loretta Young Show* would be produced by LYL Productions, Loretta's new production company. Loretta would be playing a continuing character, Christine Massey, a widowed mother with seven children, living in suburban Connecticut. James Philbrook, who had appeared on several episodes of Loretta's previous show, was cast as her love interest. His character, named Paul Belzer, was the editor of a woman's magazine, and Loretta's character was a free-lance writer.

"In many respects it will be easier for me than my first show," she said at the time, "but it won't be as much fun as changing my personality and appearance every week."

The plan was for Loretta to be the focal point of the story in alternating episodes, with the action centering around other family members on the remaining episodes.

During the same season Lucille Ball and Vivian Vance were launching a new sitcom, *The Lucy Show,* which featured the two stars as widowed women with children living in suburban Connecticut. Loretta was asked why stars such as Ball and Young were portraying themselves as widows. "First, we have statistics on our side. There's a very large percentage of women today who are trying to raise their families without the help of husbands. And secondly," the ever-practical Miss Young noted, "Lucille Ball and I are both too old not to have been married. The only way we can inject mature romance into the plot is to be widowed."

The big question among network and agency executives, of course, was whether Loretta would fail in her try at a second series as so many stars had. Eve Arden, Jack Webb, Ann Sothern, Robert Sterling, and Gale Storm had all had huge successes with their first series but only mediocre response the second time around.

Loretta pointed out that because her previous show had been an anthology series, the public didn't have a preconceived notion of a Loretta Young "character." She noted that over the long span of her thirty-seven-year career she'd never been identified with the characters she played in some ninety movies and two hundred television shows.

Most of the public actually gave no thought to what character she was going to play on an upcoming series. What they wanted to know, naturally enough, was whether Loretta was going to keep her spectacular television trademark intact— would she sweep through that door? Loretta's grand entrance was really what viewers wanted to see, and that, unbeknownst to the public, was a problem. Her sponsor, Lever Brothers, whose account was handled by the J. Walter Thompson agency, did not want Loretta to come through the doorway for her typical entrance—they felt this signature was too closely identified with Procter and Gamble products. As usual, however, Loretta argued effectively. Her entrance was *her* corporate image, she insisted; it was what people expected of her and it would stay.

There was no doubt that the premiere of *The New Loretta Young Show* was eagerly awaited. Loretta expected to succeed, for she was not accustomed to failure.

During all the years that Loretta had continued working in Hollywood, Tom Lewis had continued living in New York. It was impossible to avoid questions about the status of the Lewis marriage, although Helen Ferguson usually handled the queries and sidestepped the issue. When asked if the couple was estranged, the reply was typically, "Not as far as Loretta is concerned." Was the couple happily married? "As far as Loretta is concerned."

When an occasional interviewer was bold enough to ask Miss Young a direct question regarding the status of her marriage, he or she was given the stock reply: "No, we're not separated. Tom's work is in New York, mine is here. When possible I go to New York for visits and he comes here when possible." Although Loretta always answered sweetly, she did it in a manner that made it clear there was no room for further discussion. Writer Jane Wilkee observed, "The extended separation is adequate indication that the life as a wife which seemed to mean so much to Loretta has dwindled to nothingness."

On September 8, 1962, newspapers across the country informed an interested public that Tom Lewis and Loretta Young had "made up," at least long enough to appear together and allow themselves to be photographed. They had joined other notables on the dais at a dinner at the Beverly Hilton Hotel in Los Angeles at an event honoring Father Patrick Peyton. It was Father Peyton's twentieth anniversary as a crusader for family prayer, and he was by now perhaps second only to Bishop Fulton J. Sheen as the best-known priest in the country. President Kennedy and Pope John had both wired congratulations.

Rosalind Russell and Jack Haley were chairpersons of the event, and Danny Thomas served as master of ceremonies. Although the hundred-dollar-a-plate dinner boasted such other notables as Patricia Kennedy Lawford, the president's sister, former vice president Nixon, Irene Dunne, Raymond Burr, Dorothy Malone, and the Lennon sisters, it was Loretta and her husband who garnered all the headlines.

Reports described Peyton as "the modern priest who preaches that 'the family who prays together stays together.' '' The implication that the credo did not always succeed was both snide and strong.

The Lewis marriage still puzzled the public: Could there possibly be any truth in Loretta's statements that the couple did indeed have a long-distance marriage? And what about the lawsuits resulting from their business dealings which had been dragging on for years? Neither, of course, would comment.

At the dinner both Loretta and Tom seemed relaxed and happy in each other's company, and although they would not discuss personal matters, close friends of the couple prayed that this meeting was "a big step" in the direction of a reconciliation. It wasn't to be, however. Reliable sources state that Lewis hadn't wanted to attend the dinner—he did not want to mislead people into thinking there was a chance of a reconciliation and he knew press coverage might be unfavorable. Ultimately he was persuaded to attend, since he *was* a key factor in the broadcasting career of Father Peyton.

Everyone knew that the Lewises' contribution toward Peyton's success was incalculable. Most of the people at this gathering had been instrumental in supporting Peyton, but none had contributed more time and energy than Tom Lewis and Loretta Young Lewis.

The couple had shared so much, accomplished so much— but the reconciliation that friends hoped for would not materialize. After the award dinner Tom returned to New York and Loretta remained in Hollywood.

On Monday night, September 24, 1962, *The New Loretta Young Show* premiered. True to form, she did not disappoint her fans. She swirled through the door at ten P.M., her usual time slot, but one night later. Some noted that, like *Father Knows Best* years before, her show might be on at too late an hour to capture the family audience to which it was obviously directed. More importantly, it was Loretta's misfortune that

CBS had slotted her new show against the second season of the immensely popular hospital drama *Ben Casey*.

The first episode of Loretta's new show was a rather clever satire. To introduce the family of new characters and set up the situation, the script had Loretta and her family being interviewed on a television program very much like Edward R. Murrow's *Person to Person*. When the interviewer, in the midst of the chaos and jumble of the big family room, said, "Let's go into your living room," Loretta looked around and said, "This *is* the living room."

Her character seemed bright and refreshing, but in subsequent episodes it appeared that the scripts were trying too hard to combine Loretta's philosophical attitudes with formula sitcom, and it just wasn't working.

At first the new series seemed to be the story of a writer who was going to support herself while raising a family. Then the focus switched. During filming, it had been decided that her relationship with the editor of the magazine (Philbrook) should culminate in marriage so that he could join the family.

Their romance was, of course, depicted very demurely (one episode had them dining during their courtship and kissing behind a menu). The show then took on a serial format until they were married. Then focus switched again, from a woman making her way in the world to a sitcom concerning the amusing trials and tribulations of a large family.

Loretta Young's fans weren't buying it; they simply didn't want to see her in a predictable week-after-week characterization. Her appeal in the anthology series had obviously been her versatility. As with that show, Loretta once again immersed herself in every aspect of production. This time, however, it was even more draining because this enterprise wasn't working—the ratings were poor.

Loretta had said, "If the show is good, I see no reason why it should not run forever. If it's bad, it will go quickly, and it should."

But when the show was canceled, it came as a blow, and Loretta's peace of mind was momentarily disrupted.

She has been surrounded by the greatest scholars
in the Catholic religion. She goes on four- and
five-day retreats conducted by some of the finest
minds of the Church.

—Richard Morris

Nineteen

Loretta Young needed a rest—a long rest. "I realized there was more to life than I was experiencing inside a sound stage," she said. "I slept for almost a year when I first quit, and then I traveled. I meant to be away for just a few months, but I was gone—through the Far East, everywhere—for almost two years."

As she eased into the unaccustomed role of nonworker during those first couple of years after the cancellation of her second TV show, she enjoyed not only the opportunity to travel but also the return to her private life and family and to her charitable activities. Loretta seemed truly content to be out of "the business." Her life-style had switched gears so dramatically that the shock might have derailed a lesser woman, but she had a very strong faith to fall back on. She had always taken questions of ethics seriously, and now had the time to explore the infinite territory of philosophy.

In 1965, however, to the star's dismay, she was once again in the news. Pamela Mason was suing Loretta, charging that Portland Mason, Pamela and James Mason's daughter, had been eased out of the new Loretta Young program before it had been canceled and should be compensated for the damage suffered. In fact, Portland had made only the pilot episode for the series, but had never been signed, and that had been three years ago. Her salary was to have been four hundred dollars a week, but Mrs. Mason was claiming damages in the amount of $138,500.

The suit in itself was not particularly newsworthy and might have ended up only a blurb in a column had it not been for a tragic occurrence in the courtroom when the matter came to trial that April. Jack Murton, who had been casting director for *The New Loretta Young Show,* was on hand to testify in Loretta's behalf. After leaving the stand, Murton, who was sixty-seven, suffered a sudden heart attack as he was returning to his seat. Loretta raced to him and began crying, "Jack! Oh, Jack!" She swiftly found the medicine in Murton's pocket and pressed some nitroglycerine tablets under his tongue. A policeman in the courtroom even tried mouth-to-mouth resuscitation, but it was too late.

It was a shocking and sorrowful incident for Loretta, and it received a fair amount of coverage in the press. The suit itself was later settled when Portland Mason was awarded twenty-eight hundred dollars, seven weeks' salary.

Later in the year, Loretta traveled with her son Peter to Indiana, where he enrolled at Purdue University. The next year her other son, Christopher (a USC graduate whose best friend at the time was budding filmmaker George Lucas), was working with Tom McGowan on the production end of a film called *High Jungle,* which was to be shot in Peru. The two Lewis sons were extremely handsome young men, and either could undoubtedly have had a career as an actor if he had so chosen.

Judy Lewis was still in New York, having replaced Barbara Bel Geddes the previous year in the long-running Broadway hit *Mary, Mary.* Now she was appearing in the television daytime soap *The Secret Storm.* It seemed to some as if the second generation of the Young family was taking over. Years later,

Judy stated, "As an actress you never know what you'll be doing next. You're at the mercy of producers and agents. But I knew what I was in for from the beginning. I had seen it all happen to my mother." And she revealed, "For me there was never anything else in my life but being an actress, even though Mother did her best to discourage me."

Loretta herself was leading a full life without show business. "I honestly have trouble finding the time to do all the things I like to do," she told Bob Thomas. "I don't feel any compulsive drive to be acting again."

Her regular activities, however, seemed to be continually interrupted by litigation. One attention-getter was a lawsuit she brought against the NBC TV network. It seems that one of Loretta's former housekeepers was in Ireland, visiting relatives, when she turned on the television set one day and saw Miss Young swirling through the door in a rerun of one of the old TV shows.

She sent Loretta a note saying how wonderful it was to see an entrance of old. Miss Young, however, was aghast. In her agreement with NBC she had specifically stipulated that when the telefilms were shown abroad only the main portions of the shows would be seen. Her entrances and the closing comments, during which she wore clothes contemporary to the time the programs were filmed, were to be cut. NBC countered that Miss Young's accountant, holding her power of attorney, had authorized the use of all the material.

In her suit against NBC, Loretta claimed that she had a worldwide reputation for being "correctly and fashionably dressed in clothing in the latest period, fashion and style," and that by telecasting the episodes without deleting the introductions and closings they were holding her up to ridicule. "Most of the gowns, hairstyles and makeup, which the plaintiff wore in said openings, were outmoded, outdated and out of style," the legal complaint stated. She charged the network with breach of contract and asked for damages in excess of two and a half million dollars. The suit would drag on for years, receiving a great deal of publicity.

In 1967, Loretta received more sad news. Spencer Tracy was dead at age sixty-seven. Almost thirty-five years had passed since Loretta and Tracy had first worked together in *A Man's Castle*. Since then Tracy had gone on to become the man considered by many to be the greatest screen actor. The two-time Academy Award winner, however, had spent his life fighting alcoholism, and he had remained estranged from his wife, but never sought a divorce. His long personal and professional association with actress Katharine Hepburn would forever link their names in Hollywood legend. Tracy and Hepburn—it almost obliterates the possibility of Tracy's name being linked with any other.

During the year, Loretta moved to New York City, taking an apartment on posh Central Park South. There were vague reports that she was seeking a script as a Broadway vehicle, but the rumors were very likely unfounded. Christopher was off working, and Peter was in school. However, Judy and granddaughter Maria were in New York.

Loretta went on to Europe that year, and then in December sailed back to New York aboard the Italian luxury liner *Michelangelo*. When the ship docked, photographers were astonished when fifty-four-year-old Loretta disembarked, looking all of thirty-eight. She willingly posed for pictures.

During this period Loretta became associated in a merchandising venture with Brides Showcase International, but it was a short-lived and subsequently acrimonious union, resulting in negative publicity. The company, which franchised bridal salons throughout the country, obviously wanted Loretta for her glamorous image and PR value. She, however, must have believed that they were serious when they said they wanted her creative input. She later said—once the relationship was over—that "the wedding gowns weren't up to my standards of taste." Probably more to the point was the comment she made when discussing corporate politics, to wit, "I realized that physically I wasn't strong enough to battle four or five men."

Paul Olzman, chairman of the parent company, related his version. "She wanted to take over the company right away," he said. "I don't believe a movie star can become a retailer overnight."

There of course followed a series of lawsuits on both sides.

Loretta moved back to Hollywood and bought a new house overlooking the Beverly Hills Hotel. Finally, after ten years of litigation, Loretta and Tom at last made a settlement of their joint assets. After these financial matters were settled, Loretta took the final step. It had taken thirteen years for the Lewises to reach the courtroom, but the divorce hearing, in August 1969, lasted only five minutes. Although Loretta had been forced to charge desertion and mental cruelty, these were merely empty legal terms. To lend some credence to the hearing, however, Josie Wayne testified that Tom had told her "he had simply had it with the whole family," and that he was leaving. The divorce was granted. The Lewises had already divided all their community property, and Loretta was awarded a dollar a year token alimony.

She was quiet and introspective as she left the courtroom. One bold newsman asked, "You don't have to answer this, of course, but why did it take you so long to seek a divorce? Was it because you were hoping for a reconciliation?"

She softly replied, "Yes."

Loretta's lawyer, Louis Lee Abbott, added, "And of course there were the children." The children were now all adults.

By this time the Catholic Church's attitudes about divorce had softened somewhat. Although the Church continues to deny that any civil divorce can break the bond of marriage, it does permit divorce for the purpose of acquiring certain civil effects. According to one source book on Catholicism, "the divorce, if obtained, does not break the bond of a valid marriage."

In the summer of 1970, Loretta Young was once again in the news, this time because of a suit against Twentieth Century–Fox. Her alma mater was using clips from many old Fox films in its upcoming production of *Myra Breckinridge.* The novel, by Gore Vidal, was a spoof of Hollywood and its preoccupation with sex. The book was hilarious, vaguely pornographic, and a huge success, and Fox was pulling out all the stops to make the film version just as successful. Mae West was making a highly publicized comeback in the picture, which also starred Raquel Welch, John Huston, and critic Rex Reed in his acting debut.

By today's film standards *Myra Breckinridge* might be considered tame, but in 1970 it was a shocker. The script contained off-color language, a transsexual operation, and scenes of sodomy. As a creative device, reflecting the main character's obsession with old movies, the director tried to heighten sexual innuendo and give comic impact by intercutting scenes from classic Fox films, such as Carmen Miranda's banana number in *The Gang's All Here* and the scene in *Alexander Graham Bell* in which Loretta uttered the line "Don't move. Don't even breathe!"

Loretta was not amused.

The film was to open first in Cleveland. Loretta retained a Cleveland attorney, Richard M. Bertsch, to sue the studio for ten million dollars for the unauthorized use of her face and voice in the film. Bertsch instantly fired off a telegram to Richard Zanuck, president of Twentieth, demanding that steps be taken to delete the clip. Three weeks later a federal court judge *ordered* Fox to delete the clip, and said that the studio would face contempt of court charges if it did not comply. Fox complied. The suit was dropped.

America was in the midst of a sexual revolution, and many people laughed at Loretta for her actions, which they perceived as an effort to preserve her old-fashioned values. But many more people, though less vocal, applauded her fight to disassociate herself from the film and to try to maintain decency in the media which had seemingly gone amok.

Loretta embarked on a new adventure. She went to Phoenix, Arizona, where she lived with the nuns of St. Joseph's Hospital. She mapped out her own personal campaign to help underprivileged youth, and announced that she would underwrite a program herself—The Loretta Young Youth Project of Phoenix—in an effort to accomplish it "without red tape." Her longtime friend Sister Mary Rose Christy asserted, "We'll use no federal or state funds or United Fund contributions whatsoever. Loretta doesn't even know how much it's going to cost. It all depends on the need." Loretta made it known that she was committing part of her personal fortune to this new project.

It was a rather idealistic concept, whereby Loretta would formulate the program by talking to the underprivileged children themselves in the South Phoenix area in an effort to find out what they wanted. "She'll set up whatever the kids think they'll need. The thing is, she doesn't want to go to them and tell them what they need," Sister Mary Rose observed.

Although she had boasted, "I will succeed—I am not accustomed to failure," after much dedicated work Loretta found the project too unwieldy for her and returned to California.

Late in 1971, Loretta's suit against NBC came to trial. It was a glamorous and dramatic affair, evoking the Hollywood movie star era of the thirties and forties, as Miss Young appeared in Los Angeles Superior Court for weeks wearing a different outfit each day, thereby reinforcing her image as one of the world's best-dressed women.

On January 18, 1972, after a two-day deliberation, the jury decided in Loretta's favor and awarded her $559,000. Young personally shook the hand of each member of the jury. Although the amount was far less than the two million dollars she had sought, she had achieved an important victory of principle. It had been almost five years of litigation, but she had won.

Loretta Young has often observed, "I believe in living in the Eternal Now. In today, not in yesterday or tomorrow." As the seventies progressed, it appeared that Loretta was holding true to her philosophy. She did not look back, and although occasional film and television projects might be discussed, she was obviously not eager to reactivate her career.

She wryly noted, "The only parts being offered seemed to be weird patronesses of strange cults—and nude ones at that. Good heavens, you can't even play a maid these days without having to take your clothes off. So I kept turning down roles, and suddenly I realized time had gone by and I was retired."

Loretta's public life became primarily a life of social and charitable activities. She would make an occasional official appearance at a benefit, but for the most part she led a quiet private life. She remained, however, one of the highly sought-after guests on the Beverly Hills party circuit.

Over the next few years Young's name was continually mentioned as being connected to negotiations for some upcoming film or television project. Along with Doris Day, Loretta was mentioned for the film version of Stephen Sondheim's musical, *Follies*. The movie has yet to be made. There was talk of a biography of Mother Cabrini, the first American saint. Loretta would, of course, seem a natural for this part. That project, too, never materialized.

Although Loretta's picture often appeared on the society pages, the only time her public saw her in person was when she made a glamorous entrance at a premiere. There was the night at the Huntington Hartford Theater when Jack Klugman and Sada Thompson were opening in *All My Sons*. There is always a pack of autograph hounds outside the Huntington Hartford on premiere nights, and this night excitement was at a peak. Everyone knew that since Judy Lewis had a small part in the play, Loretta Young was sure to attend.

Young handled the situation adroitly. She arrived only moments before curtain time and politely told the autograph seekers, "I don't think we should stop right now!" as she floated past them and into the theater. Loretta had succeeded in leaving the fans breathless and exhilarated instead of angry.

Her daughter, Judy, lived in Hollywood through much of the seventies, working as an actress and occasionally directing a play. The daytime television serial she had appeared on for several years, *The Secret Storm,* was canceled in 1973. That year she had also divorced Joe Tinney, and with her teenage daughter she had moved back to Los Angeles. "I moved here because this is where most of the work is," she said at the time. "And by now I'm way past the point of being Loretta Young's daughter. I don't think of myself in those terms and neither do other people these days." But many sources say Judy moved back to be near Loretta and the other members of the close-knit Young clan.

Polly Ann Young and Sally Blane were widowed by the late nineteen seventies. Norman Foster had died in 1976. He had been active until the end, even returning to the screen as a character actor. After Foster's death, Sally received a note from her old pal Joan Crawford: "Dwell only on the joys."

Sally and Polly Ann, like Loretta, were grandmothers. Gladys—now almost ninety—was still active. She was alert as ever. Tom Lewis was in Beverly Hills one week, several years ago, staying at the Beverly Wilshire Hotel (in which he still owns a financial interest). As is his custom when at the Beverly Wilshire, Lewis drove to the Church of the Good Shepherd to attend Mass. During the course of the Mass he thought he spotted Sally across the aisle. But she did not smile or wave, and since Lewis did not have his glasses on he thought he was probably mistaken. But then when walking out of the church to the parking lot he heard the familiar, soft, southern voice of Mrs. Belzer.

"Tom?"

He walked over and greeted her.

"I told Betty Jane that was you." The trio laughed at the realization that of the three of them, Mrs. Belzer was the one to have had great eyesight. Lewis told the ninety-year-old woman, "You're still smarter than any of your daughters."

Mrs. Belzer's youngest daughter, Georgianna, had followed in Mamma's footsteps by taking an interest in interior decorating, for which she showed a great talent. Georgianna's husband embarked on the most successful phase of his career in the late seventies. Via the *Fantasy Island* series and Chrysler commercials, television would make Ricardo Montalban a household name, as it had Loretta in the nineteen fifties.

Despite her disclaimer, Judy Lewis was now not only identified as Loretta Young's daughter, but often as Ricardo Montalban's niece, a distinction she accepted stoically. When Vernon Scott interviewed Judy, he noted, "She looks strikingly like her famous mother, especially around the eyes."

Judy told Scott she was very proud of her daughter Maria and delighted that the girl had no plans for becoming a third-generation actress. "Maria has seen the hassles and struggles," Judy observed. "She is a realist. It took my mother and me much longer to become realists. I wouldn't want someone I care about to go through the ordeal of acting in pictures or television. I'm happy that Maria hasn't any interest in show business whatever.

"She doesn't resemble me or mother, although Maria does have our eyes. She is interested in social work. I'm glad she will be spared the pain of show business."

By now Judy had gone behind the cameras. She was assistant producer of ABC's Hollywood-based soap *General Hospital,* working for her old friend producer-director Gloria Monty.

In 1980, Judy returned to New York to produce a daytime serial for NBC, *Texas,* a show obviously geared to capitalize on the phenomenally successful nighttime soap *Dallas.* Although *Texas* was sexy, glitzy, and opulently produced, the contemporary drama failed to catch fire with the public, and Judy subsequently returned to Hollywood.

Although Loretta Young hadn't made a movie in twenty-seven years, she was still a much-sought-after star among fans and film buffs in Hollywood. Filmex—the Los Angeles International Film Exposition—was eager to have Loretta as the subject of a film retrospective. When they approached her, she initially declined, but later—at the urging of Irene Dunne, who herself had been the subject of a Filmex retrospective—agreed to appear. She would not, however, involve herself in the traditional question-and-answer portion of the program. Instead, she would simply take a bow.

The Filmex people obtained prints of most of her major movies, and Loretta made her telefilms—all stored in her garage—available to the committee. The program was held on Saturday, April 12, 1981, at the Goldwyn Theater, which is in the Academy of Motion Picture Arts and Sciences Building on Wilshire Boulevard in Beverly Hills, and not only did Loretta show up—for a while Filmex officials had been afraid she might back out—but so did many members of her extended family. Ninety-three-year-old Gladys was there, as were Polly Ann and Sally, brother Jack, and Peter Lewis with his wife and their son, Evan. Naturally many of Loretta's old friends attended, including Josie Wayne.

Charles Champlin, the film critic for the *Los Angeles Times,* was host. First on the agenda was the movie that had won Loretta her Oscar—*The Farmer's Daughter.* After an intermission, the audience was treated to a program of film clips compiled by David Chierichetti from eleven of Loretta's pictures —extending from the silent *Laugh, Clown, Laugh* up through her warm and ingratiating portrayal of the nun in *Come to the Stable.* Viewing these film excerpts, it was easy to see that with the exception of her role in *Born to Be Bad,* Young had been cast as basically the same character throughout her motion picture career.

Then came what the audience was really waiting for. Chierichetti had also put together scenes from Loretta's television shows. First there were ten minutes of Loretta Young's famous entrances, one after another; then came scenes from eight *Loretta Young Show* episodes, where it was obvious that she had indeed cast herself in a wide range of roles.

When Loretta was finally introduced to the audience by Charles Champlin, she received a tumultuous ovation. She was wearing a multicolored silk sheath creation, dazzling black and white pearls, and pearl drop earrings. She wore her hair in a chignon. When the applause died down, she quipped, "No wonder I was so tired that I slept most of the first year after I retired!"

She was presented with flowers, and then—to the surprise and delight of the Filmex staff—she amiably chatted with Champlin and answered questions from the audience for over an hour. It was obviously totally extemporaneous.

Champlin asked, "What would it take to lure you back into performing?" Loretta said, "I don't think there's anything." But after a slight pause she added, "Perhaps a female counterpart to *A Man for All Seasons* or *Becket.* The subject matter would be important. I'm interested in something with a point, and God knows we need pictures with a point now." But she also added, "I've done enough. Just seeing myself onscreen isn't enough of a lure anymore. Whatever it was that caused me to work so hard for so long has been satisfied now."

She told the audience that she had received much more pleasure from her TV shows than from any of her movies, because the methods of shooting were faster and there was more continuity. "For TV we shot for ten minutes straight until the film was used up, whereas in the movies you got two words out and it was 'Cut.' " She acknowledged that she had never been on the stage and hadn't had the pleasure of just playing a scene out until the conclusion. "Believe me, it is a pleasure."

Did she want to direct? "I never had the opportunity to direct, and I don't think I would have been good at it, because I was too impatient. And now I'm too lazy to start."

Ironically, Irene Dunne, who had more or less talked Loretta into the tribute, had been ill on that day and was unable to attend. A few days later Irene called a mutual friend, a costume designer, and asked, "What did you think of Loretta's dress at the tribute?"

"It was fine," he answered.

"She made it herself, you know," Miss Dunne observed.

"You're kidding!"

"No, she was out in Phoenix visiting friends and she sewed it herself from a Vogue pattern."

A month after the Filmex event, Loretta was a guest speaker at a banquet the Red Cross held to honor James Stewart. When it was her turn to speak, Loretta kidded that she wouldn't have minded if years ago Stewart had taken a romantic interest in her. But then she smiled and looked in the direction of the table where Mrs. Stewart sat, and conceded, "But perhaps he's done better."

There have been announcements of negotiations to make another film. She has talked with producer Charles Fries concerning two projects: *Potomac Jungle,* the story of the first woman president, and *Mother Angelina,* the biography of the nun who heads the Eternal World TV Network in Birmingham, Alabama. To date, nothing has come of these projects.

In the spring of 1982 Loretta was a presenter at the Academy Awards. Her dazzling appearance in a shimmering sari added a stunning note of glamour—here was a living symbol of what Hollywood had once been. She presented the best director award to Warren Beatty for *Reds,* and photographers later had a field day posing them together—one of the few genuine stars left from the past with one of the few genuine stars of the present.

Loretta enjoys her celebrity and her mobility. "I think Garbo made a mistake. She created difficulty for herself. I would hate to have to skulk around like that. The balance between privacy and public appearance is something which is often the hardest for people in Hollywood to get right."

Loretta has gotten it right.

Privately, Miss Young leads a life very much the same as any other older woman of means. She travels; she entertains and is entertained; she sees old friends—Josie Wayne, Maggie and Jean Louis, and others. The Louises, also devout Catholics, stay with her when they're in the Los Angeles area.

Loretta, who for so many years had to be up at the crack of dawn, now enjoys staying up late at night. "When I'm at home I go to bed around one-thirty or two," she said. She likes sleeping late and rarely rises before eleven-thirty. She spends time as a volunteer worker; she often goes on church retreats; and she devotes time to charitable activities, including visits to hospices. When alone, she enjoys sewing— "great therapy," she says—and has taken up painting. "Not for anyone to see," she has explained.

She spent time with her adult children. Her sons usually refer to her as Loretta, while Judy refers to her as "my mother." When Christopher and his wife, Linda, were living in Tulsa, Oklahoma, Loretta visited them. She said at the time, "I show up, and simply because I don't have to, I start doing things around the house—cooking, grocery shopping —that are pretty useful, especially since my son and his wife both work. I find when the time comes, they say, 'You don't really have to go, do you?' And I don't. So I stay a couple of weeks longer."

Loretta Young cooking? Grocery shopping? Yes, if she wants to. But she can also, when she wants to, return to the glamorous world of stardom.

She is friends with the Reagans and has visited them at the White House, and she is often present at glittering charity functions as well.

Ward Grant, who works for the Bob Hope organization, reports that he runs into Miss Young frequently at charity affairs. He says that she is as gorgeous as ever, and what's more, she has a sense of humor. When he saw her at the Hope house one evening, Loretta smiled and said, "We've got to stop meeting like this!"

Others concur that Miss Young's beauty, even close up, seems timeless. Unlike most surviving stars of her era, Miss Young has no fear of being seen or photographed. She will not, however, appear on television—when begged by her friends to at least do a talk show occasionally so her fans can get a glimpse of her, she replies, "Not me, darlings!"

There is an amusing anecdote concerning Loretta and TV talk shows. A couple of years ago, the actress and some friends were on their way to a party for designer Ted Lapidus. Their car stalled, and when a limousine stopped to give them aid, it turned out that its occupants were going to the same party. They offered Loretta and her friends a ride. However, after introductions were made, and Loretta discovered that one gentleman, Mr. Schwartz, was president of Merv Griffin Productions, she jumped to the conclusion that the Griffin show was going to film the party. Loretta wanted no part of it—in fact, she wanted them to stop the car, she would get a cab home! After many assurances from Schwartz that he, too, was only going to be a guest at the party—it was *not* being filmed for the Griffin show—the group continued on.

Late in 1982, Young swept into New York City, and while visiting Judy and Maria she made news for the next six weeks, attending many social and charity gatherings, including the Morality in Media banquet, and posing for a fashion layout in *Harper's Bazaar*.

Robert Landry of *Variety* also attended the Morality/Media banquet, and recalls that Loretta, her daughter, and granddaughter were a striking trio. Even sophisticated folk at the Plaza Hotel rushed up to Loretta to gawk and gush with compliments about her old TV shows. She was pleased to admit, "It *was* a good, clean, decent show. I set standards."

As every press agent knows, New York is the toughest town in which to get media coverage, yet here was Loretta, with no press agent and nothing to sell, garnering priceless space on the pages of New York's newspapers. Even in retirement, she remains a star.

Then, just as she had swept into town, she swept out again, off to Tulsa to spend Christmas with Chris and Linda.

In early 1983 Loretta Young was elected to the Fashion Hall of Fame. The image of Loretta as a quintessential glamour symbol is apparently indestructible.

She has made some concessions to age—there are now wisps of gray in her brunette hair. Unfortunately, she suffers a bit from arthritis and must exercise, to which end she often pedals thirty or so minutes a day on the stationary bike.

There are many who say that Loretta Young could not possibly have maintained her beauty without the aid of cosmetic surgery. When queried on how she manages to look so fantastic, her reply is, "I honestly believe people's attitudes to others have a great deal to do with what you look like." And as her close friend Maggie Louis has pointed out, "You never see Loretta with her mouth turned down, frowning, or angry. She is always in up spirits, full of joy."

Loretta's statements over the years have tended to be honest and revealing. She knows she is beautiful and has never been coy on this subject. "God gave me this face," she acknowledged, "and I made a lot of money with it. I should be grateful. And I am."

Her faith has been the mainstay of her existence and she has always been vocal about it. "I have a simple formula for everything I do," she said. "Every day, no matter what I'm doing, I say, 'Lord, I'll do the best I can and You do the rest.' " And she has perspective as well. Loretta has noted from experience, "As you grow old and mature, you realize

that what happens to you is usually your own fault. We all try
to blame others for our mistakes, but the first step to wisdom
is looking for the weaknesses within ourselves."

Pol, Bet, Gretch, and Mamma continued to see a great
deal of one another. Gladys, whose health was failing, was
living with Polly Ann. Sally lived in an apartment in Beverly
Hills and, when not traveling, Loretta lived nearby.

Extreme old age finally took its toll on the indomitable
Mamma Belzer. In the fall of 1984 the ninety-six-year-old
matriarch suffered a massive stroke, and she died on October
10. At the time of her death she was survived not only by her
five children—ages seventy-eight, seventy-six, seventy-three,
seventy-two, and sixty-one—but by thirteen grandchildren
and ten great-grandchildren.

In the year following the death of her beloved mother,
Loretta Young decided to return to acting. Producer Aaron
Spelling, whose *Dynasty* series had brought glamour back
into the American household, scored a coup by convincing
Loretta to come back to the small screen as the star of a
dramatic television movie for the ABC network, *Dark Mansions,* which would then spin off into a series. The press, from
The New York Times to the tabloids, heralded the return of
TV's former first lady. The four-million-dollar project was
touted as "the most expensive pilot show in TV history."

The financial details of the deal proved—if there had been
doubts—that Loretta Young was still a superstar. Although
she had been retired for twenty-four years, her salary was
reported to be on a par with those of *Dynasty* stars Joan Collins and Linda Evans.

To Loretta observers, however, *Dark Mansions* seemed a
peculiar vehicle for her to choose for her return. Although it
was a contemporary, currently popular genre, the nighttime
serial, the story was Gothic in character and included supernatural elements. And as on all the prime time serials, sex and
intrigue would play key roles in all the characters' story lines.

In the film, Young would be portraying a bossy mother and grandmother who is the chairman of the board of her family-owned shipping company, her fine manners concealing a hard-as-nails interior.

Aaron Spelling, a former actor-writer turned producer-mogul, is a true fan of the great stars of Hollywood's golden era. He was understandably thrilled and proud at the prospect of presenting the legendary Loretta—whom he had known socially for years—in her comeback. However, it soon became evident that there were serious—and subsequently insurmountable—problems.

Only six weeks after the announcement of the signing, Loretta dropped out of the show. Spelling said it was "because of creative differences over the way her character was developing." In the words of E. Duke Vincent, *Dark Mansions'* executive supervising producer, "Basically, the show is meant to be an ensemble piece. I think Loretta wanted to be more important in the scheme of the overall series. You have to remember that she is not only an actress and a star, but a producer-director-owner of a television series. She is not a lady who is opinionless."

"The parting between Miss Young and Aaron Spelling was an amiable one despite the story differences," said Norman Brokaw, Miss Young's longtime representative at the William Morris Agency.

"She's a great star and a great friend and I hope she always remains both," declared Spelling.

Loretta had no comment, but her replacement in the series —Joan Fontaine—did. "I'm not going to ask them to change the character or rewrite scenes," remarked Miss Fontaine. "I won't make any trouble. But if I don't like it, I'll leave." The pilot was shot. As of this writing, it hasn't sold.

To this day it seems as if Loretta Young is serious about coming out of retirement, and is searching for "the right project." Almost every year there are column blurbs in the tradepapers that she is discussing this or that upcoming role.

As this book goes to press, Tom Lewis is eighty-four and living in active retirement in Ojai. Through the years he has been the recipient of many notable awards, including the Bronze Medal from the Venice Film Festival in 1964 for outstanding service to broadcasting and the Pacific Pioneer Broadcaster award in 1967. He is a past president of the Catholic Broadcasters Association, and has won the coveted Christopher award. In addition, there is a famous award named for him: each year the Colonel Tom Lewis award is given by the Armed Forces Radio Network to an outstanding contributor to broadcasting. He travels extensively and is still very involved in Armed Forces Radio and Catholic Charities. Although friends often speak of Tom and Loretta in tandem, they have not seen each other for years.

Georgianna and Ricardo Montalban are entering their forty-third year of marriage. Georgianna, like her mother, is a talented decorator.

Polly Ann Young, Sally Blane, and their brother Jack lead quiet but active private lives.

Both Peter and Christopher Lewis have had their share of serious personal problems. Peter, who has been married several times, has lived his life outside the glare of show business. Christopher occasionally makes news because of activities which are in harsh contrast to his mother's image as a religious and moral person.

Judy Lewis travels a great deal and apparently will always work in some aspect of show business. There were reports that she was attempting to recover the rights to certain episodes of *The Loretta Young Show* and then combine them with episodes that her mother still owns in order to release the package in syndication. But more provocative news is that she is considering writing a book about her mother. Naturally, one columnist has already dubbed it *Loretta Dearest,* and claims the working title is *The Virgin Mary.* A kinder journalist noted that Loretta "trusts her daughter's judgment."

Loretta has stated that she does not plan to write her memoirs, despite rumored million-dollar offers, because, as she recently noted, "I've said everything I wanted to say."

Few individuals have possessed the self-discipline and determination of Loretta Young. Few have intrigued the fickle public for as long as Loretta—and always on her own terms.

And it is unlikely, despite recent comments to the contrary, that she will ever again reenter the arena of filmmaking. Why should she? What is there left for a woman of her accomplishments to prove? She is one of the fortunate few who can *honestly* say, "Everything I wanted to be I was." And she is intelligent enough to add, "If only for a moment."